# the food of
# ITALY

# the food of ITALY

Photography by Chris L. Jones
Recipes by Sophie Braimbridge
and Jo Glynn

MURDOCH
BOOKS

# CONTENTS

## FOOD JOURNEYS IN ITALY

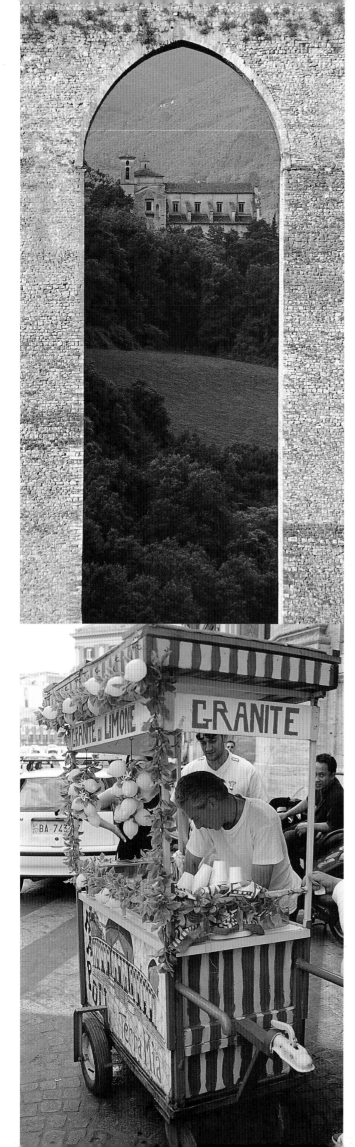

# the food of
# ITALY

THE BEAUTY OF ITALY'S FOOD IS IN ITS GASTRONOMIC DIVERSITY. EACH AREA IS LOYAL TO ITS SPECIALTIES, AND INGREDIENTS AND RECIPES CHANGE FROM THE MOUNTAINS TO THE COAST, FROM THE SOUTH TO THE NORTH, AND FROM THE MAINLAND TO THE ISLANDS.

This regionalism is historically attributed to the individualism of the sovereign states that made up Italy until the nineteenth century; to foreign influences; and to the geography that saw rice and polenta grow in the North, wild boar find a home in the forests of Central Italy and tomatoes and eggplants prosper in the sunbaked South.

Indeed, before the Second World War, Italy really could be divided geographically by its cuisine: the North ate butter, polenta, risotto and stewed meats; the Center cooked with lard and fresh pasta; and the South lived on olive oil, dried pasta, pizza, chiles and tomatoes. In the past fifty years, with the movement of people from the South to the North and from the country to the city, this has changed.

Yet *cucina regionale* (regional food) is still very much alive. Despite industrialization, the European Community and the changing face of the countryside, the artisanal skills that are the foundation for *cucina regionale* remain, and there is pride in the production of local foods like cheeses, hams, oils and pasta. Wine is also a regional specialty—at many restaurants, the choice is simply between a carafe of local red or white.

Italy is also the home of the Slow Food Movement, which champions the cause of regional food and tradition. Indeed, the whole country is undergoing a nostalgia for regional cooking and for *cucina povera* (the food of poorer southern Italy). Even in restaurants that don't specialize in regional food, dishes with traditional ingredients such as beans, chestnuts, grains and wild salad leaves are very popular.

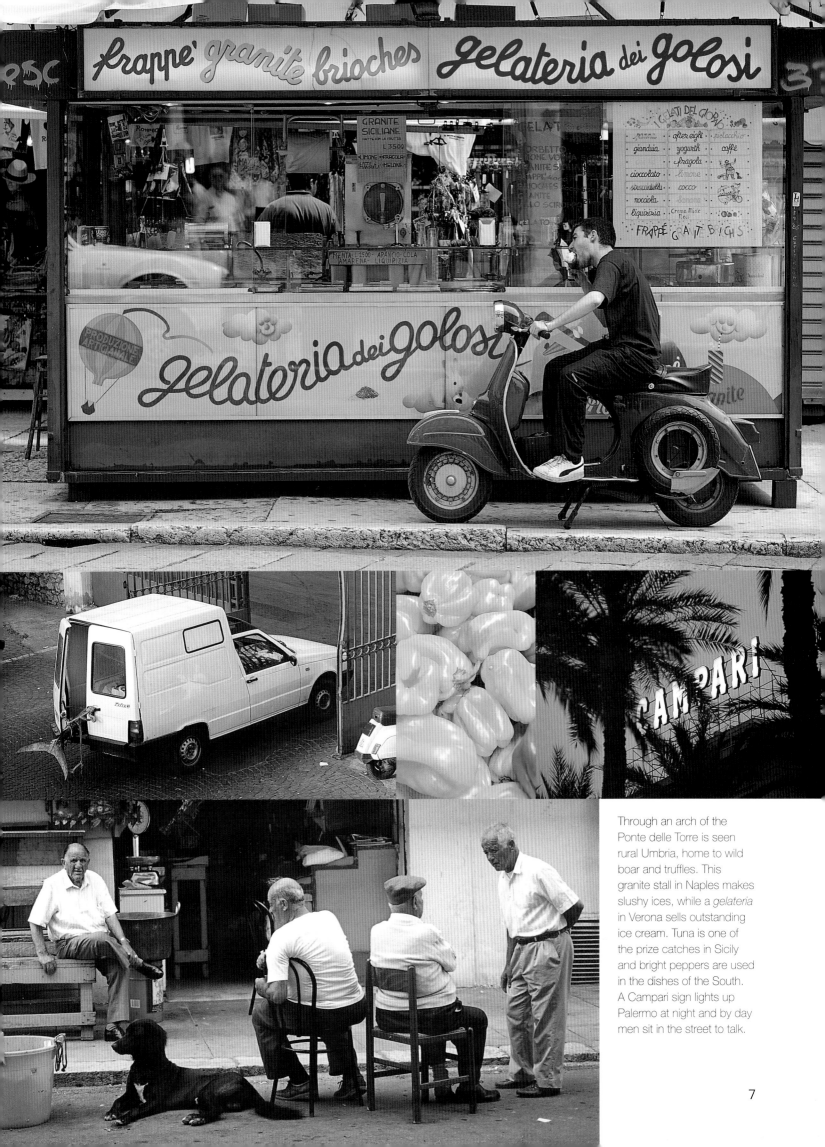

Through an arch of the Ponte delle Torre is seen rural Umbria, home to wild boar and truffles. This granite stall in Naples makes slushy ices, while a *gelateria* in Verona sells outstanding ice cream. Tuna is one of the prize catches in Sicily and bright peppers are used in the dishes of the South. A Campari sign lights up Palermo at night and by day men sit in the street to talk.

Italy's climate gives the produce intense flavor and color: purple eggplant; tiny red tomatoes; sweet cherries; meaty mushrooms and fat olives, crushed to tapenade. Food is found everywhere, from Bologna's markets to cafés in Naples' Galleria Umberto I and *salumeria* in the backstreets. A grenadine is served at Florian's in Venice and Torre Ghirlandina overlooks Modena's market.

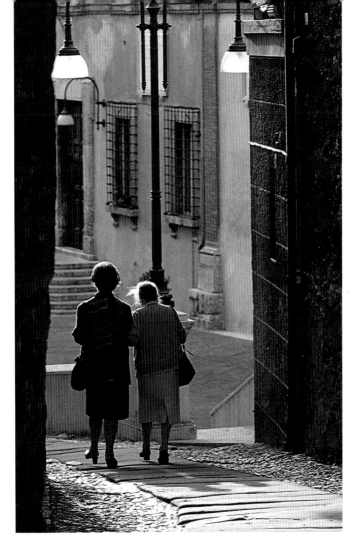

Eating and drinking well is a national pastime—from selecting fresh vegetables in the market to enjoying a mid-morning espresso in a café, lunching in a simple *trattoria* or *osteria,* and picking up some antipasto from the *salumeria* on the way home from work.

To many Italians, food shopping is practically a full-time job. Stores open twice a day so you can buy once for lunch and then again for dinner. Every city, town and village has at least one market, where the produce is more seasonal than that available in the supermarkets and standards are high as vendors compete for shoppers. Apart from the *alimentari* (general stores), there are a number of specialty food stores you would expect to find in every Italian town:

The *caseificio* and *latteria* sell dairy products and often eggs. These stores can be part of the dairy itself.
The *enoteca* sells wine by the bottle and also often by volume from huge containers.
The *macelleria (*butcher) sells fresh meat and poultry.
The *norcineria* is named for the famed butchers of Norcia (*norcini*), and sells salumi (cured pork products).
The *salumeria* also sells salumi, along with prepared foods like fresh pasta and specialty items.
The *panificio, panetteria* and *forno* sell breads and baked goods. They bake twice a day, once for each opening.
The *pasticceria* sell pastries.
The *pescheria* is the fishmonger.
The *rosticceria* is a gourmet carry-out food store, selling spit-roast chickens, meat and other prepared foods to go.
The *frantoio* is an olive oil mill or store that sells olive oil. The oil can be bought by the can or bottle or by volume like wine.
The *gelateria* is the ice-cream store, often selling ice-cream in bulk, as well as in cones and cups. Some have tables outside for serving more elaborate creations.

Italians love to buy from the source and vineyards, cheese-, pasta- and salumi-makers often have stores where you can buy straight off the shelf. Mozzarella can be purchased still warm from the dairy, pasta bought by the kilo at the factory, balsamic vinegar direct from the *acetaia* and fish off boats.

Cafés and bars are another mainstay of Italian life. In small towns they are the focus of the square and are usually occupied by a row of men drinking espresso or small shots from the bar. In and around Naples, your espresso may be sweetened by the *barista*, while in other areas it is up to you. Cappuccino is considered more of a complete breakfast than a drink and is never drunk after eleven in the morning.

9

## THE FOOD OF THE NORTH

Encompassing Piemonte, Valle d'Aosta, Lombardia and Liguria in the northwest and Trentino-Alto Adige, Veneto and Friuli-Venezia Giulia in the northeast, the food of the North has been shaped by the influence of its northern neighbors and mountainous terrain. Polenta and rice are staples and its dairy products and wines are among Italy's best.

Piemonte is home to the highly prized white Alba truffle, sprinkled over melted fontina in Piemonte's fondue-like *fonduta,* on pasta or eggs. Delicious pastries are served in Turin's famous cafés, while Alba is famed for fine chocolate. This region also produces Italy's best grissini and some of its greatest wines, including Barolo and Barbaresco.

The mountainous Valle d'Aosta is most famous for its alpine cheeses, especially fontina, Toma and Robiola, which are central to the region's cuisine.

Lombardia includes some of the richest agricultural areas in Italy and has a very diverse cuisine. Many of Italy's finest cheeses, such as Gorgonzola, Taleggio, Bel Paese and grana padano are produced here, and fresh pasta, polenta and rice are all enjoyed, including the classic *risotto alla milanese*. To the north, Valtellina is famed for bresaola (air-dried beef) and pizzoccheri, a buckwheat pasta.

Ligurian cuisine is unusual in northern Italy for its use of basil, most notably in *pesto alla genovese*. This is eaten with *trenette*, tagliatelle-like noodles, gnocchi and in minestrone. The mountains behind the Riviera provide herbs for cooking, and specialties are focaccia and walnut sauce.

Trentino-Alto Adige can be gastronomically divided into two. Alto Adige to the north is Austrian Italy and the cuisine includes speck (cured ham), *canederli* (dumplings) and *gulasch*. Trentino is more Italian, though *canederli* are popular and the excellent apples of this region are made into a local strudel. Polenta and breads accompany meals.

Outside Venice, the food of Veneto is generally simple, from bean soups, such as *pasta e fagioli,* to risotto or *risi e bisi*. Venice is known for its simple preparation of seafood, such as *moleche* (soft-shelled crabs). Veneto is also one of Italy's great wine regions, making Bardolino, Valpolicella and Soave.

Friuli-Venezia Giulia, bordering Austria and Slovenia, is known for its *prosciutto di San Daniele*—an exquisite sweet ham.

People enjoy coffee or gelati on a Sunday afternoon in a Modena bar. Fresh produce is shipped to the Rialto market in Venice by barge, then stacked up ready to sell. Asparagus is a favorite addition to risottos in the North, while at Isola della Scala, Gabriele Ferron uses his own rice to cook up wonderful dishes like this salad. These famous amaretti are made in Lombardia.

Tuscany's hillls are covered with Chianti vines, while Siena's Duomo dominates a town famed for its *panforte*. The produce of the Centre includes cherries from Emilia-Romagna, figs eaten with Parma ham and peaches from Le Marche. Bologna is famous for its restaurants; *porchetta* is sold in Spoleto, Umbria, and lentils from the hill-town of Castelluccio are enjoyed in many local dishes.

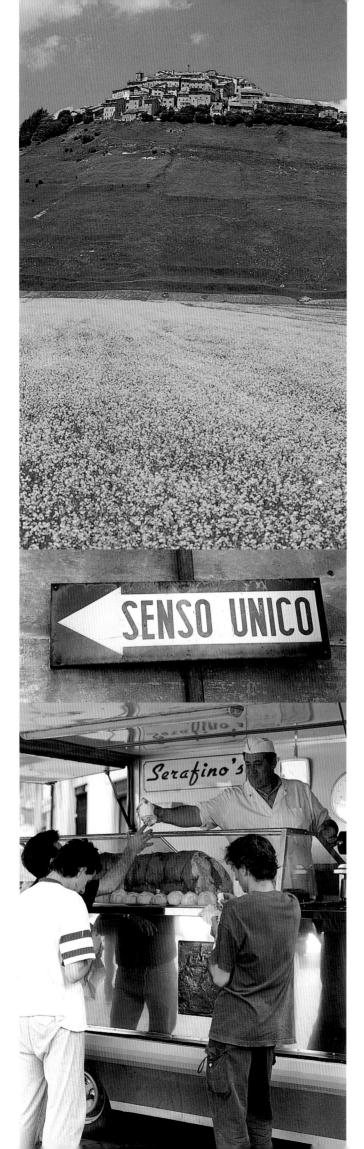

## THE FOOD OF THE CENTER

The central region of Italy encompasses Emilia-Romagna, Le Marche, Tuscany and Umbria—some of the best-known gastronomic regions of Italy. This is an area of fresh pasta, great cheeses and salumi and robust wines.

Emilia-Romagna, stretching out west from the Adriatic, is renowned both inside and beyond Italy as the country's greatest region for food. Circling out from its center, Bologna, the region produces some of Italy's best-known foods. *Prosciutto di Parma* is produced south of Parma and often served wafer-thin with bread, while the *culatello*, mortadella and *prosciutto cotto* of this area are all renowned. *Parmiggiano Reggiano* is eaten in chunks or grated over Emilia-Romagna's wonderful fresh egg pasta, which comes in more shapes and varieties than anywhere else in Italy and includes the region's favorite, tortellini. Fresh pasta is often served with Emilia-Romagna's ragù, reinterpreted worldwide as spaghetti Bolognese. *Aceto balsamico tradizionale di Modena* is an extraordinary vinegar, still made in limited quantities by ancient methods that produce an intensely concentrated flavor.

Le Marche is a self-sufficient area, separated from the rest of central Italy by the Apennines. It is renowned for its Adriatic seafood, used to produce local versions of the rich fish stew, *brodetto*. The local cuisine also makes use of its white and black truffles, wild mushrooms and fennel. Famed dishes include *porchetta* (roast suckling pig) and *vincisgrassi* (lasagne made with chicken livers and prosciutto).

Tuscan cooking is renowned as some of the simplest in Italy. The world's finest extra virgin olive oils are made here, served drizzled over Tuscany's unsalted bread. Meals are centered around meat, especially beef, soups such as *ribollita* and *papa al pomodoro,* and many bean dishes. Tuscans, in fact, are known as *i mangiafagioli*—the bean-eaters. Siena has its spicy cakes, *pan pepato* and *panforte*, that date back to medieval times, while Florence is famous for huge *bistecca alla fiorentina*. Tuscany's wines are exceptional, with Chianti being Italy's most famous red.

The only landlocked region in Italy, Umbria's food is hearty and simple. There are, however, some outstanding local products, especially the local truffles, wild mushrooms and great pecorino cheeses. Umbria is most famous for its use of pork—the town of Norcia gave its name to *norcineria,* meaning pork butcher—and its tiny lentils from Castelluccio.

## THE FOOD OF THE SOUTH

Lazio, Abruzzo, Molise, Campania, Puglia, Basilicata, Calabria, Sicily and Sardinia make up Italy's South, home to robust *cucina povera* (peasant cooking) and a wonderful cuisine created from whatever was available: sun-ripened vegetables and fruit, wheat for dried pasta and local cheeses.

Surrounding Rome, Lazio is influenced by the unique food of its capital. Roman cuisine is not delicate and makes use of pasta, beans, artichokes, meat and offal and its *spaghetti alla carbonara* and *bucatini all'amatriciana* both include the local *guanciale* (cured pig's cheek). In rural Lazio, lamb is used often in dishes like *abbacchio* (milk-fed baby lamb).

Abruzzo and Molise are mountainous areas with strong rural cooking traditions. Molise produces fine lentils, pasta and olive oils, while saffron is grown in Abruzzo, along with the *diavolilli* (tiny red chilies) that go into so many dishes.

The cuisine of Campania and Naples is famous throughout the world: spaghetti with tomatoes and basil, *spaghetti alle vongole*, pizza topped with fresh mozzarella and eggplant Parmigiana. As well as fresh mozzarella made from buffalo or cows' milk, there is good ricotta, goat cheeses and caciocavallo. Lemons are used in granite and limoncello.

Puglia has had many foreign invaders, but the food remains quintessentially Italian. Orecchiette is a delicious ear-shaped pasta, served locally with *cime di rapa* (turnip greens) and good cheeses include caciocavallo, scamorza and pecorino.

Basilicata is one of the poorest regions of Italy, but its *cucina povera,* dominated by pasta and vegetables, can be delicious. Dishes and meats are spiced with *peperoncino*.

At the tip of Italy, Calabria has two coastlines, giving it plenty of seafood, particularly swordfish and tuna. Citrus fruit grow well here, as do figs and olives. *Peperoncino* adds fire to the cooking and there is excellent provolone and caciocavallo.

Sicilian food has long been influenced by invaders, particularly the Arabs who brought sugar. The island's *dolci* (sweets), granite and gelati are still considered Italy's best. There is also an abundance of seafood, citrus fruit and capers for making caponata. The Sardinians have traditionally looked more to their inhospitable interior for food than to their once mosquito-infested coast. The food is based on sucking pig and lamb, pecorino, *pane carasu* (flat bread) and honey.

The flavors of the South: ripe tomatoes, citrus fruit, olives from twisted groves and fresh herbs. Palermo is home to both the Vucciria market, set in its backstreets, and a busy fish market, where the bellies of Sicily's famous tuna are cut out for export to Asia. Seafood is prepared simply, while marzipan fruit has been elevated to art. The grandeur of Naples is matched by its wonderful food.

15

ANTIPASTO, SALADS
& SOUPS

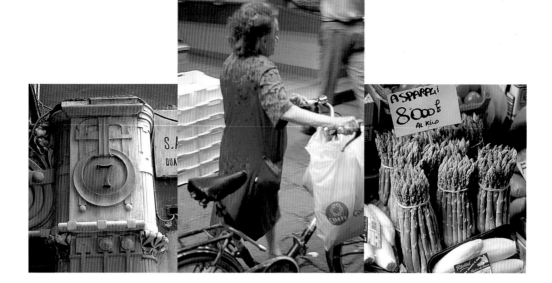

## STUFFED MUSHROOMS

8 large flat mushrooms
1¹/₂ tablespoons lemon juice
12 button mushrooms
1¹/₃ tablespoons butter
1 shallot, finely chopped
1 garlic clove, crushed
2 tablespoons white wine
3¹/₂ oz. Parmesan, grated, plus
  1 tablespoon to serve
²/₃ cup fresh bread crumbs
1 egg, lightly beaten
3 tablespoons heavy cream
1 tablespoon chopped tarragon
1 tablespoon chopped parsley

SERVES 4

PREHEAT the oven to 300°F. Wipe the large mushrooms with a damp cloth, remove and discard the stems and rub the caps with a little lemon juice to keep them white. Wipe the button mushrooms and chop them finely, then mix with the remaining lemon juice.

HEAT the butter in a small frying pan, add the shallot and garlic and cook, stirring, for 4 minutes. Add the chopped mushrooms and the wine and cook, stirring, for another 4 minutes. Remove from the heat and stir in the Parmesan, bread crumbs, egg, cream and tarragon. Season.

PLACE the mushroom caps on a lightly greased baking sheet and stuff with the filling. Bake for 12 minutes. Sprinkle with the Parmesan and parsley and serve either warm or cold.

STUFFED MUSHROOMS

## CHAR-GRILLED ASPARAGUS

24 asparagus spears
1 tablespoon extra virgin olive oil
2 tablespoons balsamic vinegar
Parmesan shavings

SERVES 4

WASH the asparagus and remove the woody ends (hold each spear at both ends and bend it gently—it will snap at its natural breaking point).

PUT the asparagus in a bowl, add the olive oil and toss well. Heat a skillet or barbecue and cook the asparagus for 10 minutes, or until *al dente*. Drizzle with balsamic vinegar and sprinkle with the Parmesan to serve.

(IF YOU DON'T have a skillet or barbecue, you can steam the asparagus or boil in salted water for 6–8 minutes until *al dente*. Drain and drizzle with the olive oil, balsamic and Parmesan.)

# STUFFED PEPPERS

STUFFED VEGETABLES ARE OF ARABIAN ORIGIN, ALTHOUGH THEY HAVE NOW BECOME ALMOST SYNONYMOUS WITH MEDITERRANEAN COOKING. IN ITALY, YOU WILL FIND VEGETABLES STUFFED WITH ALL MANNER OF INGREDIENTS, FROM RICE AND BREAD CRUMBS TO CHEESE OR MEAT.

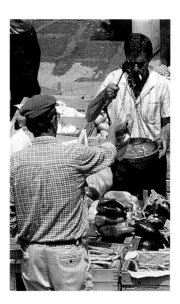

3 red or yellow peppers
1 tablespoon olive oil
1 small onion, finely chopped
2 garlic cloves, crushed
3 tablespoons butter
2 cups fresh bread crumbs
1 egg
1 oz. Parmesan, grated
2 tomatoes, peeled, seeded and
    chopped
5 oz. mozzarella, grated
2 tablespoons chopped basil
3 tablespoons extra virgin olive oil

SERVES 6

PREHEAT the oven to 325°F. Cut the peppers in half and remove the seeds. Place on a lightly oiled baking sheet.

HEAT the olive oil in a frying pan, add the onion and garlic and cook, stirring, for 5 minutes. Remove from the heat and stir in the butter and bread crumbs. Transfer to a bowl and add the egg, Parmesan, tomatoes, mozzarella, basil and 3 tablespoons water. Stir well and season.

FILL the pepper halves with the stuffing, drizzle with the extra virgin olive oil and bake for 40–45 minutes, or until the peppers are cooked through and the tops are golden brown.

# STUFFED ONIONS

8 medium white or red onions,
    peeled but left whole
3 tomatoes
1 tablespoon olive oil
1 tablespoon butter
1 onion, finely chopped
1 garlic clove, crushed
8 oz. ground beef
2 tablespoons chopped parsley
1 egg
2 oz. grated Parmesan

SERVES 4

PLACE the onions in a large saucepan, cover with water and simmer for 10 minutes. Drain and cool. Preheat the oven to 350°F. Score a cross in the top of each tomato. Plunge into boiling water for 20 seconds, then drain and peel. Chop the tomatoes, discarding the cores.

HEAT the olive oil and butter in a frying pan until butter has melted. Add chopped onion and garlic and cook, stirring, for 5 minutes or until tender. Add the tomatoes and cook for another 6 minutes over low heat. Add the beef and cook until lightly browned. Remove from the heat and cool. Add the parsley, egg and Parmesan and stir well.

CUT off the top of each onion and, using a melon baller or a spoon, remove some of the inside (being careful not to lose the shape of the onion). Place them on a baking sheet and stuff with the filling. Bake for 20 minutes and serve hot or at room temperature.

## ARTICHOKES VINAIGRETTE

There are three different sizes of artichoke. The largest are the first to appear on the plant and are known as *la mamma* (the mother). Next to grow are the *figli* (children), which are smaller and more tender. Finally, the *nipoti* (nephews) appear further down the plant, the smallest and most tender of all.

2 tablespoons lemon juice
4 young Romanesco or Violetto Toscano artichokes
1 quantity vinaigrette (page 286)

SERVES 4

MIX the lemon juice in a large bowl with 4 cups cold water. Using kitchen scissors or a sharp knife, cut off and discard the top third of each artichoke. Discard the tough outer leaves and snip off any spikes from the remaining leaves. Chop off and discard all but 1 inch of the stem and peel this with a potato peeler.

SLICE EACH artichoke in half from top to bottom, including the stem. Scrape out the furry choke and discard it. As each artichoke is prepared, place it straight into the bowl of lemon water to avoid discoloring.

SHAKE EACH artichoke half dry and arrange on a serving platter. Spoon the vinaigrette over the top and leave for at least 30 minutes before serving.

## WARM ARTICHOKES VINAIGRETTE

4 x ¾ lb. globe artichokes
juice of 1 lemon
1 quantity vinaigrette (page 286)

SERVES 4

BRING a large saucepan of salted water to a boil. Cut off the artichoke stalks at the bottom so the artichokes stand upright. Put them in the boiling water and add the lemon juice. Boil gently for 30–40 minutes or until a leaf from the bottom comes away easily. Cool quickly under cold running water and drain upside down on a baking sheet.

TO SERVE, put each artichoke on a serving plate and gently pry it open a little. Spoon the vinaigrette over the top, letting it drizzle into the artichoke and around the plate.

(WHEN eating artichokes, once you have eaten the leaves, remove the "furry choke" at the bottom with a spoon. Then you can eat the tender bottom or "heart".)

WARM ARTICHOKES
VINAIGRETTE

# BRUSCHETTA

4 large slices of "country-style"
 bread, such as ciabatta
1 garlic clove
drizzle of extra virgin olive oil

MAKES 4

BROIL, char-grill or toast the bread until it is crisp. Cut the garlic clove in half and rub the cut edge over both sides of each bread slice. Drizzle a little olive oil over each bread slice.

# TOMATO AND BASIL BRUSCHETTA

4 ripe tomatoes
1 tablespoon shredded basil
4 pieces basic bruschetta

SERVES 4

ROUGHLY chop the tomatoes and mix with the basil. Season well and pile onto the bruschetta.

Bruschetta is a traditional Italian antipasto. Use slightly stale bread (this is an excellent dish for using up leftovers) that is dense enough to stop the olive oil seeping through. Technically speaking, real bruschetta is just plain broiled bread, rubbed with garlic while it is still hot and then drizzled with good-quality olive oil.

# WILD MUSHROOM BRUSCHETTA

2 tablespoons olive oil
$4^1/_2$ cups selection of wild
 mushrooms, particularly fresh
 porcini, sliced if large, or
 chestnut mushrooms
2 garlic cloves, crushed
1 heaped tablespoon chopped
 thyme
4 pieces basic bruschetta

SERVES 4

HEAT the olive oil in a large saucepan or frying pan. When the oil is hot, add just enough mushrooms to cover the bottom of the saucepan and cook over high heat, stirring frequently. Season with salt and pepper. (Sometimes the mushrooms can become watery when cooked. Continue cooking until all liquid has evaporated.)

ADD a little crushed garlic and thyme and cook for another minute. Remove from the pan and repeat with the remaining mushrooms. Spoon over the bruschetta and serve immediately.

# EGGPLANT BRUSCHETTA

2 large eggplants, sliced
2 garlic cloves, crushed
$^1/_2$–$^2/_3$ cup extra virgin olive oil
juice of 1 small lemon
3 tablespoons roughly chopped mint
4 pieces basic bruschetta

SERVES 4

HEAT a skillet on the stove. Place a few eggplant slices on the skillet and cook over moderately high heat, turning once, until the eggplant is soft and cooked.

MIX TOGETHER the garlic, oil, lemon juice and mint and season well. Put the eggplant in a dish with the marinade and leave for 30 minutes. Place a couple of eggplant pieces on each bruschetta and spoon the marinade over the top.

EGGPLANT BRUSCHETTA

Zucchini flowers can have a baby zucchini attached, while others are simply the male flowers of the plant and have a long stem instead of a zucchini. Choose flowers that are fresh and firm.

# DEEP-FRIED ZUCCHINI FLOWERS

THOSE WHO GROW ZUCCHINIS AT HOME CAN MAKE USE OF THE YELLOW FLOWERS THAT APPEAR IN STEADY SUPPLY THROUGHOUT THE SUMMER. IF FLOWERS AREN'T AVAILABLE, YOU CAN USE THE SAME BATTER AND METHOD TO DEEP-FRY SLICES OF ZUCCHINI AND EGGPLANT.

BATTER
1/2 cup all-purpose flour
2 teaspoons olive oil
3 egg whites

8–12 zucchini flowers
oil for deep-frying
lemon wedges

SERVES 4

TO MAKE the batter, sift the flour into a bowl and stir in 1/4 teaspoon salt. Mix in the oil with a wooden spoon, then slowly add 1/4–1/2 cup warm water, changing to a whisk when the mixture becomes liquid. Continue whisking until the batter is smooth and thick. Whisk the egg whites until stiff peaks form, then fold into the batter.

CHECK that the zucchini flowers are clean and aren't hiding any stray insects. Trim the stem of each flower to 1 inch (this gives you something to hold on to when dipping).

HEAT the oil in a deep-fat fryer or deep frying pan to 350°F, or until a piece of bread fries golden brown in 15 seconds when dropped in the oil. If the oil starts to smoke it is too hot.

DIP the zucchini flowers into the batter, coating both sides. Fry the flowers in batches until golden brown, turning once to cook on both sides. Drain on paper towels and serve with a sprinkling of salt and a lemon wedge. Don't let them sit around— serve and eat immediately, preferably with a glass of chilled white wine.

# CIPOLLINE AGRODOLCE

7 cups small boiling onions
2 tablespoons brown sugar
2 tablespoons white wine vinegar
4 tablespoons butter

SERVES 8

PEEL the onions, cut off the roots and remove the first layer of skin. Heat the sugar in a large heavy-bottomed saucepan until it melts and starts to caramelize. Remove from the heat, add the vinegar and butter and stir well. Return to the heat, bring to a boil and add the onions. Add enough water to just cover the onions and simmer for 10 minutes. Cover the saucepan and simmer for another 20 minutes, or until the onions are tender. Serve hot or at room temperature.

CIPOLLINE AGRODOLCE

# CROSTINI

2 day-old ciabatta loaves
3/4 cup extra virgin olive oil

MAKES 50

TO MAKE the crostini, preheat the oven to 350°F. Thinly slice the bread, cut each piece into quarters and drizzle olive oil over both sides. Lightly toast in the oven until just crisp. The crostini will keep in an airtight container for at least a couple of days.

# TAPENADE CROSTINI

2 cups whole black olives, pitted
13/4 oz. can anchovy fillets
1 tablespoon capers, drained
2 garlic cloves, crushed
1/4 cup basil, finely chopped
grated zest and juice of 1 lemon
3/4 cup extra virgin olive oil

FINELY CHOP the olives, anchovies and capers together with a knife or food processor and place in a bowl. Add the garlic, basil, lemon zest and juice, stir in the olive oil and season well.

SPREAD on crostini to serve. (The tapenade will keep in an airtight container in the fridge for up to a month.)

Crostini are best made from slightly stale leftover bread and topped with pâté, ragù or vegetables. This is an antipasto that is particularly associated with Tuscany.

# RED PEPPER CROSTINI

3 tablespoons olive oil
1 onion, finely chopped
2 red peppers, thinly sliced
2 garlic cloves, crushed
1 tablespoon capers, drained and chopped
2 tablespoons balsamic vinegar
1 tablespoon roughly chopped flat-leaf parsley

HEAT the olive oil in a frying pan and cook the onion for a few minutes until soft. Add the peppers and cook for another 15 minutes, stirring frequently. Season. Add the garlic and cook for a minute more.

ADD the capers and vinegar and simmer gently for a few minutes to reduce the liquid. Add the parsley just before spreading onto crostini.

# CHICKEN LIVER CROSTINI

61/2 oz. chicken livers
3 tablespoons olive oil
1 small onion, finely chopped
2 garlic cloves, crushed
1 tablespoon finely chopped sage
2 tablespoons dry Marsala
2 tablespoons mascarpone

TRIM the chicken livers of any sinew. Heat the olive oil in a frying pan and gently cook the onion for 2 minutes until soft. Push the onion to the side, increase the heat and add the livers. Cook until lightly brown on both sides, add the garlic and sage and cook for 1 minute. Add the Marsala and cook briefly to reduce the liquid. Season well. Transfer to a food processor or chop by hand, and blend briefly with the mascarpone. Serve immediately, or chilled, on crostini.

Palermo's wholesale market (*Mercato Ittico*), while famous for its large tuna and swordfish, also sells local squid and shrimp.

# FRITTO MISTO DI MARE

FRITTO MISTO IS TRADITIONALLY A MIXED PLATTER. WE USUALLY THINK OF THIS AS SEAFOOD, AS IN THIS RECIPE, BUT FRITTO MISTO IS ANOTHER OF THOSE ITALIAN DISHES THAT VARIES FROM REGION TO REGION. SOME PREFER MEAT OR VEGETABLES, OTHERS USE FRUIT AND EVEN CHOCOLATE.

8 oz. baby squid
12 large shrimp
8 baby octopus
16 scallops, cleaned
12 fresh sardines, gutted and
   heads removed
8 oz. firm white fish fillets (such as
   cod or snapper), skin removed
   and cut into large cubes

GARLIC AND ANCHOVY SAUCE
$1/2$ cup extra virgin olive oil
2 garlic cloves, crushed
3 anchovy fillets, finely ground
2 tablespoons finely chopped
   parsley
pinch of dried red chile flakes

BATTER
$1^2/_3$ cups all-purpose flour
$1/_3$ cup olive oil
1 large egg white

oil for deep-frying
lemon wedges

SERVES 4

PREHEAT the oven to 275°F. Clean the squid by pulling the heads and tentacles out of the bodies along with any innards. Cut the heads off below the eyes, just leaving the tentacles. Discard the heads and set the tentacles aside. Rinse the bodies, pulling out the clear quills, and cut the bodies into rings. Peel and devein the shrimp, leaving the tails intact.

CLEAN the octopus by slitting the head and pulling out the innards. Cut out the eyes and hard beak and rinse. If the octopus seem big, cut them into halves or quarters.

TO MAKE the sauce, warm the oil in a frying pan. Add the garlic, anchovies, parsley and chile flakes. Cook over low heat for 1 minute, or until the garlic is soft but not brown. Serve warm or chilled.

TO MAKE the batter, sift the flour into a bowl and stir in $1/_4$ teaspoon salt. Mix in the oil with a wooden spoon, then gradually add $1^1/_4$ cups tepid water, changing to a whisk when the mixture becomes liquid. Continue whisking until the batter is smooth and thick. Stiffly whisk the egg white and fold into the batter. Heat the oil in a deep-fat fryer or deep frying pan to 375°F, or until a piece of bread fries golden brown in 10 seconds when dropped in the oil.

DRY the seafood on paper towels so the batter will stick. Working with one type of seafood at a time, dip the pieces in batter. Shake off the excess batter, then carefully lower into the oil. Deep-fry for 2–3 minutes, depending on the size of the pieces. Drain on paper towels, then transfer to the oven. Do not crowd the seafood. Keep warm while you fry the remaining seafood.

SERVE the seafood immediately with the lemon wedges and the sauce.

# SEAFOOD ANTIPASTI

THE GOLDEN RULE FOR COOKING SEAFOOD IS THAT ALL YOUR INGREDIENTS MUST BE ABSOLUTELY STRAIGHT-FROM-THE-SEA FRESH. BUY LIVING SHELLFISH FROM THE FISHMONGER AND BE ADVISED AS TO WHAT IS IN SEASON, A REGIONAL SPECIALTY, OR A GOOD CATCH OF THE DAY.

1 lb. mussels
1 lb. clams
8 oz. octopus
8 oz. small squid
8 oz. shrimp
1/2 cup olive oil
juice of 2 lemons
2 tablespoons finely chopped
    parsley
lemon wedges

SERVES 6

CLEAN the mussels and clams by scrubbing them thoroughly and scraping off any barnacles. Pull off the beards from the mussels and rinse well under running water. Discard any mussels or clams that are broken or open and do not close when tapped on the work surface.

CLEAN the octopus by slitting the head and pulling out the innards. Cut out the eyes and hard beak and rinse. If the flesh is still springy and has not been tenderized, beat with a mallet until soft.

PREPARE the squid by pulling the heads and tentacles out of the bodies along with any innards. Cut the heads off below the eyes, just leaving the tentacles. Discard the heads and set the tentacles aside. Rinse the bodies, pulling out the clear quills, then cut the bodies into rings. Peel and devein the shrimp, leaving the tails intact.

BRING a large saucepan of water to a boil and add the octopus. Reduce the heat and simmer for 20 minutes or until tender. Add the squid and shrimp. Cook for 2 minutes, or until the shrimp turn pink. Drain well.

PUT the mussels and clams in an even layer in a steamer. Steam over boiling water for 2 minutes or until the shells have just opened (discard any that stay closed). Pull the top shell off each mussel and clam. Arrange on a platter.

IF YOU have one octopus, cut it into pieces; if you have baby ones then leave them whole. Arrange octopus, squid, and shrimp on the platter and sprinkle with sea salt and black pepper. Mix the olive oil with the lemon juice and drizzle over the seafood. Cover with plastic wrap and leave to marinate in the fridge for at least 2 hours. Before serving, sprinkle with parsley and add the lemon wedges. Serve with bread to soak up the juices.

## OCTOPUS SALAD

Whisking the dressing for the Octopus Salad.

1¹/₄ lb. baby octopus
2 tablespoons lemon juice
¹/₂ cup olive oil
1 garlic clove, thinly sliced
1 tablespoon chopped mint
1 tablespoon chopped parsley
1 teaspoon Dijon mustard
pinch of cayenne pepper
3 cups misticanza (mixed salad
    leaves)
lemon wedges

SERVES 4

CLEAN the octopus by slitting the head and pulling out the innards. Cut out the eyes and hard beak and rinse. If the octopus seem big, cut them into halves or quarters.

BRING a large saucepan of water to a boil and add the octopus. Simmer for 8–10 minutes, or until they are tender.

MEANWHILE, make a dressing by mixing together the lemon juice, olive oil, garlic, mint, parsley, mustard and cayenne with some salt and pepper.

DRAIN the octopus well and put in a bowl. Pour the dressing over the top and cool for a few minutes before transferring to the fridge. Chill for at least 3 hours before serving on a bed of salad leaves with the lemon wedges. Drizzle a little of the dressing over the top.

## MARINATED FRESH ANCHOVIES

FRESH ANCHOVIES ARE FISHED ALL OVER THE MEDITERRANEAN, AS WELL AS THE ATLANTIC COASTS OF FRANCE AND SPAIN. YOU WILL NEED VERY FRESH FISH FOR THIS SIMPLE DISH, WITH PERHAPS JUST SOME BREAD TO SOAK UP JUICES. THE DISH CAN BE KEPT REFRIGERATED FOR UP TO THREE DAYS.

³/₄ lb. fresh anchovies
¹/₄ cup olive oil
1 tablespoon extra virgin olive oil
3 tablespoons lemon juice
2 garlic cloves, crushed
2 tablespoons finely chopped
    parsley
2 tablespoons finely chopped basil
1 small red chile, seeded and
    chopped

SERVES 4

FILLET the anchovies by running your thumbnail or a sharp knife along the backbone, then pulling the head upwards. The head, bones and guts should all come away together, leaving you with the fillets. Carefully wash under cold water and pat dry with paper towels. Place the fillets in a shallow serving dish.

MIX ALL the remaining ingredients together with some salt and pepper and pour over the anchovies. Cover with plastic wrap and marinate in the fridge for at least 3 hours before serving.

MARINATED FRESH ANCHOVIES

**SALAME** is the generic Italian term for a cured sausage. Salami is usually made from pork and pork fat, often with chiles and spices added for flavoring, then cured and eaten raw.

**COGLIONI DI MULO** the literal translation for this pork salami is "mules' balls", so-named apparently because this is something a mule lacks, rather than because of its content.

**FINOCCHIONA SBRICIOLONA** a typical Tuscan salami made from pork and pork fat and flavored with garlic and wild fennel seeds. It is used in Tuscan antipasto plates.

**SALAME UMBRO** a local Umbrian pork salami with pieces of pork fat running through it. It is eaten in chunks or sliced as part of an antipasto platter.

**CIAUSCOLO** a smooth and very soft spreadable salami made from pork. This salami is a specialty of Le Marche.

**SALSICCIA** the general name for sausages. Classically made with ground pork, pork fat, spices and herbs, though some varieties are made with other meats.

**SALAME DI NAPOLI** a long salami made from pork, beef and pork fat, seasoned with garlic, pepper, wine, chile and paprika, making it a much more strongly flavored salami than most.

**MORTADELLA** this very large Bolognese salami is a *salame cotto* (cooked salami). Made from ground pork and pork fat, which shows up as white spots, it is often cut into cubes to eat.

**SALSICCIA AL TARTUFO** a specialty salami from Umbria, an area famous for its black truffles. The salami are delicately flavored with truffle and cut into chunks for eating.

**SOPPRESSATA** a large salami made with pig's brawn. It is sometimes lightly smoked before being pressed into shape. The shape of various soppressata may vary and some are flatter.

**SALSICCIA DI CINGHIALE** an Umbrian salami made from wild boar. This is a *cacciatori,* hunter-style, salami—a small salami that can be easily carried when out hunting for the day.

**SALAME MILANO** this fine-textured pork, or often now pork and beef, salami has a mild flavor and sometimes has added garlic. It is also known as *crespone*.

NORCIA, in Umbria, is famous for its pork butchers and the town gives its name to *norcini*, a term used throughout Italy to mean pork butchers. *Norcini* from this area traditionally traveled all over Italy during the butchering and curing season in November to ply their trade, returning home in April. Butcher shops in Central Italy are also known as *norcineria* and specialize in local cured pork and wild boar products.

# SALUMI

SALUMI IS A GENERAL TERM REFERRING TO ALL ITALY'S FAMOUS CURED OR PRESERVED PORK PRODUCTS, FROM SALAMI AND SALSICCE (SAUSAGES) TO CURED HAMS SUCH AS PARMA AND COOKED HAMS SUCH AS PROSCIUTTO COTTO, AND TO INGREDIENTS SUCH AS LARD, PANCETTA AND COPPA.

Curing was once the only way in which meat could be enjoyed all year round. A family would keep a pig to be butchered in the winter, then turn it into salumi to be eaten throughout the year. Though beef, wild boar and venison are used for making cured meats, pork has always predominated, made popular by the fact that every scrap of the animal can be used. When the pig was butchered, the fat would be rendered into lard, the best meat turned into hams and pancetta, the rest of the pig used to make salami and sausages, the blood used for sausages and the bones saved for stock. The meats would then be cured, usually by drying, smoking or preserving them in fat. In Italy, you can still buy just about every part of the pig, including *guanciale*, cured pig's cheek; trotters, boned and stuffed to make *zampone*; and the neck, cured and made into *coppa*.

## SALAMI

In Italy, butchers display their salami marked as pork (*suino*) or beef (*bovino*), and some may be labeled *salsicce* rather than salami. A salami can be sold under its own name or marked "*nostrano*", meaning that it is from the area or

# CHAR-GRILLED OCTOPUS

BUY SMALL OCTOPUS IF YOU CAN FIND THEM—THEY ARE MORE TENDER THAN THE LARGE ONES. IF ONLY LARGE ARE AVAILABLE, TENDERIZE THEM BY BEATING WITH A ROLLING PIN BEFORE COOKING. IN SOME COASTAL REGIONS, YOU CAN SEE OCTOPUS BEING TENDERIZED IN A CEMENT MIXER.

16 small octopus (about 3 lb.)
2/3 cup extra virgin olive oil
4 thyme sprigs
2 bay leaves
2 garlic cloves, crushed
lemon wedges

SERVES 4

CLEAN the octopus by slitting the head and pulling out the innards. Cut out the eyes and hard beak and rinse. If the flesh is still springy and has not been tenderized, beat with a mallet until soft. Skin the octopus tentacles and make small diagonal cuts along their length, cutting about a third of the way through the tentacle. Place in a bowl and pour over the oil. Add the thyme, bay leaves and garlic and toss well. Cover with plastic wrap and marinate in the refrigerator overnight. Leave four wooden skewers to soak in water.

HEAT a skillet or a barbecue. Drain the excess oil from the octopus and thread onto the skewers. Cook for 5–7 minutes on each side or until the octopus is golden and the tip of a knife slips through a tentacle. Season with salt and pepper and drizzle with some extra marinade or extra virgin olive oil if you like. Leave for a few minutes and then serve with lemon wedges.

CHAR-GRILLED OCTOPUS

# GARLIC SHRIMP

20 large shrimp
1/4 cup olive oil
1/3 cup butter
1/2 red chile, finely chopped
10 garlic cloves, crushed
1/4 cup white wine
3 tablespoons chopped parsley

SERVES 4

PEEL and devein the shrimp, leaving the tails intact if you like. Put the olive oil in a large frying pan and add the butter, chile and half the garlic. Cook, stirring, for 3 minutes. Add the shrimp and sprinkle with the remaining garlic.

COOK for 3 minutes or until the shrimp are pink. Turn the shrimp, add the wine and cook for another 4 minutes. Add the parsley, season well with salt and pepper and serve with bread.

**PARMA HAM** Italy's best-known *prosciutto crudo* (cured ham), it must conform to regulations on pig-rearing, diet, curing and air-drying. The pigs are fed on whey left over from making Parmesan.

**TUSCAN HAM** a *prosciutto crudo* that is stronger and saltier than sweeter types of prosciutto like Parma or San Daniele. This chewy, tasty ham is eaten with Tuscan bread and wine.

**SAN DANIELE** another fine-grade *prosciutto crudo* from Friuli. It has a redder color and sweeter flesh than Parma ham and is best eaten on its own or thinly sliced with bread.

**PROSCIUTTO COTTO** means "cooked ham". The cut of ham is the same as for *prosciutto crudo* and is made by being pressed into a mold and steamed. It is eaten as antipasto or in cooking.

**CULATELLO** a ham from Emilia-Romagna made from the top of a pig's leg cured in brine and then air-dried inside a casing. It has a very sweet flavor and can be served on its own.

**PANCETTA** this bacon is made from cured belly pork and is available unsmoked, smoked (*affumicata*) and rolled. It is usually chopped and used as an ingredient in soups and sauces.

**PANCETTA ARROTOLATA** is bacon made from belly pork, which is known as *pancia*. Pancetta comes both as a flat piece or rolled (*arrotolata*), as shown here.

**GUANCIALE** the cured cheek of a pig, guanciale tastes and resembles pancetta and is the traditional ingredient in *spaghetti carbonara* and *all'Amatriciana*.

**LOMBO DI MAIALE** cured loin of pork, a particularly lean and tender cut from below the rib-cage. It can be sliced and used for antipasto plates or in pasta sauces and soups.

**ZAMPONE** a boned pig's trotter stuffed with pork, nutmeg, cinnamon and cloves. To eat, the sausage is simmered for a few hours to give it a slightly gelatinous texture.

**LARDO** the cured lard from pork, it is often flavored with herbs, pepper and salt. Lard is used as a flavoring in cooking, or is sometimes finely shaved and eaten on its own.

**COPPA** made from the collar of pork, salt-cured in brine, then air-dried. It is a mixture of meat and fat, with the best having equal amounts of each. It is sliced thinly for antipasto.

SAN NICOLA'S PARMA HAM is made from pigs' hind legs that have been preserved by having sea salt massaged into them for a month. The exposed ends are then treated with pork fat and the legs air-dried in the pure air of the Alta val Parma for a year. Each ham is tested by smell with a piece of bone and any rejects sold as prosciutto. Certified hams are double-stamped with a crown and have their birthday written on them.

homemade. Salami change in flavor and texture according to where they are made. The Northeast tends towards heavier, more Austrian-tasting salami, the Center prefers a more refined texture, while in the South salami are often spicy. Flavorings may also be added to standard salami — in Tuscany this is often fennel seed and in Umbria truffles are used. The larger the salami, the thinner it should be sliced.

## PROSCIUTTO

*Prosciutto crudo* is a cured ham made from an air-dried pig's leg and sliced paper-thin for antipasto. Parma ham is just one type of prosciutto and many regions produce their own hams. *Prosciutto salato*, salted hams, are cured heavily with salt. Tuscan ham is one of the finest and these robust hams can be excellent with unsalted bread. Parma and San Daniele hams are both *prosciutto dolce*, sweet hams, whose subtle curing and longer hanging give them a sweet, refined flavor.

THIS BUTCHER in Norcia proudly displays its title as an *artigiani norcini* (artisan pork butchers). Nowadays, many *norcini* work on large pig farms, producing salami and other pork products.

Fresh tuna has a dark meaty flesh that is delicious both raw and cooked. Tuna is fished off the coasts of Sicily and Calabria where the fish come to spawn. The better-tasting red flesh indicates that the tuna was caught by hand, killed and bled quickly, while muddy-brown flesh means the fish drowned and so probably was caught by net.

# CARPACCIO

CARPACCIO IS NAMED AFTER THE RENAISSANCE PAINTER WHOSE USE OF REDS AND WHITES IS REFLECTED IN THE DISH. IT WAS CREATED IN HARRY'S BAR IN VENICE FOR A FAVORITE CUSTOMER WHOSE DOCTOR HAD PLACED HER ON A DIET FORBIDDING COOKED MEAT.

1 1/2 lb. good-quality beef fillet
1 egg yolk
3 teaspoons Dijon mustard
3 tablespoons lemon juice
2 drops Tabasco
1/4–1/3 cup olive oil
1 tablespoon light cream
2–3 tablespoons baby capers, rinsed

SERVES 6

PLACE the beef in the freezer for about half an hour, or until it is firm. Using a sharp knife or mandoline, cut the beef into paper-thin slices. Cover six serving plates with the beef in an even layer.

BLEND together the egg yolk, mustard, lemon juice and Tabasco. With the motor running, add the olive oil in a thin stream until fully mixed in. Transfer to a bowl and whisk in the cream. Season to taste with salt and pepper. Drizzle over the beef slices and sprinkle with capers.

# TUNA CARPACCIO

3/4 lb. sashimi-quality tuna
1 cup basil leaves
1 garlic clove
1/3 cup extra virgin olive oil
1 teaspoon lemon juice

SERVES 4

PLACE the tuna in the freezer for about half an hour, or until it is firm. Using a sharp knife or a mandolin, cut the tuna into paper-thin slices. Cover four serving plates with the slices in a thin even layer.

BLANCH the basil leaves in salted boiling water for 10 seconds, then drain well. Place the leaves in a food processor or blender with the garlic, olive oil and lemon juice and mix well. Season with salt and pepper. Drizzle over the tuna and serve with bread.

TUNA CARPACCIO

# AFFETTATI MISTI

USE A GOOD SELECTION OF MEATS THAT CONTRAST IN FLAVOR AND APPEARANCE, BUT STICK TO JUST ONE TYPE OF FRUIT. INSTEAD OF MELON OR FIGS YOU COULD TRY THIN SLICES OF PEAR. CIPOLLINE AGRODOLCE CAN BE REPLACED BY PICKLED ONIONS, AND BLACK OLIVES INSTEAD OF GREEN ARE FINE.

8 slices mortadella
8 slices prosciutto
12 slices coppa
15 slices bresaola (air-dried beef)
15–20 slices casalinga-type (coarse) salami or 15–20 slices finocchiona (Tuscan or Florentine-type salami with fennel seeds)
young arugula leaves
lemon wedges
extra virgin olive oil
quartered fresh figs or slices of honeydew melon or cantaloupe
cipolline agrodolce (page 26)
green olives
cetriolini (small pickles)
"country-style" bread, such as ciabatta

SERVES 6

ARRANGE the meat around a large platter. Vary the presentation by rolling up the mortadella, for instance, or folding large salami slices into a half-moon shape. Use the arugula as a bed for the coppa or bresaola.

PLACE the lemon wedges by the prosciutto and drizzle extra virgin olive oil over the bresaola. Arrange the figs or slices of melon next to the prosciutto.

SERVE the cipolline, olives and cetriolini separately in bowls, and provide plenty of sliced bread. Also have on hand the bottle of extra virgin olive oil and plenty of black pepper.

Italian cured meat is very much regionally based, with each area making its own affettati misti. If you are putting together an antipasti platter, you can match up local products—try Parma ham with mortadella and a local Bolognese salami. For the best flavor, slice large salami and meat very thinly.

# BROILED TOMATOES

4 large ripe tomatoes
2 garlic cloves, crushed
1/4 cup olive oil
1 tablespoon chopped parsley

SERVES 4

CUT the tomatoes in half horizontally. Place them on a baking sheet, skin side up, and broil them for 2 minutes, then turn. Mix together the garlic, olive oil and parsley and drizzle over the tomatoes. Season with salt and pepper.

PLACE the tomatoes back under the broiler and cook for 6 minutes or until cooked. Serve hot or warm.

BROILED TOMATOES

# PINZIMONIO

8 scallions
4 small artichokes
2 baby fennel bulbs
8 celery stalks
8 radishes
8 baby carrots
1 red pepper
1 cup extra virgin olive oil

SERVES 4

TRIM the scallions at both ends and peel off any loose bits of skin. If the artichokes are the type you can eat raw, then cut them in half and remove the chokes; if not, boil them until they are tender and then cut them in half and remove the chokes. Trim the tops of the fennel and cut them into quarters. Trim the celery and radishes. Peel or rub the skin off the carrots but leave any greenery attached. Cut the red pepper into strips, trimming off any membrane and scraping out the seeds.

PUT 1/4 cup of olive oil into each of four small dishes and add a pinch of salt and a grinding of pepper to each. Arrange the vegetables on a large platter. Give each person a bowl of olive oil of their own to dip vegetables into.

# BAGNA CAODA

A FONDUE BOWL AND BURNER WORKS VERY WELL TO HEAT THE BAGNA CAODA (THE NAME MEANS LITERALLY "HOT BATH"). THIS PIEMONTESE SPECIALTY IS A POPULAR GROUP MEAL ALL YEAR ROUND, BUT IS ESPECIALLY ASSOCIATED WITH THE VIBRANT ATMOSPHERE OF THE GRAPE HARVEST.

40 pieces assorted raw vegetables
  (carrots, celery, scallions, fennel
  or cauliflower florets)
3/4 cup olive oil
6 garlic cloves, crushed
4 oz. anchovy fillets, finely ground
6 tablespoons butter
"country-style" bread, such as
  ciabatta

SERVES 4

TRIM, wash and dry the vegetables and cut them into strips for dipping.

PUT the oil, garlic and anchovies in a saucepan and place over moderately low heat. Cook gently, stirring once or twice, until the anchovies dissolve. Do not let the garlic brown. Add the butter and leave over low heat until it has melted. Season with pepper.

TRANSFER the sauce to a heated flameproof bowl and keep warm at the table, e.g. by placing on a food warmer. Serve the vegetables and bread arranged on a platter. Guests dip their choice of vegetable into the bagna caôda and use a piece of bread to catch any stray drips.

BAGNA CAODA

# CAPONATA

2 lb. eggplants
1/2 tablespoon salt
3/4 cup olive oil
1 large onion, roughly chopped
2 celery stalks, sliced
1 small red pepper, cut into short
  strips
2 tablespoons pine nuts
14 oz. can chopped tomatoes
4 tablespoons red wine vinegar
1 tablespoon sugar
2 tablespoons capers, rinsed and
  chopped if large
24 green olives, pitted and halved
4 tablespoons finely chopped
  parsley

SERVES 6

CUT the eggplant into 1-inch cubes and place in layers in a colander, sprinkling each layer with salt as you go. Leave to drain for 30 minutes. Rinse and squeeze the eggplant dry with your hands.

HEAT 1/3 cup of the oil in a large frying pan. Brown the eggplant in batches over high heat, adding oil as needed. Drain on paper towels.

ADD MORE oil to the pan, reduce the heat and cook the onion and celery for 5 minutes, or until softened but not brown. Add the red pepper and pine nuts and cook for 2 minutes. Spoon off any excess oil and add the tomatoes and 1/4 cup water. Simmer for 10 minutes or until the mixture is quite dry. Season well with black pepper.

ADD the vinegar, sugar, capers and olives and cook for 2–3 minutes over low heat. Add the eggplant, cook for another 5–6 minutes, then remove from the heat and leave to cool. Taste for pepper and toss the parsley through to serve.

Olive oil and red wine vinegar are found on every restaurant table in Italy for dressing your salad, as well as being used together in many dishes. The acidity of the wine vinegar cuts through the oiliness.

# PANZANELLA

1 garlic clove, cut in half
1 loaf "country-style" bread, such as
  ciabatta
6 ripe tomatoes
1 small yellow pepper
1/2 cucumber, peeled
1/2 white salad onion
2 tablespoons shredded basil
  leaves
1/3 cup olive oil
2 tablespoons red wine vinegar

SERVES 4

RUB the cut side of the garlic around the inside of a large salad bowl. Remove the crust from the bread and cut it into cubes. Put the bread in the bowl and sprinkle it with enough cold water to moisten.

CUT the tomatoes, pepper and cucumber into chunks and dice the onion. Add the vegetables to the bread with the basil and then sprinkle with the olive oil and vinegar. Toss well and leave for 30 minutes before serving.

PANZANELLA

# CHAR-GRILLED EGGPLANT SALAD

2 large eggplants, thinly sliced
 lengthwise
2 garlic cloves, crushed
1/2 cup extra virgin olive oil
juice of 1 small lemon
1/2 red chile, finely chopped
1/4 cup basil or mint leaves, roughly
 chopped

SERVES 4

HEAT a skillet on the stove and cook the eggplant, a few slices at a time, over moderately high heat, turning once until it is soft and cooked. (There is no need to add oil or to salt the eggplant first.) As you remove the eggplant slices from the skillet, put them on a plate on top of each other— this helps them to steam a little and soften further.

IF you do not have a skillet, preheat the oven to 400°F. Drizzle a couple of tablespoons of olive oil over a baking sheet and place the eggplant slices on top. Drizzle with a little more oil and cook the eggplant until soft.

MIX TOGETHER the garlic, olive oil, lemon juice, chile and herbs. (If you have baked the eggplant, use a little less oil.) Place the eggplant in a flat dish and pour over the marinade. Mix briefly without breaking up the eggplant and marinate for at least 30 minutes before serving.

# CHAR-GRILLED VEGETABLE SALAD

4 long thin eggplants
4 zucchinis
4 plum tomatoes
1 small red pepper
1 small green pepper
1 small yellow pepper
1/4 cup olive oil
2 garlic cloves, halved

DRESSING
1/4 cup extra virgin olive oil
1 tablespoon balsamic vinegar
1 garlic clove, crushed
3 tablespoons chopped parsley
1/4 teaspoon superfine sugar

SERVES 4

SLICE the eggplants and zucchinis diagonally into 1/2-inch thick pieces. Halve the tomatoes lengthwise and slice the peppers into short strips. Place all the vegetables in a bowl and add the olive oil and the garlic. Toss well.

PREHEAT a skillet and brush with oil. Cook the eggplant and zucchini for 2–4 minutes on each side, or until browned. Transfer to a shallow serving dish. Cook the tomatoes and peppers for 1–2 minutes on each side, or until the peppers start to smell sweet and their skins blister. Transfer to the serving dish and set aside to cool.

TO MAKE the dressing, mix together all the ingredients and then season. Drizzle the dressing over the vegetables and toss lightly. Serve at room temperature.

CHAR-GRILLED
VEGETABLE SALAD

# INSALATA CAPRESE

INSALATA CAPRESE IS TRADITIONALLY SERVED WITH NO OTHER DRESSING THAN A DRIZZLE OF EXTRA VIRGIN OLIVE OIL. HOWEVER, IF YOU'RE NOT ABSOLUTELY CONFIDENT THAT YOUR TOMATOES HAVE THE BEST FLAVOR, A LITTLE BALSAMIC VINEGAR WILL HELP THEM ALONG.

6 ripe plum tomatoes
3–4 balls mozzarella
2 tablespoons extra virgin olive oil
15 young basil leaves
1/2 teaspoon balsamic vinegar
(optional)

SERVES 4

SLICE the tomatoes, pouring off any excess juice, and cut the mozzarella into slices of a similar thickness.

ARRANGE alternating rows of tomato and mozzarella on a serving plate. Sprinkle with salt and pepper and drizzle the olive oil over the top. Tear the basil leaves into pieces and scatter over the oil. To serve, take to the table and sprinkle with the balsamic vinegar, if you're using it.

Caprese is also known as *insalata tricolore*—the mozzarella, ripe tomatoes and basil reflect the colors of the Italian flag.

# INSALATA DI RINFORZO

1/2 lb. carrots
11/4 cups green beans
1/2 red onion
21/2 cups white wine vinegar
1 tablespoon sea salt
1 tablespoon sugar
1 bay leaf
21/2 cups cauliflower florets

DRESSING
1/3 cup extra virgin olive oil
2 tablespoons lemon juice
1 tablespoon finely chopped parsley
1 tablespoon chopped capers
1 garlic clove, halved

4 anchovy fillets, halved lengthwise
1/2 cup small black olives (Niçoise
or Ligurian)
1 tablespoon roughly chopped
parsley
1–2 tablespoons extra virgin olive oil

SERVES 4

CUT the carrots into lengths the size of your little finger, slice the beans into similar lengths and slice the onion into rings.

COMBINE the vinegar, salt, sugar and bay leaf in a saucepan with 2 cups water and bring to a boil. Cook the carrots until crisply tender. Transfer to a bowl with a slotted spoon. Add beans to the saucepan and cook until similarly done. Add to the carrots in the bowl. Add the onions and cauliflower to the saucepan and cook until the cauliflower just starts to soften. Drain, add to the bowl and cool.

TO MAKE the dressing, mix together the olive oil, lemon juice, parsley, capers and garlic and season well. Pour over the cooled vegetables and toss gently. The salad can be stored in an airtight container for up to 2 weeks at this stage.

TO SERVE toss through the anchovy fillets, olives, parsley and oil.

INSALATA DI RINFORZO

PARMIGIANO REGGIANO The Co-op, Casearia Castelnovese uses milk from all over Modena to make its Parmigiano Reggiano. The milk is brought to the cooperative by each farm, then rested so the cream comes to the top and can be skimmed off. Two hundred and sixty-four gallons of both skimmed and some unskimmed milk are then poured into one of the co-op's huge copper cauldrons, rennet is added

# CHEESE

AS WELL AS MAKING FAMOUS CHEESES LIKE PARMIGIANO REGGIANO OR MOZZARELLA, ITALIAN CHEESEMAKERS CREATE HUNDREDS OF REGIONAL CHEESES, FRESH AND AGED, AND MANY THAT ARE NEVER FOUND OUTSIDE ITALY.

The history of cheese in Italy is very closely related to the country's varied geography. The rich mountainous pastures of the North produce hundreds of cheeses like fontina, Gorgonzola, mascarpone, Asiago, *grana padano* and Taleggio. In the Center, Emilia-Romagna is the home of Parmigiano Reggiano (Parmesan), perhaps Italy's most famous cheese. Tuscany and Umbria produce fresh pecorinos, while the sparser and hotter South is more suited

to farming sheep and goats than cows. These sheep and goats cheeses are usually harder than the French *chèvre chaud* and are even suitable for grating, though you can also find some soft, fresh cheeses like sheeps ricotta. The South is also the home of *pasta filata*, cheeses made from stretched out curds like mozzarella, *scamorza*, *caciocavallo* and provolone.

## DENOMINAZIONE DI ORIGINE CONTROLLATA

Many of the traditional methods for making cheese are safeguarded by *consorzi* (cooperatives), which impose their own rules for production to ensure that their cheeses are made to the highest quality, using the best milk in each area. The rules for production can include methods passed down through centuries, such as milking Parmesan cows by hand, and this explains the often higher cost of these cheeses. Cheeses from these cooperatives are usually awarded a DOC (*Denominazione di Origine Controllata*) rating in the form of a brand or stamp on the rind.

When a crust begins to form, the cheese is wrapped in a sheet of plastic that imprints the brand number and Parmigiano Reggiano stamp onto its rind, while a metal band over the top holds the shape. After being branded, the cheeses are placed in saline for three days, then arranged on wooden shelves to dry. The drying process takes place in a huge room called a cathedral, where the cheeses are left to mature for up to

**TALEGGIO** aged in caves, this cheese has a rich, soft texture with tiny holes. Buy fresh, as it gets stronger and more acidic as it ages. A delicious table cheese.

**ASIAGO** made in the Veneto, Asiago comes in two types: a whole-milk one with a sweet flavor, and Asiago d'Allevo, a skimmed-milk one matured slowly with a sharper flavor.

**GRANA PADANO** tastes like and is made in a similar way to Parmigiano Reggiano, but unlike Parmigiano, it can be produced in areas outside of Emilia-Romagna. Eaten young or grated when aged.

**MOZZARELLA** a fresh cheese made from buffalo or cows milk (*fior di latte*). *Mozzata* means tearing, and the curds are torn, then shaped in hot water. Fresh mozzarella is perfectly white.

**BEL PAESE** Italy's first truly commercialized cheese, Bel Paese is soft with a high fat content. It melts very well when cooked and is also eaten as a table cheese.

**PARMIGIANO REGGIANO** this great cheese is sold at different ages for different uses. Young ones are eaten as a table cheese and older ones are grated and used in cooking.

**BURRINO** this *pasta filata* cheese encloses a ball of butter. When the pear-shaped ball is broken open, the butter is spread on bread and the cheese eaten in slices.

**CACIOTTA** meaning 'small cheese', caciotta is a generic name for many small, mostly farm-produced, cheeses. They can be young or aged, and are made in a variety of styles.

**TARTUFO** truffled cheese is a specialty of Umbria. The truffles through them give an earthy flavor to the cheeses.

**FONTINA** made in the Valle d'Aosta in the North, this semi-soft and sweet-flavored cheese melts beautifully. Usually used in cooking, it can also be eaten as a table cheese.

**PECORINO** this is an Umbrian variety of a cheese that is made all over Italy. A sheeps milk cheese, pecorino is used as a table cheese and for cooking. The rind darkens as it ripens.

**MONTASIO** a cows milk cheese from the Veneto that can be eaten fresh straight after it is made, or after it has been aged for 4–12 months. It goes well with polenta.

# MINESTRONE ALLA GENOVESE

JUST ABOUT EVERY REGION OF ITALY HAS ITS OWN MINESTRONE. THIS VERSION HAS A SPOONFUL OF PESTO STIRRED THROUGH AT THE END; OTHERS HAVE RICE OR POTATOES INSTEAD OF PASTA, TO THICKEN. FOR *MINESTRONE ALLA MILANESE*, ADD 1 CUP ARBORIO RICE INSTEAD OF THE PASTA.

1 cup dried borlotti beans
1/4 cup lard or butter
1 large onion, finely chopped
1 garlic clove, finely chopped
1/4 cup parsley, finely chopped
2 sage leaves
4 oz. pancetta, cubed
2 celery stalks, halved then sliced
2 carrots, sliced
3 potatoes, peeled but left whole
1 teaspoon tomato paste
14 oz. can chopped tomatoes
8 basil leaves
12 cups chicken or vegetable stock
2 zucchinis, sliced
1 1/2 cups shelled peas
1 cup green beans, cut into
   1 1/2-inch lengths
1/4 cabbage, shredded
1 3/4 cups ditalini, avemarie or other
   small pasta
1 batch pesto (page 285)
grated Parmesan

SERVES 6

PUT the dried beans in a large bowl, cover with cold water and leave to soak overnight. Drain and rinse under cold water.

TO MAKE the *soffritto*, melt the lard in a large saucepan and add the onion, garlic, parsley, sage and pancetta. Cook over low heat, stirring once or twice, for about 10 minutes, or until the onion is soft and golden.

ADD the celery, carrots and potatoes and cook for 5 minutes. Stir in the tomato paste, tomatoes, basil and borlotti beans. Season with plenty of pepper. Add the stock and bring slowly to a boil. Cover and leave to simmer for 2 hours, stirring once or twice.

IF the potatoes haven't already broken up, roughly break them up with a fork against the side of the saucepan. Taste for seasoning and add the zucchini, peas, green beans, cabbage and pasta. Simmer until the pasta is *al dente*. Serve with a dollop of pesto and the Parmesan.

The soup base is called a *soffritto*, which means "underfried". The slow-cooked mixture of onion, garlic, pancetta and herbs gives the soup its base flavor. Other types of minestrone simmer the vegetables in stock without frying them first, then add olive oil towards the end for flavor.

and the milk heated to form curds. After cutting the curds into tiny pieces, the mixture is heated further until the curds collect together again at the bottom of the cauldron. Then they are scooped up into a linen cloth. Extremely heavy, the curds must be cut into two cheeses, each one wrapped in its own cloth to drain. The new cheeses are lifted into white molds to be shaped, then turned every few hours for one day.

### MILK FOR CHEESE

Italian cheeses can be made from cows, buffalos, goats and sheeps milk. Cows milk is used more in the North, while buffaloes are farmed just around Naples and almost all the milk is used for *mozzarella di bufala* (although most mozzarella production in Italy is now in fact made with cheaper cows milk). Goat and sheep cheeses are increasingly popular, and most are produced in Tuscany, Umbria and the South. Both pasteurized and unpasteurized cheeses are made in Italy, with unpasteurized or partly unpasteurized cheeses, such as *caciocavallo* and provolone, being known as *pasta cruda* and continuing to develop as they age.

### HARD AND SOFT CHEESES

Italian cheeses are also divided into hard and soft cheeses. Hard cheeses (*formaggi a pasta dura*) have a water content of less than 40 percent and include cheeses used mainly for cooking like *grana padano* and pecorino. Soft cheeses (*formaggi a pasta molle*) have a water content of more than 40 percent and are best eaten as soon as possible after being made. They include cheeses like mascarpone and mozzarella, which should be eaten the day they are made.

Unlike French cheeses, Italian cheeses are more famous worldwide for their use in cooking than for being eaten as a separate cheese course. In Italy though, cheeses are often eaten at every course, in cooking and as table cheeses. Cooking cheeses are known as *formaggio per cucina* and perhaps the most famous is Parmigiano Reggiano, rarely eaten as part of a cheese platter outside of Italy. Table cheeses are known as *formaggio da tavola* and in Italy both fresh and hard cheeses are eaten on their own. A piece of Parmigiano Reggiano eaten with just a fresh fig or thinly sliced prosciutto; a ball of fresh buffalo mozzarella with some very ripe tomatoes and basil; or a tub of fresh ricotta sweetened with a little honey are some of the simplest and most delicious treats to be had in Italian cuisine.

a year, while being turned and cleaned every few days by robots. There are strict rules covering the quality of the cheeses, and before they can be sold they are tested by experts, who tap each cheese to listen for "faults" inside. A faulty cheese is marked with a cross and sold young. If a cheese passes the test, it can be branded as DOC. Parmesan are never cut, but instead are cracked open by pushing small knives into the rind.

PROVOLONE a *pasta filata* cows milk cheese shaped into cylinders and pear shapes. It can be eaten young and sweet, or matured to give a sharper flavor. Eaten plain and used in cooking.

ROBIOLA this soft cheese is a specialty of Piemonte and Lombardia and there are several versions. It can be eaten as a table cheese and small versions are called robioline.

CACIOCAVALLO this southern cheese is molded into a pear shape, then dried. Eaten as a table or melting cheese when young, and grated over dishes like a Parmesan when aged.

CRESCENZA a white, soft cheese from Lombardia that must be eaten very fresh. It has a rich but delicate flavor and is most often used in cooking.

CAPRINO a subtly flavored goats cheese eaten fresh or left to marinate in olive oil and vinegar, either plain or with flavorings. There is also an aged version with a yellower skin.

RICOTTA a by-product of cheesemaking, this fresh, sweet-flavored cheese is created by skimming off milk solids left in the whey. It can be eaten on its own or used to fill pastas or in desserts.

RICOTTA SALATA a salted dried cheese that has a firmer texture than ordinary ricotta. It is sometimes sold from a tub of wheat husks. Can be grated or eaten in chunks.

RICOTTA AL FORNO small rounds of ricotta that have been baked to give them a caramelized edge and a sweet flavor. It can be eaten with pasta or bread.

DOLCELATTE a soft and mild blue cheese like Gorgonzola, but with a more delicate flavor. A good melting and table cheese that goes very well with pasta or polenta.

GORGONZOLA a pungent blue cheese originating in Gorgonzola in Lombardia. A good eating cheese, but also melts well in gnocchi, sauces and risottos.

SCAMORZA a stretched curd cheese similar to provolone and used for cooking or eaten fresh. The smoked version shown here is the most popular and is often used in pasta sauces.

MASCARPONE made by coagulating curds from cream, this very creamy cheese is used for cooking rather than eating, and is an essential ingredient in tiramisù and some pasta dishes.

# ZUPPA DI PESCE

FOR A COUNTRY WHERE ALMOST EVERY REGION HAS A SEA COAST, IT IS HARDLY SURPRISING THAT ITALY HAS ALMOST AS MANY VERSIONS OF THIS SOUP AS THERE ARE FISH IN THE SEA. THE RECIPE INCLUDES SUGGESTIONS FOR FISH VARIETIES, BUT ASK YOUR FISHMONGER WHAT'S BEST ON THE DAY.

Score a criss-cross pattern into the squid to make it curl.

### FISH STOCK

10 oz. firm white fish fillets, such as monkfish, red mullet or cod, skin removed, cut into large cubes, bones reserved
12 shrimp
1 small onion, roughly chopped
1 carrot, roughly chopped
1/4 cup parsley

1/2 lb. squid tubes
4 tablespoons olive oil
1 onion, finely chopped
1 celery stalk, finely chopped
1 carrot, finely chopped
2 garlic cloves, finely chopped
pinch of cayenne pepper
1 fennel bulb, trimmed and thinly sliced
1/2 cup dry white wine
14 oz. can chopped tomatoes
1/2 lb. scallops, cleaned

### CROSTINI

3 tablespoons extra virgin olive oil
2 garlic cloves, crushed
4 slices "country-style" bread, such as ciabatta

SERVES 4

TO MAKE the fish stock, rinse the fish bones in cold water, removing any blood or innards. Peel and devein the shrimp and put the fish bones and shrimp shells in a large saucepan with just enough water to cover. Bring slowly to a simmer, skimming any froth from the surface. Add the onion, carrot and the stems from the parsley, then simmer gently for 20 minutes. Strain through a fine colander and measure 6 cups stock. If there is less than this, add a little water; if there is more than this, put the strained stock back into the saucepan and simmer until reduced to 6 cups.

LIE the squid out flat, skin side up, and score a criss-cross pattern into the flesh, being careful not to cut all the way through. Slice diagonally into bite-sized strips.

HEAT the oil in a large saucepan and cook the onion, celery, carrot, garlic and roughly chopped parsley over moderately low heat for 5–6 minutes, or until softened but not browned.

ADD the cayenne pepper and season well. Stir in the fennel and cook for 2–3 minutes. Add the white wine, increase the heat and cook until it has been absorbed. Stir in the tomatoes, then add the fish stock and bring to a boil. Reduce the heat and simmer for 20 minutes.

ADD the squid to the pan with the fish pieces and simmer for 1 minute. Add the scallops and shrimp and simmer for another 2 minutes. Taste and add more seasoning if necessary.

TO MAKE the crostini, heat the olive oil and crushed garlic in a large frying pan over moderately low heat. Add the slices of bread and fry on both sides until golden. Place a slice of bread into each of four warmed serving bowls. Ladle the soup on top and serve immediately.

# LA RIBOLLITA

RIBOLLITA MEANS 'REBOILED' BECAUSE THIS TUSCAN BEAN SOUP IS BEST MADE A DAY IN ADVANCE TO LET THE FLAVORS DEVELOP, THEN REHEATED. IT SHOULD THEN BE THICK ENOUGH TO EAT WITH A FORK RATHER THAN A SPOON.

Make sure the cabbage stems are thoroughly softened before adding the other vegetables—this gives the cabbage a chance to really soak up the flavor of the *soffritto*.

4 tablespoons olive oil
1 onion, finely chopped
1 large carrot, finely chopped
3 celery stalks, finely chopped
2 large garlic cloves, crushed
3 cups cavolo nero or Savoy cabbage
1 zucchini, finely chopped
2 cups cooked cannellini or borlotti beans
14 oz. can tomatoes
3/4 cup red wine
4 cups chicken stock or water
3/4 cup stale "country-style" bread, such as ciabatta, crusts removed and broken into 1-inch cubes
drizzle of extra virgin olive oil

SERVES 4

TO MAKE the *soffritto*, pour the olive oil into a large saucepan and add the onion. Cook the onion gently—use this time to chop the carrot and celery and add them to the saucepan as you go along. Once you have added the garlic, leave to cook for a few minutes.

STRIP the leaves of the cavolo from the stems or cut away the thick stem of the Savoy. Wash and finely chop the stems and roughly chop the leaves. Add the cabbage stems and zucchini to the *soffritto* and cook, stirring occasionally, for 5 minutes, or until the vegetables have changed to an opaque color and soaked up some of the olive oil.

STIR in the beans and cook for 5 minutes more, then add the tomatoes and cook for another 5 minutes to reduce the liquid.

ADD the cabbage leaves and mix into the soup, stirring until just wilted. Add the wine and stock or water and gently simmer for 40 minutes.

ADD the bread to the saucepan (if the bread is very fresh, dry it out a little in the oven first to prevent it disintegrating into the soup). Mix briefly and remove the saucepan from the heat. Leave for 30 minutes. This rests the soup and allows the flavors to mingle. Serve hot but not boiling with a generous drizzle of extra virgin olive oil.

IF REHEATING the soup, make sure it comes to a boil but then remove it from the heat and leave to cool for 5 minutes. Serve in cold bowls. The soup should be warm, rather than piping hot.

# CHESTNUT, PANCETTA AND CABBAGE SOUP

1 1/3 cups cavolo nero or Savoy
   cabbage, roughly chopped
2 tablespoons olive oil
1 large onion, finely chopped
6 oz. pancetta, diced
3 garlic cloves, crushed
1/4 cup rosemary, chopped
2 cups cooked peeled chestnuts
1/2–2/3 cup red wine
drizzle of extra virgin olive oil

SERVES 4

COOK the cabbage in 6 cups boiling salted water for about 10 minutes. Drain, reserving the water. Rinse the cabbage in cold water if too hot to handle, and chop more finely.

HEAT the olive oil in a large saucepan and cook the onion and pancetta over moderately high heat until the onion is soft and the pancetta lightly browned. Add the garlic and rosemary and cook for a few minutes. Break up the chestnuts a little and add to the pan with the cabbage. Stir to infuse the flavors, season, then add the wine. Bring to a boil and cook for a couple of minutes. Finally add the cabbage water and simmer for 15 minutes.

PUREE HALF of the soup, leaving the remainder unpuréed to create a little texture. Serve hot with a drizzle of extra virgin olive oil over each bowl.

Spoleto town center.

Farro is a grain also known as "spelt". It was widely used by the Romans to make porridge, soups and, in its ground form, bread.

# MINESTRA DI FARRO

1 cup dried borlotti beans
2 tablespoons olive oil
1 small onion, thinly sliced
2 garlic cloves, crushed
6 cups chicken stock
8 mint leaves, roughly torn
1 1/3 cups farro (spelt)
1 cup Parmesan, grated
1 tablespoon finely chopped mint
4 teaspoons extra virgin olive oil

SERVES 4

SOAK the borlotti beans in cold water overnight. Drain and place in a large saucepan with plenty of cold water. Bring to a boil and simmer until tender (approximately 1 1/2 hours, depending on the age of the beans). Drain.

HEAT the olive oil in a large saucepan and cook the onion over low heat for 6 minutes, or until soft. Season. Add the garlic and cook without browning for 20–30 seconds. Add the stock and torn mint and bring to a boil.

STIR in the farro a little at a time so that the stock continues to boil, then lower the heat and simmer for 15 minutes. Add the borlotti beans and simmer for 30 minutes, or until the farro is tender and the soup thick. Purée half the soup. Return to the pan and stir in the Parmesan and chopped mint. Season and stir in 1/2–1 cup of hot water to give a spoonable consistency. Serve immediately, with a teaspoon of extra virgin olive oil stirred through each bowl.

MINESTRA DI FARRO

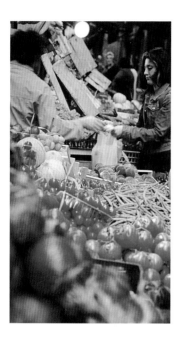

## ZUPPA DI VERDURE

3 tablespoons olive oil
2 small onions, chopped
2 celery stalks, chopped
4 small carrots, chopped
2 large potatoes, diced
2 leeks, sliced
2 garlic cloves, crushed
1 cup green beans
$2/3$ cup shelled green peas
7 cups vegetable stock
2 cups cavolo nero or cabbage
12 asparagus spears
6 slices "country-style" bread, such
   as ciabatta, crusts removed
1 garlic clove, cut in half
$1/3$ cup Parmesan, grated
drizzle of extra virgin olive oil

SERVES 6

HEAT the olive oil in a large saucepan and add the onions, celery, carrots, potatoes, leeks and crushed garlic. Cook over low heat for 5–6 minutes, or until the vegetables are softened but not browned. Season, add $1^1/2$ cups water and bring to a boil. Reduce to low heat and simmer for 30 minutes.

SLICE the beans diagonally and add to the saucepan. Add the peas and stock and simmer for another 30 minutes. Finely shred the cabbage and slice the asparagus diagonally. Add both to the saucepan and simmer for another 5 minutes.

TOAST the bread and, while still hot, rub on both sides with the cut edge of the halved garlic clove.

STIR the Parmesan into the soup and taste for seasoning. Place a slice of toast in the bottom of each bowl and ladle the soup over the top. Drizzle with a little olive oil and serve at once.

## PAPPA AL POMODORO

PAPPA AL POMODORO IS A TUSCAN SOUP MADE, AS SO MANY GREAT ITALIAN DISHES ARE, TO USE UP LEFTOVERS—IN THIS CASE BREAD AND TOMATOES. *PAPPA* MEANS "MUSH" AND THAT IS THE SOUP'S CONSISTENCY. SIMILAR DISHES ARE CALLED *PANCOTTO* AND *AQUACOTTA*, "COOKED WATER".

2 tablespoons olive oil
3 garlic cloves, crushed
1 white onion, finely chopped
2 lb. ripe tomatoes, peeled and
   finely chopped
2 thick slices stale "country-style"
   bread, such as ciabatta, crusts
   removed
$3^1/3$ cups hot chicken stock
20 basil leaves, shredded
drizzle of extra virgin olive oil

SERVES 4

HEAT the olive oil in a large saucepan. Add the garlic and onion and cook over low heat for 6–8 minutes, or until softened but not browned. Add the tomatoes and season. Cover and simmer for 30 minutes. Break the bread into pieces and add to the saucepan. Simmer, stirring once or twice, for 5 minutes.

GRADUALLY stir in the stock. Cook, stirring, until the bread has broken down and the soup is thick. Remove from the heat and add the basil. Cover and leave for 1 hour. Serve at room temperature or reheat. Drizzle extra virgin olive oil into each bowl before serving.

PAPPA AL POMODORO

# ARTICHOKE FRITTATA

ALMOST AN OMELET, BUT FLASHED UNDER THE BROILER TO FINISH OFF THE COOKING, THE FRITTATA VARIES FROM THIN AND PANCAKE-LIKE, TO THICKER, WITH A GOLDEN CRUST AND CREAMY CENTER. IT IS A FAVORITE THROUGHOUT ITALY, BUT THE ARTICHOKE FRITTATA IS A SPECIALTY OF TRENTINO.

1 cup fava beans, fresh or frozen
1 onion
14 oz. can artichoke hearts, drained
3 tablespoons olive oil
6 eggs
2 tablespoons chopped parsley
1/2 cup pecorino, grated
pinch of nutmeg

SERVES 4

BRING a small saucepan of water to a boil and add a large pinch of salt and the fava beans. Boil for 2 minutes, then drain and rinse under cold water. Peel off the skins from the beans.

HALVE the onion and slice thinly. Cut the artichoke hearts from bottom to top into slices about 1/4 inch wide. Discard any slices that contain the tough central choke.

HEAT the oil in a 12-inch frying pan and fry the onion over low heat for 6–8 minutes, without allowing it to brown. Add the artichoke slices and cook for 1–2 minutes. Stir in the fava beans.

PREHEAT the broiler. Lightly beat together the eggs, parsley, pecorino and nutmeg and season well with salt and pepper. Pour into the frying pan and cook over low heat until three-quarters set, shaking the pan often to stop the frittata sticking.

FINISH the top off under the broiler and leave to cool before serving in wedges.

Preparing artichokes by hand at the Rialto market in Venice.

# RED PEPPER AND ZUCCHINI FRITTATA

1 tablespooon olive oil
1 onion, sliced
1 red pepper, sliced
2 zucchinis, sliced
6 eggs
1 tablespoon chopped basil
1/2 cup Parmesan, grated

SERVES 4

HEAT the olive oil in a 12-inch frying pan and cook the onion until soft. Add the red pepper and zucchini and fry until soft. Preheat the broiler.

LIGHTLY beat the eggs, basil and Parmesan and season well. Pour into frying pan and cook over low heat until three-quarters set, shaking the pan to stop the frittata from sticking. Finish the top off under the broiler and leave to cool before serving in wedges.

The zucchini is one of Italy's favorite vegetables. In the north it is baked in béchamel, in the south fried with tomatoes and basil. These long ones are from Sicily.

# OMELET WITH FRESH HERBS AND PARMESAN

1 tablespoon butter
1¹/2 tablespoons olive oil
6 eggs
2 tablespoons finely chopped mixed
   basil, parsley and chives
1¹/3 tablespoons Parmesan
   shavings

SERVES 2

HEAT the butter and oil in a small frying pan. Beat the eggs and stir in the herbs. Season well.

POUR the eggs into the frying pan and cook gently over high heat, pulling the mixture in from the sides until it begins to set in small, fluffy clumps. Reduce the heat and shake the pan from side to side to prevent the omelet sticking.

WHEN the omelet is almost set but still soft on the surface, scatter the Parmesan onto one half and fold the other half over to encase it. Cook for another 10–12 seconds, shaking the pan once or twice. Slide onto a warm plate and serve at once.

ZUCCHINI AND
PARMESAN OMELET

# ZUCCHINI AND PARMESAN OMELET

¹/2 tablespoon butter
1 tablespoon olive oil
1 small zucchini, sliced
1 small leek, white part only, sliced
small pinch of nutmeg
¹/2 teaspoon finely chopped basil

1 tablespoon butter
1¹/2 tablespoons olive oil
6 eggs
1¹/3 tablespoons Parmesan shavings

SERVES 2

HEAT the butter and olive oil in a small frying pan. Gently fry the zucchini and leek for 5–6 minutes, or until golden. Season with salt, pepper and the nutmeg, stir in the basil and remove from the pan.

MAKE the omelet as above (without the herbs). Spoon the zucchini and leek mix on top of the Parmesan, then fold the omelet over to encase it. Cook for another 10–12 seconds, shaking the pan once or twice. Slide onto a warm plate and serve at once.

MUSHROOM AND
FENNEL OMELET

# MUSHROOM AND FENNEL OMELET

2 tablespoons butter
1 cup button mushrooms, sliced
1 baby fennel bulb, thinly sliced
   (reserving the fronds)

1 tablespoon butter
1¹/2 tablespoons olive oil
6 eggs

SERVES 2

HEAT the butter in a small frying pan and cook the mushrooms and fennel for 4–5 minutes, until the fennel has softened and the mushrooms are lightly golden. Season and remove from the pan. Make the omelet as above, using 1¹/2 tablespoons of chopped fennel fronds instead of the herbs. Spoon the mushroom mix onto one half, then fold the omelet over. Cook for 10–12 seconds, shaking the pan once or twice. Slide onto a warm plate and serve at once.

# SUPPLI

WHEN THESE CROQUETTES ARE BITTEN INTO, THE MOZZARELLA PULLS OUT TO RESEMBLE STRANDS OF TELEPHONE WIRES, HENCE THE ITALIAN NAME FOR THIS DISH, *SUPPLI AL TELEFONO*. SUPPLI ARE EXCELLENT FOR USING UP LEFTOVER RISOTTO.

3 tablespoons butter
1 small onion, finely chopped
6 cups chicken stock
3³/₄ cups risotto rice (vialone nano, arborio or carnaroli)
³/₄ cup Parmesan, grated
2 eggs, beaten
9 basil leaves, torn in half
1 cup mozzarella, cut into 18 cubes (¹/₂ inch square)
1¹/₂ cups dried bread crumbs
oil for deep-frying

SERVES 6

MELT the butter in a large saucepan. Add the onion and cook over low heat for 3–4 minutes until softened but not browned. Heat the stock to a simmer in another saucepan.

ADD the rice to the onion and cook, stirring, for 1 minute to seal the rice. Add several ladles of the hot stock, stirring continuously so that the rice cooks evenly. Keep adding enough stock to just cover the rice, stirring frequently. Continue in this way for 20 minutes, or until the rice is creamy on the outside but still *al dente*.

REMOVE from the heat and stir in the Parmesan and eggs. Season with salt and pepper. Spread out on a large baking sheet to cool completely.

DIVIDE the rice into 18 portions. Take one portion in the palm of your hand and place a piece of basil and a cube of mozzarella in the center. Fold the rice over to encase the cheese and at the same time mold the croquette into an egg shape. Roll the croquette in bread crumbs and place on a baking sheet while you make the rest.

HEAT enough oil in a deep-fat fryer or deep frying pan to fully cover the croquettes. Heat the oil to 350°F, or until a piece of bread fries golden brown in 15 seconds when dropped in the oil. Deep-fry the suppli in batches, without crowding, for about 4 minutes, or until evenly golden brown. Drain on paper towels and serve at once, as they are or with tomato sauce.

Shaping the suppli takes a little practice but, if the rice is the right consistency, it is fairly easy. Make sure the basil and mozzarella filling is fully enclosed so it doesn't spill out when the suppli are fried.

The risotto made for the arancini must be thick enough for the balls to hold their shape while they are being fried.

# ARANCINI

ARANCINI—THE NAME MEANS "LITTLE ORANGES"—ARE A SPECIALTY OF SICILY. THE SAFFRON RISOTTO IS TRADITIONAL. IF YOU CAN FIND IT, USE VIALONE NANO OR ANOTHER SEMI-FINE RICE—THE GLUTINOUS TEXTURE KEEPS THE GRAINS OF RICE TOGETHER.

large pinch of saffron threads
1 cup white wine
7 tablespoons butter
1 onion, finely chopped
1 large garlic clove, crushed
3 cups chicken stock
2 tablespoons thyme
1 cup risotto rice (vialone nano, arborio or carnaroli)
1/2 cup Parmesan, grated

2/3 cup mozzarella or fontina, cut into cubes
3/4 cup dried bread crumbs
oil for deep-frying

MAKES 20

LEAVE the saffron to soak in the wine while you prepare the risotto. Melt the butter in a large saucepan. Add the onion and garlic and cook over low heat for 3–4 minutes until softened but not browned. Heat the stock to a simmer in another saucepan.

ADD the thyme and rice to the onion and cook, stirring, for 1 minute to seal the rice. Add the wine and saffron and stir until the wine is all absorbed. Add several ladles of the hot stock, stirring continuously so that the rice cooks evenly. Keep adding enough stock to just cover the rice, stirring frequently. Continue in this way for 20 minutes, or until the rice is creamy.

FOR ARANCINI it is not so essential to keep the rice al dente. Add more water or chicken stock if the rice is not fully cooked. Make sure all this liquid is absorbed. Remove from the heat and stir in the Parmesan, then spread out onto a baking sheet covered with plastic wrap. Leave to cool and, if possible, leave in the fridge overnight.

TO MAKE the arancini, roll a small amount of risotto into a walnut-sized ball. Press a hole in the middle with your thumb, place a small piece of cheese inside and press the risotto around it to enclose in a ball. Repeat with the rest of the risotto. Roll each ball in the bread crumbs, pressing down to coat well.

HEAT enough oil in a deep-fat fryer or deep frying pan to fully cover the arancini. Heat the oil to 350°F, or until a piece of bread fries golden brown in 15 seconds when dropped in the oil. Deep-fry the arancini in batches, without crowding, for 3–4 minutes. Drain on paper towels and leave for a couple of minutes before eating. Serve hot or at room temperature.

Ravida Estate in Menfi, Sicily.

# PIZZA RUSTICA

THE NAME IS MISLEADING, BECAUSE PIZZA RUSTICA IS A PIE, NOT A PIZZA. THIS MEDIEVAL RECIPE IS UNUSUAL IN ITS COMBINATION OF A SWEET PASTRY CASE WITH A SAVORY FILLING AND, LIKE MANY RICH PIES, PROBABLY BEGAN ITS LIFE AS A CELEBRATION DISH FOR COUNTRY FESTIVALS.

PASTRY
1³/₄ cups all-purpose flour
1/2 teaspoon baking powder
pinch of salt
7 tablespoons butter, chilled
1/4 cup superfine sugar
1 egg yolk
1/4 cup light cream

FILLING
2 cups ricotta
3 eggs
2/3 cup pecorino Romano, grated
1 cup mozzarella, grated
4 oz. prosciutto, finely shredded
2 tablespoons finely chopped
  parsley

SERVES 6

TO MAKE the pastry, sift the flour, baking powder and salt into a large bowl. Cut the butter into cubes and add it to the bowl, then rub it in with your fingertips until the mixture resembles fine bread crumbs. Stir in the sugar.

MIX the egg yolk and cream together and pour this into the pastry mixture. Mix together and then knead once or twice until you have a soft dough. Refrigerate until needed.

TO MAKE the filling, mix the ricotta with the eggs, cheese, prosciutto and parsley and season well with pepper—you probably won't need to add any salt if the prosciutto is salty. Preheat the oven to 400°F.

CUT one third off the pastry and roll out remainder on a floured surface. Line an 8 x 1½ inch pie pan and trim off any excess pastry. Fill the pastry case with the filling and smooth the top.

ROLL OUT the remaining pastry and cover the pie. Trim the edges and bake for 20 minutes, then reduce the temperature to 350°F and bake for another 20 minutes, or until the filling is cooked through.

A metal pie pan will give your pastry a good crisp finish and help it brown nicely on the outside. When putting in the filling, make sure you squash out any air bubbles so the pie is packed full.

SEAFOOD

Skim the froth from the surface of the fish stock as it simmers.

Monkfish being skinned in the Vucciria market in Palermo.

# LIGURIAN FISH STEW

THE FISH SUGGESTIONS BELOW ARE MERELY A GUIDELINE. TAKE YOUR FISHMONGER'S ADVICE ON WHAT IS FRESH AND SEASONAL. ASK FOR THE FISH TO BE PREPARED AND CUT INTO LARGE CHUNKS, THOUGH YOU WILL NEED THE BONES FOR YOUR STOCK (THIS CAN BE MADE IN ADVANCE AND FROZEN).

FISH STOCK

$1/2$ lb. red mullet or red snapper, cut into chunks, bones removed and reserved

$1/2$ lb. cod, halibut or turbot, cut into chunks, bones removed and reserved

$1/2$ lb. monkfish, or any other firm white fish, cut into chunks, bones removed and reserved

6 large shrimp

1 small onion, roughly chopped

1 carrot, roughly chopped

$1/2$ cup flat-leaf parsley, roughly chopped, stems reserved

$1/2$ cup olive oil

1 red onion, halved and thinly sliced

1 large fennel bulb, thinly sliced

3 garlic cloves, thinly sliced

1lb 10 oz. can tomatoes

$1 1/4$ cups dry white vermouth or wine

large pinch of saffron threads

1 lb. waxy potatoes, quartered lengthwise

1 lb. mussels

SERVES 6

TO MAKE the fish stock, rinse the fish bones in cold water, removing any blood or innards. Peel and devein the shrimp and put the fish bones and shrimp shells in a large saucepan with just enough water to cover. Bring slowly to a simmer, skimming any froth from the surface. Add the onions, carrots and the stems from the parsley, then simmer gently for 20 minutes. Strain through a fine colander and measure 4 cups stock. If there is more, put the strained stock back into the saucepan and simmer until reduced to 4 cups.

TO MAKE the soup base, heat the olive oil in a large saucepan and cook the onions and fennel for about 5 minutes to soften. Add the garlic and tomatoes. Bring to a boil, then reduce the heat and simmer until the tomatoes have reduced to a thick sauce. Season and add $3/4$ cup of the vermouth, the saffron and potatoes. Increase the heat and boil for about 5 minutes, then add the fish stock, reduce the heat and simmer for 10 minutes, or until the potatoes are cooked.

SCRUB the mussels, pull off the beards and discard any that are broken or cracked or don't close when tapped on the work surface. Bring $1/3$ cup vermouth to a boil in another saucepan and add the mussels. Cover with a lid and cook quickly for about 1 minute, or until the shells have just opened (discard any that stay closed). Remove the mussels from their shells and place in a bowl. Pour over the remaining cooking liquid, discarding any sediment left in the saucepan.

ADD the shrimp and fish to the soup. Stir briefly, season and simmer for 5 minutes, until the fish is cooked. Add the mussels at the last moment to reheat. Remove from the heat and leave for at least 10 minutes before serving. Add the parsley and serve in hot bowls with crostini.

# CALAMARI RIPIENI

IF YOUR FISHMONGER HAS HAD A CATCH OF SMALL TENDER SQUID, SNAP THEM UP—THIS IS THE PERFECT RECIPE FOR THEM. IF YOU ARE HAVING TO MAKE DO WITH LARGER SQUID, YOU MIGHT NEED TO INCREASE THE COOKING TIME AND TAKE CARE THAT THE LIQUID DOES NOT EVAPORATE.

TOMATO SAUCE
1 lb. 10 oz. can tomatoes
1/3 cup red wine
2 tablespoons chopped flat-leaf
    parsley
pinch of sugar

STUFFING
1 1/4 lb. small squid
1/3 cup olive oil
1 small onion, finely chopped
1 small fennel bulb, finely chopped
2 garlic cloves, crushed
1/3 cup risotto rice (arborio, vialone
    nano or carnaroli)
large pinch of saffron threads
1/2 large red chile, chopped
1/2 cup white wine
2 tablespoons chopped flat-leaf
    parsley

SERVES 4

TO MAKE the sauce, put the tomatoes, red wine, parsley and sugar in a saucepan. Season and simmer until some of the liquid has evaporated.

TO MAKE the stuffing, prepare the squid by pulling the heads and tentacles out of the bodies with any innards. Cut the heads off below the eyes, just leaving the tentacles. Rinse the bodies, pulling out the transparent quills. Finely chop the tentacles and set aside with the squid bodies.

HEAT the oil in a saucepan, add the onion, fennel and garlic and cook gently for 10 minutes until soft. Add the rice, saffron, chile and chopped tentacles and cook for a few minutes, stirring frequently until the tentacles are opaque. Season and add the white wine and 6 tablespoons of the tomato sauce. Cook, stirring frequently, until the tomato and wine has reduced into the rice. Add 1/2 cup water and continue cooking until the rice is tender and all the liquid has been absorbed. Add the parsley and cool for a few minutes.

STUFF the squid with the filling, using a teaspoon to push the filling down to the bottom of the squid sacks. Do not overfill—you need to close the tops of the sacks easily without any filling squeezing out. Seal the tops with wooden cocktail picks.

PUT the remaining tomato sauce in a saucepan with 3/4 cup water. Cook for 2 minutes, then add the stuffed squid, cover the saucepan and simmer gently for 30–45 minutes, depending on the size of the squid, until soft and tender. Don't stir, or the filling may fall out (if a little filling does fall out it will merely add flavor to the sauce). Shake the pan a little if you are worried about sticking.

REMOVE the wooden cocktail picks and serve calamari with a salad and some bread.

Don't overfill the squid with stuffing or you'll find it leaking out into the tomato sauce.

Outdoor fish stall in Palermo, Sicily.

# SARDINE RIPIENE

TO MAKE A SARDINE DISH MEMORABLE THE FISH MUST BE REALLY FRESH. SARDINES, LIKE MACKEREL, DO NOT LAST LONG OUT OF THE WATER SO DON'T ATTEMPT THIS RECIPE IF THE FISH LOOK TIRED. THIS RECIPE WILL SERVE TWO AS A MAIN COURSE OR FOUR AS AN ANTIPASTO.

8 medium-sized sardines, heads
   removed, scaled and gutted
4 tablespoons olive oil
1 small onion, thinly sliced
1 fennel bulb, thinly sliced
$1/3$ cup pine nuts
4 tablespoons flat-leaf parsley,
   roughly chopped
$1/4$ cup fresh bread crumbs
1 large garlic clove, crushed
juice of $1/2$ lemon
extra virgin olive oil
lemon wedges

SERVES 4

BUTTERFLY the sardines by pressing your fingers on either side of the backbone and gently easing it away from the flesh, following the line of the bone as you go. Remove the bone, leaving the tail attached to the flesh for a more attractive look. The fresher the fish, the harder this is to do, so you might want to ask your fishmonger to butterfly the sardines for you. (Alternatively, use fillets and put them back together to form a whole after cooking, although the result will not be as attractive.) Rinse the fish in cold water and drain on paper towels. Leave in the fridge until needed.

PREHEAT the oven to 400°F. To prepare the stuffing, heat the olive oil in a frying pan and add the onion, fennel and pine nuts. Cook over moderately high heat until soft and light brown, stirring frequently. Mix 1 tablespoon of parsley with 1 tablespoon of bread crumbs and set aside. Add the garlic and remaining bread crumbs to the pan and cook for a few minutes more. Add the rest of the parsley, season and set aside.
(This mixture can be made in advance and kept in the fridge, but bring back to room temperature before cooking.)

DRIZZLE a little olive oil in a flameproof dish that will fit eight sardines in a single layer. Arrange the fish in the dish, skin side down, and season with salt and pepper. Spread the stuffing over the sardines and fold over to encase. (If you are using fillets, spread half with stuffing, then place the other fillets on top, skin side up, tail to tail like a sandwich.) Season again and sprinkle with the parsley and bread crumb mixture. Drizzle with the lemon juice and a little extra virgin olive oil.

BAKE FOR 5–10 minutes, depending on the size of the sardines. (If the filling is still warm the sardines will cook faster.) Serve immediately or at room temperature with lemon wedges.

# RED MULLET WITH FENNEL

2 fennel bulbs
2 tablespoons butter
2 tablespoons olive oil
1 onion, chopped
1 garlic clove, crushed
4 red mullet, gutted and scaled
extra virgin olive oil
1 lemon, quartered
2 teaspoons chopped oregano,
    or ¹/₂ teaspoon dried oregano
lemon wedges

SERVES 4

PREHEAT the oven to 375°F and grease a large shallow flameproof dish. Finely slice the fennel, keeping the green fronds.

HEAT the butter and olive oil in a large frying pan and gently cook the fennel, onion and garlic for 12–15 minutes until softened but not browned. Season with salt and pepper.

STUFF EACH fish with a heaped tablespoon of the fennel mixture and a quarter of the fennel fronds. Brush with extra virgin olive oil, squeeze a lemon quarter over each one and season well.

SPOON the remainder of the cooked fennel into the dish and sprinkle with half of the oregano. Arrange the fish, side by side, on top. Sprinkle the remaining oregano over the fish and cover the dish loosely with foil. Bake for 25 minutes, or until just cooked through. Serve with lemon wedges.

Brushing the fish with oil prevents the skin from drying out while it bakes and helps the seasoning to stick to the fish skin.

# BAKED SWORDFISH SICILIANA

FISHED MAINLY OFF THE COAST OF SICILY, SWORDFISH HAS A FIRM MEATY TEXTURE. WHILE MANY MORE DELICATE FISH WOULD BE OVERPOWERED BY THE STRONG MEDITERRANEAN FLAVORS OF THIS DISH, THE MORE ROBUST FLESH OF THE SWORDFISH CAN HOLD ITS OWN. YOU CAN ALSO USE TUNA.

¹/₃ cup olive oil
2 tablespoons lemon juice
2¹/₂ tablespoons finely chopped
    basil
4 swordfish steaks
¹/₂ cup pitted black olives, chopped
1 tablespoon baby capers
¹/₂ teaspoon finely chopped
    anchovies in olive oil
1 lb. tomatoes, peeled, seeded and
    chopped
2 tablespoons dried bread crumbs

SERVES 4

MIX half the olive oil with the lemon juice and 1 tablespoon of the basil. Season and pour into a shallow flameproof dish, large enough to hold the swordfish in a single layer. Arrange the swordfish in the dish and leave to marinate for 15 minutes, turning once. Preheat the oven to 450°F and preheat the broiler.

COMBINE the olives, capers, anchovies and tomatoes with the remaining olive oil and basil and season well. Spread over the swordfish and sprinkle the bread crumbs over the top. Bake for 20 minutes, or until the fish is just opaque. Finish off by placing briefly under the hot broiler until the bread crumbs are crisp. Serve with bread to soak up the juices.

BAKED SWORDFISH SICILIANA

Cod from Northern Europe was traditionally preserved in salt for consumption inland. Its popularity in Mediterranean countries is a legacy of meatless "humility" days observed by the Catholic Church.

TUNA WITH BEANS

# SALT COD FRITTERS

1/2 lb. salt cod
1 small onion, sliced
2 garlic cloves, sliced
1 bay leaf
1²/3 cups milk
1/3 cup dry white vermouth or white wine
1/2 lb. potatoes, chopped
2 tablespoons flat-leaf parsley, roughly chopped
pinch of nutmeg
1 egg yolk
1 tablespoon all-purpose flour, plus a little extra for dusting
2 cups oil for frying

SERVES 4

SOAK the salt cod in cold water for 24 hours, changing the water four times.

PUT the onion, garlic, bay leaf, milk and vermouth in a saucepan, season with pepper and bring to a boil. Add the salt cod, reduce the heat and simmer, covered, for 10–15 minutes until the fish is cooked and flakes away from the skin. Leave in the liquid until cool enough to handle. Meanwhile, boil the potatoes until tender, then drain and cool.

PLACE the fish on a board and flake the flesh away from the skin and bones. Put the flaked fish in a bowl and add the potatoes, parsley, nutmeg, egg yolk, flour and a little pepper. Mix well and taste for seasoning—you should not need to add any more salt. Leave in the fridge for 15 minutes and then roll into small balls and flatten slightly.

HEAT the oil in a frying pan. Dust the fritters with flour and fry in batches in the hot oil for 2 minutes on each side. Drain on paper towels and serve warm, perhaps with a tomato sauce.

# TUNA WITH BEANS

2 cups dried beans, such as cannellini
1 bay leaf
1 garlic clove
1/2 cup olive oil
1 small red onion, finely sliced
2 tablespoons finely chopped parsley
1 lb. can tuna in olive oil, drained

SERVES 4

SOAK the beans overnight in plenty of cold water. Rinse them and transfer to a very large saucepan. Cover with plenty of cold water and bring to a boil. Add the bay leaf, garlic and 1 tablespoon olive oil, cover and simmer for 1–1¹/2 hours or until tender, depending on the age of the beans. Salt the water for the last 15–20 minutes of cooking. The beans should keep their shape and have a slight bite rather than be soft.

DRAIN WELL, remove the bay leaf and garlic and transfer the beans to a shallow serving dish. Add the onion and remaining olive oil and season with salt and pepper. Toss well, then chill.

TOSS through two-thirds of the parsley and taste for seasoning. Break the tuna up into bite-sized pieces and toss through the beans. Sprinkle the remaining parsley over the top and serve.

# CHAR-GRILLED SHELLFISH

THIS RECIPE CALLS FOR DUBLIN BAY PRAWNS BUT, IF YOU CAN'T FIND THEM, ANY LARGE SHRIMP WILL

DO. USING A ROSEMARY TWIG FOR BASTING GIVES THE MARINADE A SUBTLE HERB FLAVOR, WITHOUT

ALLOWING IT TO BECOME OVERPOWERING.

$^1/_2$ cup extra virgin olive oil

2 garlic cloves

1 tablespoon finely chopped basil

$^1/_3$ cup lemon juice

12 Dublin Bay prawns or large
  shrimp

12 scallops in the half shell

16 shrimp

long sturdy rosemary twig, for
  basting

16 large clams

SERVES 4

COMBINE the oil, garlic cloves, basil and lemon juice in a bowl and season well. Set aside to infuse for 15–20 minutes.

REMOVE the claws and heads from the Dublin Bay shrimp, then butterfly by splitting them down the underside with a sharp knife and opening them out.

REMOVE the scallops from their shells, reserving the shells, and pull away the white muscle and digestive tract around each one, leaving the roes intact if you like. Peel and devein the shrimp, leaving the tails intact.

PREHEAT a skillet or barbecue until hot. Using the rosemary twig as a brush, lightly brush the cut surfaces of the Dublin Bay prawns with the oil dressing. Brush the skillet or barbecue plate with the dressing (be careful of the flame flaring) and place the Dublin Bay prawns on to cook, shell sides down.

AFTER 30 seconds, brush the scallops with the dressing and add them to the skillet with the shrimp and clams (discard any clams that are broken or don't close when tapped). Turn over the Dublin Bay prawns and cook for another minute. Turn the shrimp once. Baste with more dressing once or twice. All the shellfish should be ready within 3–4 minutes—the clams can be moved to the side and brushed with a little dressing as they open. Put them back on the shells.

DISCARD the garlic cloves and pour the oil dressing into a small serving bowl. Transfer the shellfish to a warm serving platter. Serve at once with bread and finger bowls.

Dublin Bay prawns are particularly meaty. Butterflying allows the flesh to cook through the shell and take on the flavor of the rosemary.

The stuffing of parsley, bread crumbs and garlic is bound together with beaten egg. The mussels are filled with the stuffing and tied with lengths of kitchen string, then simmered in tomato sauce. Remove the string before you serve.

# STUFFED MUSSELS

MUSSELS ARE ESPECIALLY POPULAR IN THE PUGLIA REGION—THE HEEL OF ITALY'S "BOOT". THIS DISH, FLAVORED WITH OLIVE OIL, GARLIC, TOMATO AND BASIL, EPITOMIZES THE FLAVORS OF THAT STRETCH OF MEDITERRANEAN COAST.

24 mussels
3 tablespoons olive oil
4 garlic cloves, crushed
2 cups tomato passata
1 1/2 tablespoons roughly chopped basil
1/4 cup parsley, finely chopped
1/2 cup fresh white bread crumbs
2 eggs, beaten
pinch of cayenne pepper

SERVES 4

CLEAN the mussels by scrubbing them thoroughly. Discard any that are broken or cracked or do not close when tapped. Insert a sharp knife at the point where the beard protrudes and pry the shell open, leaving the mussel intact inside and keeping the two shells attached. Pull out the beard and discard. Rinse the mussels.

HEAT the oil in a large saucepan and gently cook half the garlic for 15–20 seconds, without browning. Add the passata and basil, season lightly with salt and pepper and bring to a boil. Reduce the heat and simmer for 5 minutes, then add 1 1/4 cups cold water. Return to a boil, cover and keep at a low simmer until needed.

COMBINE the parsley, bread crumbs and the remaining garlic, then blend in the eggs. Add the cayenne pepper and season. Using a teaspoon, fill each mussel with a little of this mixture. Tie the mussels closed with kitchen string as you go, to prevent the filling from escaping.

WHEN the mussels have all been stuffed, place them in the tomato sauce and simmer, covered, for 10 minutes.

LIFT OUT the mussels with a slotted spoon and remove the string. Pile on a warm platter and serve with the tomato sauce, bread and finger bowls.

# ROAST EEL WITH BAY LEAVES

2 x 1³/₄ lb. eels or 1 x 2¹/₂ lb. eel,
  skin removed
2 lemons, halved
4 garlic cloves
25–30 large bay leaves (fresh, not
  dried)
coarse sea salt

SERVES 4

PREHEAT the oven to 400°F. Lightly brush a large shallow casserole with oil. Rub the eel with a cloth to wipe off some of the shine, then rub it with the cut side of half a lemon. Cut the eel into 2-inch sections, discarding the head and the section behind it that contains the innards.

ARRANGE HALF the eel pieces in a single layer in the casserole. Scatter with the garlic cloves and squeeze some lemon juice over the top. Sprinkle lightly with pepper. Scatter half the bay leaves over the top, then liberally sprinkle with salt. Repeat the layers with the remaining ingredients. Bake for 35–40 minutes, or until the eel is tender.

ROAST EEL WITH BAY LEAVES

# CHAR-GRILLED MACKEREL

4 small mackerel, cleaned
4 tablespoons olive oil
2 garlic cloves, roughly chopped
¹/₂ teaspoon paprika
1 tablespoon lemon juice
8 small rosemary sprigs, plus
  4 more to serve
lemon wedges

SERVES 4

BUTTERFLY the mackerel by pressing your fingers on either side of the backbone and gently easing it away from the flesh, following the line of the bone as you go. Remove the bone, leaving the tail attached to the flesh for a more attractive look.

COMBINE the olive oil, garlic, paprika and lemon juice in a shallow bowl large enough to take the mackerel side by side. Season well. Make two diagonal cuts on each side of the fish and leave in the marinade for 30 minutes, turning once.

PREHEAT a grillpan or barbecue. Brush the garlic from the fish. Secure a rosemary sprig on each side of the mackerel with wooden toothpicks or, if using a barbecue, use four small fish grill baskets (the rosemary will be kept in place by the basket, and the fish can be turned easily).

BRUSH the grillpan with olive oil, adjust the heat to moderate and add the mackerel. Grill, turning once, for 5 minutes each side or until they are cooked through. Gently remove the rosemary. Serve each fish with a wedge of lemon and garnish with a fresh sprig of rosemary.

Leave the heads on the mackerel if you prefer to serve whole fish.

POULTRY, MEAT
& GAME

# CHICKEN CACCIATORA

JUST LIKE THE FRENCH *CHASSEUR*, CACCIATORA MEANS "HUNTER'S STYLE". THE DISH IS ORIGINALLY FROM CENTRAL ITALY, BUT LIKE SO MUCH ITALIAN FARE, EVERY REGION HAS PUT ITS OWN SPIN ON THE RECIPE. THIS ONE, WITH TOMATOES, IS PROBABLY THE MOST WIDELY TRAVELED.

3 tablespoons olive oil
1 large onion, finely chopped
3 garlic cloves, crushed
1 stalk celery, finely chopped
5 oz. pancetta, finely chopped
1 1/3 cups button mushrooms, thickly sliced
4 chicken drumsticks
4 chicken thighs
1/3 cup dry vermouth or dry white wine
2 x 14 oz. cans chopped tomatoes
1/4 teaspoon brown sugar
1 oregano sprig, plus 4–5 sprigs to garnish
1 rosemary sprig
1 bay leaf

SERVES 4

HEAT half the oil in a large casserole. Add the onion, garlic and celery and cook, stirring from time to time, over moderately low heat for 6–8 minutes until the onion is golden.

ADD the pancetta and mushrooms, increase the heat and cook, stirring occasionally, for 4–5 minutes. Spoon out onto a plate and set aside.

ADD the remaining olive oil to the casserole and lightly brown the chicken pieces, a few at a time. Season them as they brown. Spoon off any excess fat and return all the pieces to the casserole. Add the vermouth, increase the heat and cook until the liquid has almost evaporated.

ADD the tomatoes, sugar, oregano, rosemary, bay leaf and 1/4 cup cold water. Bring to a boil then stir in the reserved pancetta mixture. Cover and leave to simmer for 20 minutes, or until the chicken is tender but not falling off the bone.

IF the liquid is too thin, remove the chicken from the casserole, increase the heat and boil until thickened. Discard the sprigs of herbs and taste for salt and pepper. Toss in the additional oregano sprigs and the dish is ready to serve.

Early morning shopping in Bologna.

# POLLO ALLA DIAVOLA

DEVIL'S CHICKEN ORIGINATED IN THE TUSCAN KITCHEN. THE CHICKEN IS BUTTERFLIED, THEN MARINATED IN OLIVE OIL AND CHILE. TRADITIONALLY THE BIRD WOULD BE COOKED ON A GRILL OVER AN OPEN FIRE—THE FLAMES LICKING UP FROM BELOW LIKE THE FIRES OF THE DEVIL.

2 x 2 lb. chickens
1/2 cup olive oil
juice of 1 large lemon
2 sage leaves
3–4 very small red chiles, finely minced, or 1/2 teaspoon dried red chile flakes
2 shallots
2 garlic cloves
4 tablespoons chopped parsley
2 1/2 tablespoons softened butter
lemon slices

SERVES 4

SPLIT EACH chicken through the breastbone and press open to form a butterfly, joined down the back. Flatten with your hand to give a uniform surface for cooking. Place in a shallow casserole large enough to take both chickens side by side.

MIX TOGETHER the olive oil, lemon juice, sage and chile in a bowl and season well with salt and pepper. Pour over the chicken and leave to marinate in the fridge for 30 minutes. Turn the chickens and leave for another 30 minutes.

MEANWHILE, chop the shallots, garlic, parsley and butter in a blender or food processor until fine and paste-like. (If you have to do this by hand, chop the vegetables and then mix them into the softened butter.) Season with salt and pepper. Preheat the broiler.

PLACE the chickens, skin side down, on a broiler pan. Position about 4 inches below the heat and broil for 10 minutes, basting with the marinade once or twice. Turn the chickens and broil, basting occasionally, for another 10–12 minutes, or until the juices run clear when a thigh is pierced deeply with a skewer.

SPREAD the butter paste over the skin of the chickens with a knife. Reduce the heat and broil for 3 minutes until the coating is lightly browned. Serve hot or cold, with lemon wedges.

Wild chiles have been eaten in Mexico since 7000 BC. It is likely that the plants were brought to Europe by Columbus—the chile reached southern Italy in 1526 and, as in many other countries, was absorbed into local dishes.

Monti Sibillini, Umbria

# ROAST CHICKEN WITH ROSEMARY

TURNING THE CHICKEN REGULARLY DURING ROASTING KEEPS THE BREAST MEAT BEAUTIFULLY MOIST—THE JUICES RUN INTO IT INSTEAD OF DRAINING AWAY INTO THE PAN. THE REGULAR TURNING ALSO KEEPS THE BIRD FROM FLATTENING ON ANY ONE SIDE.

2 rosemary sprigs
3 garlic cloves
1 teaspoon balsamic vinegar
1 x 3 lb. chicken
2 tablespoons extra virgin olive oil
2 tablespoons olive oil
1/2 cup chicken stock

SERVES 4

PREHEAT the oven to 400°F. Put one rosemary sprig, the garlic and balsamic vinegar inside the cavity of the chicken. Add a large pinch of salt and a few grinds of black pepper. Truss the legs together.

RUB the extra virgin olive oil over the chicken skin. Pour the olive oil into a roasting pan and put the chicken in the pan, breast up. Place the second sprig of rosemary on top.

TRANSFER TO the oven and roast for 1 hour, turning the chicken and basting with the pan juices every 15 minutes.

PUT the chicken on a warm serving plate and discard the rosemary sprig. Spoon off the fat from the roasting pan and place it over high heat on the stovetop. Add the chicken stock and deglaze the pan. Boil until reduced and thickened. Taste for salt and pepper, then pour into a gravy boat to accompany the chicken. Serve with roast rosemary potatoes.

Markets in Italy are usually held in a special square known as the *Piazza Erbe*.

# VINEGAR-POACHED CHICKEN

LIKE A LOT OF ITALIAN FOOD, THE SIMPLICITY OF THIS DISH MEANS YOU REALLY DO NEED TO USE THE BEST-QUALITY INGREDIENTS. BUY A FREE-RANGE BIRD—YOU'LL FIND IT HAS A GREAT DEAL MORE FLAVOR FOR JUST A LITTLE MORE EXPENSE. USE ANY LEFTOVER POACHING LIQUID FOR SOUP STOCK.

4 x 1 lb. small chickens or poussin
1 large carrot, chopped
1 large onion, chopped
1 celery stalk, chopped
bouquet garni
1 1/2 tablespoons sugar
2 cups white wine vinegar
3 tablespoons balsamic vinegar
1 tablespoon butter
1 tablespoon all-purpose flour
1/2 cup chicken stock
4 rosemary sprigs

SERVES 4

TRIM ANY fat from the chickens and season well with salt and pepper, both inside and out. Tie the legs together and tuck the wings behind the chicken. Spread out the carrot, onion and celery in a casserole large enough to take the chickens side by side (don't add the chickens yet, though). Add the bouquet garni, sugar, white wine vinegar and balsamic vinegar and bring to a boil. Reduce the heat and simmer for 5 minutes.

PLACE the chickens on top of the vegetables, breast up. Add enough boiling water to cover the birds, put the lid on the casserole and simmer for 25 minutes, or until they are just cooked. Turn off the heat and leave the chickens in the casserole for 10 minutes.

MELT the butter in a small saucepan. Add the flour and cook, stirring, for 30 seconds. Gradually stir in the chicken stock and simmer until smooth and thickened. Stir in 3–4 tablespoons of the chicken poaching liquid and then taste. Continue adding a little poaching liquid (probably about 1/2 cup in total) until the sauce is to your taste. Increase the heat and boil until slightly thickened. Season with salt and pepper.

REMOVE the chickens from the casserole, drain well and arrange on a warm serving platter. Spoon just enough sauce over the chickens to glaze the skin, garnish with the rosemary sprigs and serve.

The chickens are simmered in liquid to keep the flesh moist and infuse it with the vinegar flavor.

The home of balsamic vinegar is Modena, where authentic vinegars are labeled *aceto balsamico tradizionale di Modena*. Originally made only by wealthy families who could afford to wait for their vinegar to mature, a version is now made commercially and sold at between eight and fifty years old.

Blanch fresh grape leaves in boiling water before use.

Marinating the quail with lemon juice and olive oil.

# QUAILS WRAPPED IN GRAPE LEAVES

4 rosemary sprigs
4 quails
2 tablespoons olive oil
4 teaspoons balsamic vinegar
2 teaspoons brown sugar
4 large grape leaves

SERVES 4

PREHEAT the oven to 350°F. Stuff a sprig of rosemary into each quail and then tie its legs together. Tuck the wings behind the back.

HEAT the olive oil in a frying pan and add the quails. Brown them all over and then add the vinegar and sugar and bubble everything together. Remove from the heat.

BLANCH the grape leaves in boiling water for 15 seconds and then wrap one around each quail. Put the wrapped quail in a roasting pan, seam side down, and bake for 15 minutes.

# BROILED QUAILS

QUAILS REALLY ARE BEST COOKED SIMPLY AND WITHOUT MUCH FUSS. IN THIS RECIPE THE TINY BIRDS ARE JUST MARINATED AND BROILED. THE COOKING TIME IS SHORT, BUT THE GOLDEN RULE WITH QUAILS IS NOT TO OVERCOOK THEM. THIS RECIPE ALSO WORKS WELL WITH SQUAB.

4 quails
2$^{1}/_{2}$ tablespoons lemon juice
4 tablespoons olive oil
8 small sage leaves
2 garlic cloves, halved
1 small red chile, seeded and
   roughly chopped
2 tablespoons chopped parsley
lemon wedges

SERVES 4

SPLIT EACH quail through the breastbone with a sharp knife and then turn it over. Press open hard with the heel of your hand to flatten it out. Transfer the quails to a shallow dish large enough to hold all the birds side by side.

MIX TOGETHER the lemon juice, olive oil, sage leaves, garlic and chile, and season with salt and pepper. Pour over the quails and leave to marinate for 30 minutes, turning the birds after 15 minutes. Preheat the broiler.

PLACE the quails, skin side up, in a broiler pan. Position them 5–6 inches below the heat and broil for about 5 minutes on each side, or until golden and cooked through.

SERVE hot or cold, with a sprinkling of chopped parsley and lemon wedges.

BROILED QUAILS

# ROAST DUCK WITH PARMA HAM

PARMA HAM WAS SUPPOSEDLY SERVED TO HANNIBAL AT A BANQUET IN THE CITY IN 217 BC. TODAY ITS PRODUCTION IS A LICENSED INDUSTRY, WITH ONLY HAM FROM THE EMILIA-ROMAGNA REGION TAKING THE NAME. THESE HAMS HAVE THE DUCAL CROWN OF PARMA BRANDED ON THEIR SKIN.

2 thick slices "country-style" bread, such as ciabatta, crusts removed
1/2 cup milk
1 x 41/2 lb. duck
6 thick slices Parma ham
3 garlic cloves, crushed
4 oz. ground pork
4 oz. ground veal
2 shallots, finely chopped
2 tablespoons grated Parmesan
1 tablespoon finely chopped parsley
1 egg
1/4 cup olive oil
4 tablespoons lard or butter
2 rosemary sprigs
4 tablespoons grappa or brandy
1 cup chicken stock
3 tablespoons heavy cream

SERVES 4

PREHEAT the oven to 425°F. Soak the bread in the milk. Remove any excess skin and fat from the duck, leaving just enough skin to sew up the cavity later.

BRING a large saucepan of water to a boil. Prick the skin of the duck all over and put it into boiling water with a teaspoon of salt. Boil for 12 minutes. Remove and place, cavity side down, in a colander to drain for 10 minutes. Dry well all over, inside and out, with paper towels.

FINELY CHOP 2 slices of Parma ham and mix with the garlic, ground pork and veal, shallots, Parmesan and parsley. Squeeze the bread dry and add to the mixture. Add the egg, season and mix well. Fill the duck cavity with the stuffing then sew up with kitchen string. Tie the wings and legs together with string.

PUT the olive oil, lard and rosemary in a roasting pan and heat in the oven for 5 minutes. Put the duck in the middle, breast up, and roast for 10 minutes. Baste with the pan juices and lay the remaining slices of Parma ham over the breast, covering the legs as well. Reduce the temperature to 375°F and roast for another hour, basting several times. Remove the Parma ham, increase the heat to 415°F and return to the oven for 10 minutes.

TRANSFER the duck to a carving plate and leave to rest for 10 minutes. Spoon all the fat out of the roasting pan, leaving just the duck juices, and place the pan over high heat on the stove. Add the grappa and cook until it is syrupy and almost evaporated, then add the chicken stock. Continue boiling until slightly thickened, then add the cream. Season well and strain into a gravy boat. Remove the string, carve the duck and stir any juices into the sauce before serving.

Stuff the duck, then stitch up the opening with kitchen string—you can buy special large needles from kitchen stores. The ham slices prevent the duck from drying out.

Pistachios ripen on a tree in Sicily.

Marsala is a fortified wine, taking its name from the town in Sicily where the grapes are grown. It was created by an English wine shipper in 1773, who added grape spirit to the wine to prevent it spoiling during the sea journey.

# ROAST TURKEY WITH PISTACHIO STUFFING

ITALIAN ROAST TURKEY IS TRADITIONALLY SERVED WITH *MOSTARDA DI CREMONA*, A TYPE OF ITALIAN CHUTNEY, MADE FROM CANDIED FRUIT SUCH AS PEAR, APRICOT, MELON AND ORANGE PRESERVED WITH MUSTARD, HONEY, WINE AND SPICES. YOU CAN ALSO USE THIS RECIPE TO ROAST GUINEA FOWL.

STUFFING
1/3 cup shelled pistachio nuts
4 oz. prosciutto, finely chopped
7 oz. ground pork
7 oz. ground chicken
1 egg
1/3 cup heavy cream
1/2 cup chestnut purée
1/2 teaspoon finely chopped sage or
   1/4 teaspoon dried sage
pinch of cayenne pepper

1 x 6 1/2 lb. turkey
1 1/4 cups butter, softened
1 onion, roughly chopped
4 sage leaves
1 rosemary sprig
1/2 celery stalk, cut into 2–3 pieces
1 carrot, cut into 3–4 pieces
1 cup dry white wine
1/2 cup dry Marsala
1 cup chicken stock

SERVES 8

TO MAKE the stuffing, preheat the oven to 325°F. Spread the pistachio nuts on a baking sheet and toast for 6–8 minutes. Place in a bowl with the other stuffing ingredients, season well and mix together thoroughly.

FILL the turkey cavity with the stuffing and sew up the opening with kitchen string. Cross the legs and tie them together, and tuck the wings behind the body. Rub the skin with one third of the butter. Put the onion in the center of a roasting pan and place the turkey on top, breast up. Add another third of the butter to the pan with the sage, rosemary, celery and carrot. Pour the white wine and Marsala over the top. Roast for 2 1/2–3 hours, basting several times. Cover with buttered parchment paper when the skin becomes golden brown.

TRANSFER the turkey to a carving plate and leave to rest in a warm spot. Put the vegetables from the pan into a food processor and blend, or push them through a sieve. Add the pan juices and scrapings from the bottom of the pan and blend until smooth. Transfer the mixture to a saucepan, add the remaining butter and the chicken stock and bring to a boil. Season and cook until thickened to a good gravy consistency. Transfer to a gravy boat.

CARVE the turkey and serve with stuffing and gravy, and preferably *mostarda di Cremona*.

# VENISON CASSEROLE

A DARK GAMEY MEAT LIKE VENISON NEEDS STRONG FLAVORS TO BALANCE IT. THIS CASSEROLE CONTAINS CLOVES, JUNIPER AND ALLSPICE—ALL ROBUST FLAVORINGS IN THEIR OWN RIGHT. SERVE WITH CREAMY POLENTA OR POTATOES TO SOAK UP THE RICH GRAVY.

1 rosemary sprig
1 large onion
1 garlic clove
3 oz. prosciutto
7 tablespoons butter
2 lb. venison, cut into large cubes
4 cups beef stock
1/4 cup red wine vinegar
1/2 cup robust red wine
2 cloves
4 juniper berries
pinch of allspice
1 bay leaf
3 tablespoons all-purpose flour
2 tablespoons dry Marsala or
    brandy
1 1/2 teaspoons grated lemon zest
1 1/2 tablespoons finely chopped
    parsley

SERVES 4

STRIP the leaves off the rosemary and chop them finely with the onion, garlic and prosciutto. Heat half the butter in a large heavy saucepan with a lid. Add the chopped mixture and soften over moderately low heat for 5 minutes. Season with pepper. Increase the heat, add the venison and cook for 10 minutes, or until brown on all sides.

PUT the stock in another saucepan and bring to a boil, then reduce the heat and keep at a low simmer.

INCREASE the heat under the venison, add the vinegar and cook until the liquid becomes thick and syrupy. Pour in the red wine. When that becomes syrupy, stir in half of the simmering stock. Add the cloves, juniper berries, allspice and bay leaf and cover the pan. Simmer for 1 hour, stirring once or twice and adding a little hot water if necessary to maintain the liquid level.

MEANWHILE, melt the remaining butter in a saucepan. Stir in the flour and cook over moderately low heat for 1 minute. Slowly stir in the remaining stock and cook until the sauce thickens slightly.

STIR the sauce into the venison casserole, then add the Marsala. Uncover the pan and simmer for another 20 minutes. Taste for salt and pepper. Mix together the lemon zest and parsley and sprinkle over the top before serving.

La Kalsa, Palermo.

# VEAL SALTIMBOCCA

8 small veal cutlets
8 slices prosciutto
8 sage leaves
2 tablespoons olive oil
4 tablespoons butter
3/4 cup dry white wine or dry
   Marsala

SERVES 4

PLACE the veal between two sheets of plastic wrap and pound with a meat mallet until even in thickness. Season lightly. Cut prosciutto slices to the same size as the veal. Cover each veal piece with a slice of prosciutto and place a sage leaf on top. Secure in place with a wooden cocktail pick.

HEAT the oil and half the butter in a large frying pan. Add the veal in batches and fry, prosciutto up, over moderately high heat for 3–4 minutes, or until the veal is just cooked through. Transfer each batch to a hot plate as it is done.

POUR OFF the oil from the pan and add the wine. Cook over high heat until reduced by half, scraping up the bits from the bottom of the pan. Add the remaining butter and, when it has melted, season. Spoon over the veal to serve.

The wooden cocktail pick will hold together the sage, prosciutto and veal. Take it out just before serving.

# VEAL ALLA MILANESE

8 veal chops
2 eggs
2/3 cup fine dried bread crumbs
3 tablespoons grated Parmesan
3 tablespoons butter
1 tablespoon oil
4 lemon wedges dipped in finely
   chopped parsley

SERVES 4

CUT ALL the fat from the veal chops and trim the lower rib bone until it is clean of all fat and flesh. Place each chop between two sheets of plastic wrap and pound the flesh with a meat mallet until it is half its original thickness.

LIGHTLY BEAT the eggs with salt and pepper and pour into a dish. Combine the bread crumbs and Parmesan and place in another dish. Dip each chop into the egg, coating it on both sides. Shake off the excess egg, then coat the chop with the bread crumb mix, pressing each side firmly into the crumbs. Place all the chops on a plate and chill for 30 minutes.

HEAT the butter and oil in a large frying pan. As soon as the butter stops foaming, add the chops and fry gently for 4 minutes on each side, until the bread crumbs are deep golden. Serve immediately with the lemon wedges.

VEAL ALLA MILANESE

# OSSO BUCO ALLA MILANESE

OSSO BUCO IS A MILANESE DISH AND TRADITIONALLY TOMATOES ARE NOT USED IN THE COOKING OF NORTHERN ITALY. THE ABSENCE OF THE ROBUST TOMATO ALLOWS THE MORE DELICATE FLAVOR OF THE GREMOLATA TO COME THROUGH IN THIS CLASSIC OSSO BUCO. SERVE WITH *RISOTTO ALLA MILANESE*.

12 pieces veal shank, about
  1 1/2 inches thick
all-purpose flour, seasoned with salt
  and pepper
1/4 cup olive oil
4 tablespoons butter
1 garlic clove
1 cup dry white wine
1 bay leaf or lemon leaf
pinch of allspice
pinch of ground cinnamon

GREMOLATA
2 teaspoons grated lemon zest
6 tablespoons finely chopped
  parsley
1 garlic clove, finely chopped

thin lemon wedges

SERVES 4

TIE EACH piece of veal shank around its middle to secure the flesh, then dust with the seasoned flour. Heat the oil, butter and garlic in a large heavy saucepan big enough to hold the shanks in a single layer. Put the shanks in the pan and cook for 12–15 minutes until well browned. Arrange the shanks, standing them up in a single layer, pour in the wine and add the bay leaf, allspice and cinnamon. Cover the saucepan.

COOK AT a low simmer for 15 minutes, then add 1/2 cup warm water. Continue cooking, covered, for about 45 minutes to 1 hour (the timing will depend on the age of the veal) until the meat is tender and you can cut it with a fork. Check the volume of liquid once or twice and add more warm water as needed. Transfer the veal to a plate and keep warm. Discard the garlic clove and bay leaf.

TO MAKE the gremolata, mix together the lemon zest, parsley and garlic. Increase the heat under the saucepan and stir for 1–2 minutes until the sauce is thick, scraping up any bits off the bottom of the saucepan as you stir. Stir in the gremolata. Season with salt and pepper if necessary and return the veal to the sauce. Heat through, then serve with the lemon wedges.

The pan for osso buco must be large enough to fit the shank pieces in a single layer so that they cook through evenly.

Ask your butcher to cut the osso buco from the hind shin of the veal where the meat is more tender. The pieces should have a high proportion of meat to bone.

Tying herbs together as a bouquet garni means they are much easier to lift out when the dish is cooked.

# OSSO BUCO WITH TOMATOES

THE TOMATO-BASED VERSION OF OSSO BUCO MAY NOT BE COMPLETELY AUTHENTIC. BUT ITS ENDURING POPULARITY VOUCHES FOR ITS FLAVOR. SERVE WITH CREAMY POLENTA TO CATCH THE JUICES.

10 pieces veal shank, about
   1¹/₂ inches thick
all-purpose flour, seasoned with salt
   and pepper
¹/₄ cup olive oil
4 tablespoons butter
1 garlic clove
1 small carrot, finely chopped
1 large onion, finely chopped
¹/₂ celery stalk, finely chopped
1 cup dry white wine
1¹/₂ cups veal or chicken stock
14 oz. can chopped tomatoes
bouquet garni

SERVES 4

TIE EACH piece of veal shank around its middle to secure the flesh, then dust with the seasoned flour. Heat the oil, butter and garlic in a large heavy saucepan big enough to hold the shanks in a single layer. Put the shanks in the saucepan and cook for 12–15 minutes until well browned. Remove the shanks from the saucepan and set aside. Discard the garlic.

ADD the carrot, onion and celery to the saucepan and cook over moderate heat for 5–6 minutes, without browning. Increase the heat to high, add the wine and cook for 2–3 minutes. Add the stock, tomatoes and bouquet garni. Season with salt and pepper.

RETURN veal shanks to the saucepan, standing them up in a single layer. Cover the saucepan, reduce the heat and simmer for 1 hour, or until the meat is tender and you can cut it with a fork.

IF YOU prefer a thicker sauce, remove the veal shanks and increase the heat. Boil the sauce until reduced and thickened, then return the veal to the saucepan. Discard the bouquet garni, and taste for salt and pepper.

# VITELLO TONNATO

THERE ARE TWO VERSIONS OF THIS NORTH ITALIAN DISH, BOTH FEATURING A SAUCE OF MASHED TUNA AND ANCHOVIES. IN THE OLDER MILANESE VERSION THE SAUCE IS THINNED WITH CREAM; THIS RECIPE IS FOR THE PIEMONTESE DISH, WHICH USES MAYONNAISE RATHER THAN CREAM.

1 x 2½ lb. boneless rolled veal roast
2 cups dry white wine
2 cups chicken stock
2 garlic cloves
1 onion, quartered
1 carrot, roughly chopped
1 celery stalk, roughly chopped
2 bay leaves
3 cloves
10 peppercorns

SAUCE
3 oz. can tuna in olive oil
½ oz. anchovy fillets
2 egg yolks
2 tablespoons lemon juice
½ cup olive oil

parsley sprigs
capers
thin lemon slices

SERVES 4

PUT the veal, wine, stock, garlic, onion, carrot, celery, bay leaves, cloves and peppercorns in a stockpot or very large saucepan. Add enough water to come two-thirds of the way up the veal and bring to a boil. Reduce the heat, cover the saucepan and simmer for 1¼ hours, or until tender. Leave to cool for 30 minutes, then remove the veal from the saucepan and strain the stock. Pour the stock into a saucepan and boil rapidly until reduced to 1 cup.

TO MAKE the sauce, purée the tuna and its oil with the anchovy fillets in a blender or small food processor. Add the egg yolks and 1 tablespoon of the lemon juice and process until smooth. With the motor running, slowly pour in the oil. Gradually add the reduced stock until the sauce has the consistency of a thin mayonnaise. (If you are doing this by hand, chop the tuna and anchovy finely, mix in the egg yolks and lemon juice and then whisk in the oil and stock.) Blend in the remaining lemon juice and season well.

TO SERVE, thinly slice the cold veal and arrange in overlapping slices down the center of a serving platter. Spoon the sauce over the top and garnish with the parsley, capers and lemon slices.

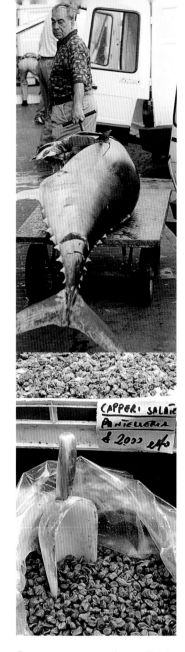

Capers are usually available preserved in vinegar (and are best rinsed before use) but you will find that those preserved in salt are of a superior quality. Rinse well and pat dry before using.

The veal can be cooling in the stock while you make the sauce.

Veal cutlets are usually pounded with a meat mallet before use, giving a thin tender meat that can be wrapped around fillings and fried quickly. Tie the involtini with kitchen string to prevent them unraveling while you're frying.

# VEAL INVOLTINI

INVOLTINI MEANS "LITTLE BUNDLES" AND IF YOU TRAVEL AROUND ITALY YOU'LL FIND THIS RECIPE IN MANY GUISES. TRADITIONALLY INVOLTINI WERE MADE WITH MEAT OR FISH, STUFFED WITH BREAD CRUMBS, PINE NUTS AND CURRANTS. YOU COULD ALSO USE TURKEY OR CHICKEN BREAST.

8 asparagus spears
4 veal cutlets
4 thin slices mortadella (preferably
   with pistachio nuts)
4 thin slices Bel Paese
all-purpose flour, seasoned with salt
   and pepper
3 tablespoons butter
1 tablespoon olive oil
3 tablespoons dry Marsala

SERVES 4

WASH the asparagus and remove the woody ends (hold each spear at both ends and bend it gently—it will snap at its natural breaking point). Blanch the asparagus in boiling salted water for 3 minutes. Drain, reserving 3 tablespoons of the liquid.

PLACE EACH veal cutlet between two sheets of plastic wrap and pound with a meat mallet to make a 5 x 7 inch rectangle. Season lightly with salt and pepper. Trim both the mortadella and cheese slices to just a little smaller than the veal.

COVER EACH piece of veal with a slice of mortadella, then a slice of cheese. Place an asparagus spear in the center, running across the shortest width, with the tip slightly overhanging the veal at one end. Place another asparagus spear alongside, but with its tip overhanging the other end. Roll each veal slice up tightly and tie in place at each end with kitchen string. Roll in the seasoned flour to coat.

HEAT 2 tablespoons of the butter with the olive oil in a frying pan. Fry the rolls over low heat for about 10 minutes, turning frequently, until golden and tender. Transfer to a hot serving dish and keep warm.

ADD the Marsala, the reserved asparagus liquid and the remaining butter to the pan and bring quickly to a boil. Simmer for 3–4 minutes, scraping up the bits from the base of the pan. The juices will reduce and darken. Taste for seasoning, then spoon over the veal rolls and serve immediately.

# UCCELLETTI SCAPPATI

THE NAME MEANS LITERALLY "LITTLE BIRDS THAT GOT AWAY" AND REFERS TO THE SMALL GAME BIRDS THAT WERE ONCE COOKED LIKE THIS. YOU CAN ALSO GRILL THE SKEWERS IF YOU PREFER: MELT THE BUTTER IN A SMALL SAUCEPAN AND USE IT TO BASTE THE SKEWERS FREQUENTLY.

1$^1/_4$–1$^1/_2$ lb. sliced leg of veal
3 oz. pancetta, thinly sliced
40–60 sage leaves
3 oz. pancetta, cubed
5 tablespoons butter

SERVES 6

SOAK 12 bamboo skewers in cold water for 1 hour.

PLACE the veal between two sheets of plastic wrap and pound with a meat mallet until even in thickness. Cut into 2$^1/_2$ x 1$^1/_4$ inch rectangles and trim the pancetta slices to the same size.

WORKING in batches, place the veal pieces flat on a board and season with pepper. Place a slice of pancetta on each rectangle of veal and then half a sage leaf on top. Roll up each veal slice, starting from one of the short ends.

THREAD a cube of pancetta onto a skewer, followed by a sage leaf. Thread the skewer through a veal roll to prevent it unrolling. Thread four more veal rolls onto the skewer, followed by a sage leaf and, finally, another cube of pancetta. Continue in this way with more skewers until all the ingredients are used.

HEAT the butter in a large frying pan. When it foams, add the skewers in batches and cook over high heat for 12 minutes, or until cooked through, turning several times during cooking. Season lightly and serve with fried polenta.

Soak the skewers in water before you start to prevent them scorching (unless you're using metal skewers). Roll up the tiny bundles of veal, pancetta and sage and thread onto the skewers so they can't unroll. Wedge them in place at either end with a sage leaf and cube of pancetta.

## PICCATA AL LIMONE

4 large veal cutlets
all-purpose flour, seasoned with salt
    and pepper
1 tablespoon olive oil
2 tablespoons butter
1/3 cup dry white wine
1 cup chicken stock
3 tablespoons lemon juice
2 tablespoons capers, rinsed and
    chopped if large
1 tablespoon finely chopped parsley
8 caperberries

SERVES 4

PLACE the veal between two sheets of plastic wrap and pound with a meat mallet until it is an even thickness. Lightly dust each side with flour.

HEAT the olive oil and butter in a large frying pan. Fry the cutlets over moderately high heat for 2 minutes on each side, or until golden. Season and transfer to a warm plate.

ADD the wine to the pan, increase the heat to high and boil until there are just 3–4 tablespoons of liquid left. Pour in the stock and boil for 4–5 minutes, or until it has reduced and slightly thickened. Add the lemon juice and capers and cook, stirring, for 1 minute. Taste for seasoning, then return the cutlets to the pan and heat through for 30 seconds. Sprinkle with parsley and serve at once, garnished with caperberries.

Streets behind the Bay of Naples.

## BISTECCA ALLA PIZZAIOLA

4 rib or rump steaks
4 tablespoons olive oil
1–1 1/4 lb. tomatoes
3 garlic cloves, crushed
3 basil leaves, torn into pieces
1 teaspoon finely chopped parsley

SERVES 4

BRUSH the steaks with 1 tablespoon of the olive oil and season well. Put on a plate and set aside.

SCORE a cross in the top of each tomato. Plunge into boiling water for 20 seconds, then drain and peel away the skin from the cross. Chop the tomatoes, discarding the cores.

HEAT 2 tablespoons of the olive oil in a saucepan over low heat and add the garlic. Soften without browning for 1–2 minutes, then add the tomato and season. Increase the heat, bring to a boil and cook for 5 minutes. Stir in the basil.

HEAT the remaining oil in a large frying pan with a tight-fitting lid. Brown the steaks over moderately high heat for 2 minutes on each side (cook in batches rather than crowding the pan). Place in a slightly overlapping row down the center of the pan and spoon the sauce over the top, covering the steaks completely. Cover the pan and cook over low heat for about 5 minutes, or until the steaks are cooked to your taste. Sprinkle the parsley over the top and serve at once.

BISTECCA ALLA PIZZAIOLA

# BOLLITO MISTO

THIS MEAL REQUIRES A TRIP TO A REALLY GOOD BUTCHER. IF YOU ARE LUCKY ENOUGH TO FIND A

ZAMPONE (PORK SAUSAGE STUFFED INTO A PIG'S TROTTER), USE IT INSTEAD OF THE COTECHINO. YOU

WILL ONLY NEED A LITTLE OF THE COOKING LIQUID FOR SERVING—KEEP THE REST FOR MAKING SOUP.

1 x 1³/₄ lb. cotechino sausage
1 x 2¹/₂ lb. small beef tongue
3 parsley sprigs
4 baby carrots
1 celery stalk, sliced
2 onions, roughly chopped
10 peppercorns
2 bay leaves
1 x 2¹/₂ lb. beef brisket
1 tablespoon tomato paste
1 x 2 lb. chicken
12 whole baby turnips
18 small onions, such as pickling
   or pearl onions

SERVES 8

BRING a saucepan of water to a boil. Prick the casing of the cotechino sausage and add to the pan. Reduce the heat, cover the saucepan and simmer for about 1¹/₂ hours, or until tender. Leave in the cooking liquid until ready to use.

MEANWHILE, bring a stockpot or very large saucepan of water to a boil. Add the tongue, parsley, carrots, celery, chopped onions, peppercorns, bay leaves and 1 teaspoon salt. Bring back to a boil, skim the surface and add the beef brisket and tomato paste. Cover the saucepan, reduce the heat and simmer for 2 hours, skimming the surface from time to time.

ADD the chicken, turnips and onions to the stockpot and simmer for another hour. Top up with boiling water if necessary to keep the meat always covered. Add the cotechino for the last 20 minutes of cooking.

TURN OFF the heat and remove the tongue. Peel, trim and slice it, then arrange the slices on a warm platter. Slice the cotechino and beef and quarter the chicken. Arrange all the meats on the platter and surround them with the carrots, turnips and onions. Moisten with a little of the cooking liquid then take to the table. Serve with salsa verde (page 285) and *mostarda di Cremona*.

"Boiled meats" is a tradition in prosperous northern Italy, where cows and pigs are plentiful, with Piemonte generally accepted as the home of the best bollito misto. There, grand restaurants serve seven different meats with three sauces from a special cart. Elsewhere, and when cooked at home for large family gatherings, the dish is a little less flamboyant, containing only two or three different meats.

Wrapping the beef in prosciutto serves the dual purpose of sealing in the flavors of the garlic and rosemary and protecting the beef from the heat of the oven so it remains moist and juicy.

# BEEF BRAISED IN RED WINE

IF YOU ARE FORTUNATE ENOUGH TO HAVE A WHOLE FILLET (RATHER THAN A PIECE OF ONE) THEN FOLD THE THIN END UNDER SO THE BEEF IS AN EVEN THICKNESS AND INCREASE THE QUANTITIES OF THE OTHER INGREDIENTS ACCORDINGLY. SERVE WITH CREAMY POLENTA.

1¹/₂ lb. trimmed thick beef fillet
3 garlic cloves, thinly sliced
2 tablespoons chopped rosemary
8–10 thin slices prosciutto, pancetta or smoked bacon
2 tablespoons olive oil
4 dried wild mushrooms, such as porcini
1 onion, halved and sliced
¹/₂ cup red wine such as Barolo
14 oz. can chopped tomatoes

SERVES 4

MAKE SEVERAL small incisions around the beef. Push a slice of garlic into each incision, using up one of the garlic cloves. Scatter 1 tablespoon of rosemary over the beef and season with salt and pepper. Lay the prosciutto slices on a board in a line next to each other, creating a sheet of prosciutto to wrap the beef in. Put the beef fillet across them and fold the prosciutto over to enclose the fillet. Tie several times with kitchen string to keep the beef and prosciutto together. Leave in the fridge to rest for at least 15 minutes.

PREHEAT the oven to 375°F. Heat the olive oil in a casserole. Add the beef and sear on all sides until the prosciutto is golden brown, but not burnt. A little of the prosciutto might fall off, but it doesn't matter: just make sure the beef is well sealed. Remove from the casserole.

LEAVE the mushrooms to soak in ³/₄ cup hot water for 10 minutes. Add the onion to the casserole, reduce the heat and gently cook until soft. Add the remaining garlic and rosemary and cook for a few minutes more.

REMOVE the mushrooms from the water and add to the onion, reserving the water. Cook the mushrooms for a couple of minutes, then add the mushroom water, discarding any sediment at the bottom of the bowl, and boil until nearly all the liquid is reduced. Add the wine and cook for a few minutes, then add the tomatoes and cook for another 5–10 minutes to reduce to a thick sauce.

SEASON WITH salt and pepper and add the beef to the casserole, turning over in the sauce to coat all sides. Cover the casserole with a lid and place in the oven. Cook the beef for 15 minutes for rare or 20 minutes for medium-rare. Remove from the oven and leave to rest, covered, for at least 15 minutes.

# BEEF COOKED IN RAGU

THIS DISH IS BOTH STARTER AND MAIN COURSE IN ONE POT. SERVE THE RAGU ON SPAGHETTI OR

BUCATINI AS A FIRST COURSE, AND THE BEEF WITH VEGETABLES OR A SALAD FOR THE MAIN. RAGU IS

THE TRADITIONAL TOMATO-BASED SAUCE OF BOLOGNA.

1 x 3 lb. piece of beef, such as
  boneless sirloin tip or round
1/4 cup pork fat, cut into small thin
  pieces
2 tablespooons butter
3 tablespoons olive oil
pinch of cayenne pepper
2 garlic cloves, finely chopped
2 onions, finely chopped
2 carrots, finely chopped
1 celery stalk, finely chopped
1/2 red pepper, finely chopped
3 leeks, sliced
3/4 cup red wine
1 tablespoon tomato paste
11/2 cups beef stock
3/4 cup strained tomatoes
8 basil leaves, torn into pieces
1/2 teaspoon finely chopped
  oregano leaves, or 1/4 teaspoon
  dried oregano
2 tablespoons finely chopped
  parsley
1/4 cup heavy cream

SERVES 6

MAKE DEEP incisions all over the beef with the point of a sharp knife, then push a piece of pork fat into each incision.

HEAT butter and olive oil in a large casserole and brown beef for 10–12 minutes, until it is browned all over. Season with salt and add the cayenne, garlic, onions, carrots, celery, pepper and leeks. Cook over moderate heat for 10 minutes until the vegetables are lightly browned.

INCREASE the heat, add the wine and boil until it has evaporated. Stir in the tomato paste, then add the stock. Simmer for 30 minutes. Add the strained tomatoes, basil and oregano and season with pepper. Cover the casserole and cook for 1 hour, or until the beef is tender.

REMOVE the beef from the casserole and allow to rest for 10 minutes before carving. Taste the sauce for salt and pepper and stir in the parsley and cream.

The casserole needs to be large enough to hold the beef without it touching the side, so the sauce can cover the beef completely. Finish the sauce off with a little cream to make it velvety.

Putting the garlic and sage in the pan and laying the pork on top makes a rack for the meat to prevent it boiling in its own juices instead of roasting. Pour the milk over the pork and roast uncovered so the skin crisps.

# PORK BRAISED IN MILK

ASK YOUR BUTCHER TO CHINE AND SKIN THE PORK LOIN (CHINING MEANS REMOVING THE BACKBONE FROM THE RACK OF RIBS SO THAT YOU CAN CARVE BETWEEN THE RIBS). THE MILK AND LEMON SAUCE WILL APPEAR LUMPY AND CURDLED, BUT TASTES DELICIOUS—YOU CAN STRAIN IT IF YOU LIKE.

1 x 5 lb. pork loin, chined and skin
   removed
$1/4$ cup olive oil
4 garlic cloves, cut in half
   lengthwise
$3/4$ cup sage or rosemary leaves
4 cups milk
grated zest of 2 lemons
juice of 1 lemon

SERVES 6

PREHEAT the oven to 400°F. Prepare the pork by trimming the fat to leave just a thin layer. The bone and fat keep the pork moist.

HEAT the olive oil in a large roasting pan. Add the pork and brown the meat on all sides. Remove the pork and pour away the fat from the roasting pan. Add the garlic and sage to the pan and place the pork on top of them. Season with salt and pepper and pour the milk over the pork. Return to the heat and bring just to a boil. Remove the pan from the heat again, add the lemon zest and drizzle with the lemon juice.

TRANSFER to the oven and roast for 20 minutes. Reduce the temperature to 300°F and cook for another $1–1 1/4$ hours, depending on the thickness of the meat. If necessary, add a little more milk every so often, to keep the meat roasting in liquid. Baste the meat with the juices every 30 minutes. Do not cover, so that the juices reduce and the fat on the pork becomes crisp.

TO TEST if the pork is cooked, insert a skewer into the middle of the meat, count to 10 and pull it out. Touch it on the inside of your wrist and, if it feels hot, the meat is cooked through. Leave the meat to rest for 10 minutes before carving.

STRAIN the sauce if you like (you don't need to, but it may look curdled) and serve with the meat. Delicious with braised fennel, cavolo nero or roasted vegetables.

# FLORENTINE ROAST PORK

3 large fennel bulbs
1/2 tablespoon finely chopped
  rosemary
4 garlic cloves, crushed
1 x 3 lb. pork loin, chined and skin
  removed
3 white onions
1/3 cup olive oil
3/4 cup dry white wine
1/3 cup extra virgin olive oil
1 cup chicken stock
3–4 tablespoons heavy cream

SERVES 6

PREHEAT the oven to 400°F. Cut the green fronds from the tops of the fennel and chop to give 2 tablespoons. Mix with the rosemary, garlic and plenty of salt and black pepper. Make deep incisions with a sharp knife all over the pork and rub this mixture into the incisions and the splits in the pork bone. Cut two of the onions in half and place in a roasting pan. Put the pork on top of the onion halves and drizzle the olive oil over the top.

ROAST in the oven for 30 minutes. Baste the pork with the pan juices, then reduce the temperature to 350°F. Roast for another 30 minutes. Baste and lightly salt the surface of the pork. Pour in half the white wine. Continue roasting for another 30–45 minutes, basting once or twice.

MEANWHILE, remove the tough outer leaves of the fennel and discard. Slice the bulbs vertically into 1/2-inch sections and place in a large saucepan. Thinly slice the remaining onion and add to the saucepan with the extra virgin olive oil and a little salt. Add enough water to cover, put the lid on and bring to a boil. Simmer for about 45 minutes, or until the fennel is creamy and soft and almost all the liquid has evaporated.

REMOVE the pork from the pan and leave to rest in a warm spot. Spoon off the excess oil from the pan and discard the onion. Place the pan over high heat on the stovetop and stir in the remaining wine to deglaze. Add the stock and boil the sauce until slightly thickened. Remove from the heat, season with salt and pepper and stir in the cream. Slice the pork and serve on the fennel, with the sauce.

Scoring the pork all over and pressing the fennel, garlic and rosemary into the cuts ensures that the flavor infuses the meat while it cooks. Cook the chopped fennel separately until it is creamy.

Use your hands to combine the meatball mixture—it's the easiest and most efficient method.

Lunching *al fresco* in Bologna.

# ITALIAN MEATBALLS WITH TOMATO SAUCE

JUST ABOUT EVERY ITALIAN HOME WILL HAVE ITS OWN FAMILY RECIPE FOR MEATBALLS, OR *POLPETTE*, AS THEY ARE KNOWN. THEY CAN BE SERVED WITH PASTA OR BREAD. THE DISH IS BEST MADE A DAY IN ADVANCE TO LET THE FLAVORS BLEND TOGETHER.

$^3/_4$ cup olive oil
1 onion, finely chopped
$^2/_3$ cup pine nuts, roughly chopped
3 garlic cloves, crushed
$1^1/_3$ cups flat-leaf parsley, roughly chopped
1 tablespoon basil or rosemary, roughly chopped
2 teaspoons fennel seeds, ground
$^2/_3$ cup fresh bread crumbs
1 cup ricotta
$^1/_4$ cup Parmesan, grated
grated zest of 1 large lemon
1 egg
1 lb. ground pork or beef

SAUCE
$1^3/_4$ lb. tomatoes or
    2 x 14 oz. cans tomatoes
$^1/_2$ cup red wine

SERVES 4

HEAT half the olive oil in a saucepan and cook the onion and pine nuts until the onion is soft and the pine nuts are light golden brown. Add the garlic and cook for a few minutes more, then set aside to cool.

PUT the herbs, fennel seeds, bread crumbs, ricotta, Parmesan, lemon zest and egg in a bowl and add the ground meat. Add cooled onion and pine nuts, season with salt and pepper and mix briefly until all the ingredients are combined. Test for correct seasoning by frying one small meatball and tasting for flavor. Leave the mixture to rest in the fridge for at least 30 minutes or overnight.

TO MAKE the meatballs, roll about 2 tablespoons of mixture into a ball about the size of a walnut and then flatten slightly to make it easier to cook on both sides. Repeat with the rest of the mixture.

HEAT the remaining olive oil in a large saucepan and fry the meatballs until golden brown on both sides. If necessary, cook them in two batches to prevent the pan from crowding. Make sure there is enough oil to prevent the meatballs from sticking to the bottom of the saucepan. Remove all the meatballs from the saucepan.

TO MAKE the sauce, if you are using fresh tomatoes, score a cross in the top of each one, plunge them into boiling water for 20 seconds, then drain and peel the skin away from the cross. Finely chop the flesh. Add the tomatoes and wine to the saucepan, season with salt and pepper and simmer for 5 minutes. Gently add the meatballs to the sauce and reduce the heat to a gentle simmer. Cover the saucepan and cook for another 10 minutes. Leave for 10 minutes before serving.

# ROAST LAMB

THIS RECIPE CAN ALSO BE USED FOR ROASTING A LEG OF VEAL OR A RIB OR LOIN OF LAMB OR VEAL.
FOR LAMB, FOLLOW THE COOKING TIMES IN THE RECIPE. YOU WILL NEED TO ROAST THE VEAL FOR
25 MINUTES PER POUND, PLUS AN EXTRA 10 MINUTES.

2 rosemary sprigs
3 garlic cloves
2$^{1}/_{2}$ oz. pancetta
1 x 4$^{1}/_{2}$ lb. leg of lamb, shank bone
   cut off just above the joint and
   trimmed of excess fat
1 large onion, cut into 4 thick slices
$^{1}/_{2}$ cup olive oil
1$^{1}/_{2}$ cups dry white wine

SERVES 4

PREHEAT the oven to 450°F.

STRIP the leaves off the rosemary sprigs and chop with the garlic and pancetta until fine and paste-like (a food processor works well for this). Season with a little salt and plenty of pepper.

WITH the point of a sharp knife, make incisions about $^{1}/_{2}$ inch deep all over the lamb. Rub the rosemary filling over the surface of the lamb, pressing it into the incisions.

PUT the onion slices in the center of a roasting pan. Place the lamb on top and gently pour the olive oil over it. Roast for 15 minutes. Reduce the temperature to 350°F and pour in 1 cup of the wine. Roast for 1 hour for medium-rare, or longer if you prefer. Baste a couple of times and add a little water if the juices start to burn in the pan. Transfer the lamb to a carving platter and leave to rest for 10 minutes.

DISCARD the onion and spoon off the excess fat from the pan. Place over high heat on the stovetop, pour in the remaining wine and cook for 3–4 minutes, or until the sauce reduces and slightly thickens. Taste for seasoning. Slice the lamb and serve on a warm serving platter with the sauce spooned over the top.

Firmly but gently push the knife $^{1}/_{2}$ inch into the meat at regular intervals. Baste a couple of times while the meat is roasting.

A butcher trims a leg of lamb in a Sicilian market.

# SPICY LAMB CASSEROLE

THE PINCH OF CHILE SIGNIFIES THIS AS A SOUTHERN DISH, PROBABLY FROM BASILICATA, WHERE SHEEP WERE THE MAIN SOURCE OF INCOME. SUCH DISHES OFTEN ORIGINATED WITH SHEPHERDS, WHO USED WILD HERBS AND VEGETABLES FOUND AROUND THEIR CAMP.

3 tablespoons olive oil
2¹/₂ lb. lamb leg or shoulder, cut into 1¹/₂-inch cubes
1 small onion, finely chopped
1 celery stalk, finely chopped
3 garlic cloves, crushed
¹/₂ cup dry Marsala
³/₄ teaspoon dried red chile flakes
1 tablespoon crushed juniper berries
2 tablespoons tomato paste
1 cup chicken stock
1 rosemary sprig
12 small onions, such as pickling or pearl onions
2 potatoes, cut into cubes
2 tablespoons finely chopped parsley

SERVES 4

PREHEAT the oven to 350°F.

HEAT the olive oil in a large casserole. Add the lamb in batches, so that you don't crowd the pan, season with salt and pepper and brown lightly over high heat. Remove each batch from the casserole as it browns. Once all the lamb is browned and has been removed from the casserole, add the onion, celery and garlic, reduce the heat and cook for 4–5 minutes until softened.

RETURN the lamb to the casserole. Pour in the Marsala and cook over high heat until it is dark brown and reduced by half. Add the dried red chile flakes and juniper berries and cook, stirring, for just 10–15 seconds. Add the tomato paste, chicken stock, rosemary and about 1 cup water, or enough to just cover.

COVER the casserole with a lid and bake in the oven for 45 minutes. Add the pearl onions and potato and cook for another 45 minutes. Stir the parsley through just before serving.

# SAUSAGE AND LENTIL STEW

3 tablespoons olive oil
1³/₄ lb. Italian sausages
1 onion, chopped
3 garlic cloves, thinly sliced
1¹/₂ tablespoons chopped
  rosemary
28 oz. can chopped tomatoes
16 juniper berries, lightly crushed
pinch of grated nutmeg
1 bay leaf
1 dried red chile, crushed
³/₄ cup red wine
¹/₂ cup green lentils

SERVES 4

HEAT the oil in a large saucepan and cook the sausages for 5–10 minutes, until browned. Remove the sausages from the saucepan and reduce the heat. Add the onion and garlic to the saucepan and cook gently until the onion is soft.

STIR IN the rosemary, then add the tomatoes and cook gently until reduced to a thick sauce. Add the juniper berries, nutmeg, bay leaf, dried red chile, wine and 1²/₃ cups water. Bring to a boil, then add the lentils and sausages. Give the stew a good stir, cover the saucepan and simmer gently for 40 minutes, or until the lentils are soft. Stir a couple of times to prevent the lentils sticking to the bottom of the pan. Add a little more water if the lentils are still not cooked.

Umbria is the fertile heart of Italy and the tiny lentils that come from Castelluccio are regarded as the country's best. Traditionally, they are eaten on New Year's Eve to bring wealth in the coming year.

# SAUSAGES WITH BROCCOLI

1³/₄ lb. Italian sausages
1¹/₄ lb. broccoli florets
1 teaspoon olive oil
2 shallots, finely chopped
3 garlic cloves, crushed
¹/₄ dried red chile, finely chopped
¹/₂ cup chicken stock
1 tablespoon lemon juice
6 pitted black olives

SERVES 4

PRICK the sausages several times, place in a single layer in a deep non-stick frying pan and add cold water to a depth of ¹/₂ inch. Bring to a boil, then reduce the heat and simmer for 20 minutes. Turn the sausages from time to time and add a little extra water should it evaporate too quickly—when the sausages are cooked, all the water will have evaporated, leaving just a little sausage fat in the pan.

MEANWHILE, bring a large saucepan of water to a boil. Add the broccoli with a teaspoon of salt. Simmer for 4–5 minutes, or until the florets are barely tender. Drain and set aside.

ADD the oil to the frying pan and evenly brown the sausages. Push to one side and add the shallots, garlic and chile to the pan. Cook over low heat for 3–4 minutes, stirring from time to time. Add the stock and lemon juice, increase the heat and cook until reduced by half. Add the broccoli and olives, spoon the sauce over the broccoli and serve when it has heated through.

SAUSAGES WITH BROCCOLI

Saint Theodore taming the dragon in the Piazzetta San Marco, Venice.

# LAMB KIDNEYS WITH FENNEL

20 lamb kidneys
1/3 cup vinegar
2 tablespoons olive oil
2 tablespoons butter
2 large onions, finely sliced
1 small fennel bulb, finely sliced
3 tablespoons finely chopped
  parsley
4 slices day-old "country-style"
  bread, such as ciabatta, crusts
  removed
1 garlic clove, halved

SERVES 4

CUT the kidneys in half and place in a glass bowl. Add the vinegar and enough cold water to cover. Leave for at least 30 minutes.

MEANWHILE, heat the olive oil and butter in a large frying pan. Add the onions and fennel, season well and cook over very low heat without browning for 20–25 minutes. Transfer to a bowl.

CORE the kidneys and cut into thin slices. Add to the dry pan and cook over medium heat until they release their red liquid and turn brown. Drain through a colander, discarding the liquid. Rinse the kidneys under cold water and drain well.

WIPE the pan dry with paper towels, then add the cooked onion mixture and kidneys. Add the parsley and season well. Cook over moderately high heat, stirring often, for 3–4 minutes or until the kidneys brown.

TOAST the bread and rub with the cut side of the garlic. Serve with the kidneys.

# VENETIAN LIVER

VENETIAN LIVER

2 tablespoons olive oil
4 tablespoons butter
2 large onions, halved and thinly
  sliced
1 1/4 lb. calves liver, very thinly sliced
1 tablespoon finely chopped parsley
lemon wedges

SERVES 4

HEAT the olive oil and half the butter in a large frying pan and add the onions. Cover and cook over low heat for 30–40 minutes, stirring from time to time, until very soft and golden. Season well with salt and pepper and transfer to a bowl.

MELT the remaining butter in the frying pan, increase the heat and fry the liver quickly until brown on all sides. Return the onions to the pan and cook, stirring often, for 1–2 minutes more, or until the liver is cooked. Remove from the heat, stir in the parsley and check for seasoning. Serve with lemon wedges.

VEGETABLES

# EGGPLANT PARMIGIANA

PARMIGIANA IS A DECEPTIVE NAME FOR THIS DISH, AS THE RECIPE DOES NOT, IN FACT, HAIL FROM THAT CITY. INSTEAD ITS CREATION IS CLAIMED BY ALMOST EVERY REGION OF ITALY, BUT THE USE OF MOZZARELLA AND TOMATOES INDICATES A DISH FROM THE SOUTH.

3 lb. eggplants
all-purpose flour
1 1/3 cups olive oil
2 cups strained tomatoes
2 tablespoons roughly torn basil
   leaves
1 2/3 cups mozzarella, grated
1 cup Parmesan, grated

SERVES 8

THINLY SLICE the eggplants lengthwise. Layer the slices in a large colander, sprinkling salt between each layer. Leave for 1 hour to extract the bitter juices. Rinse and pat the slices dry on both sides with paper towels. Coat the eggplant slices lightly with flour.

PREHEAT the oven to 350°F and grease a 13 x 8 inch shallow casserole or baking sheet.

HEAT 1/2 cup of the olive oil in a large frying pan. Quickly fry the eggplant in batches over moderately high heat until crisp and golden on both sides. Add more olive oil as needed, and drain well on paper towels as you remove each batch from the pan.

MAKE a slightly overlapping layer of eggplant slices on the bottom of the casserole. Season with pepper. Spoon 4 tablespoons of strained tomatoes over the eggplant and scatter a few pieces of basil on top. Sprinkle with some mozzarella, followed by some Parmesan. Continue with this layering until you have used up all the ingredients.

BAKE FOR 30 minutes. Remove from the oven and allow to cool for 30 minutes before serving.

Frying the eggplant slices first adds flavor to the finished dish.

# LA BANDIERA

LA BANDIERA IS THE NAME OF THE ITALIAN FLAG. THIS DISH, FROM PUGLIA IN ITALY'S SOUTH, CONTAINS TOMATOES, ARUGULA AND PASTA—THE RED, GREEN AND WHITE INGREDIENTS MIMIC THE COLORS OF THE FLAG.

The colors of the Italian flag are reflected in many dishes, as tomatoes, peppers and green vegetables are often eaten with white mozzarella and pasta.

2 potatoes, cut into 1-inch cubes
3 1/3 cups ditali, pennette or maccheroncini rigati
4 tablespoons olive oil
3 garlic cloves, crushed
1/2 teaspoon ground anchovy fillets
2 x 14 oz. cans tomatoes, roughly chopped
1/4 teaspoon sugar
2 tablespoons chopped basil leaves
2 cups arugula leaves, torn into small pieces if large
2 tablespoons grated pecorino, plus a little extra for serving

SERVES 4

PUT a large saucepan of water on to boil. Add the potato with 1 teaspoon salt. When the potato has been boiling for 3–4 minutes, stir the pasta into the water.

MEANWHILE, heat the oil, garlic and anchovies in a large frying pan over low heat for 30 seconds. Before the garlic colors, add the tomato, sugar and basil. Increase the heat, season with salt and pepper and simmer until the pasta in the other pan has finished cooking.

DRAIN the potato and pasta and add to the tomato sauce. Add the arugula and pecorino, toss to coat and serve at once, with a little extra grated pecorino over the top.

# BEANS WITH RED PEPPER

1 cup fava beans
3 1/3 cups ditali, pennette or maccheroncini rigati
1/3 cup oil
2 garlic cloves, crushed
1 red pepper, julienned
pinch of cayenne pepper
1 1/3 cups mozzarella, diced
3 tablespoons grated pecorino

SERVES 4

BRING a large saucepan of water to a boil. Add the fava beans and cook for 2 minutes. Using a slotted spoon, transfer the beans to a bowl and cover with a plate. Stir the pasta into the boiling water with 1 teaspoon salt and cook until *al dente*. Meanwhile, peel off the fava bean skins.

HEAT the oil in a large frying pan and add the garlic and red pepper. Cook over low heat, without browning, for 2–3 minutes then add the cayenne pepper.

DRAIN the pasta and add to the frying pan with the fava beans, mozzarella and pecorino. Toss to coat and heat until the mozzarella just begins to melt. Season and serve.

BEANS WITH RED PEPPER

The popularity of the bean has spread from its home region of Tuscany (whose inhabitants are affectionately known as the "bean-eaters") to embrace the whole country. Many varieties of bean are bought dried and need to be soaked overnight before use.

# FAGIOLI ALL'UCCELLETTO

1³/₄ cups dried cannellini beans
bouquet garni
¹/₂ cup olive oil
2 garlic cloves
1 sage sprig, or ¹/₂ teaspoon dried sage
4 ripe tomatoes, peeled and chopped
1 tablespoon balsamic vinegar

SERVES 6

SOAK the beans in cold water overnight, then drain. Place in a large saucepan of cold water with the bouquet garni and bring to a boil. Add 2 tablespoons of the olive oil, reduce the heat and simmer for 1 hour. Add 1 teaspoon of salt and 2 cups boiling water and cook for a further 30 minutes, or until tender. Drain.

CUT the garlic cloves in half and put in a large saucepan with the sage and the remaining oil. Gently heat to infuse the flavors, but do not fry. Add the tomato and simmer for 10 minutes, then discard the garlic and the sprig of sage.

ADD the beans, season well and simmer for 15 minutes. Add a little boiling water at first to keep the saucepan moist, but then let the liquid evaporate towards the end of cooking. Stir the vinegar through just before serving. Serve hot.

# BRAISED BORLOTTI BEANS

BETTER KNOWN AS CRANBERRY BEANS IN THE U.S., THESE ARE BEST EATEN WARM OR COLD RATHER THAN PIPING HOT STRAIGHT FROM THE STOVE. THEY KEEP WELL IN THE FRIDGE FOR UP TO SIX DAYS, BUT, IF YOU ARE MAKING THEM IN ADVANCE, DON'T ADD PARSLEY UNTIL YOU ARE READY TO SERVE.

BRAISED BORLOTTI BEANS

1³/₄ cups dried borlotti (cranberry) beans
1³/₄ cups dry red wine
1 small onion, finely chopped
3 cloves
¹/₂ cup olive oil
1 rosemary sprig
3 garlic cloves, crushed
pinch of dried red chile flakes
3 tablespoons chopped parsley

SERVES 4–6

SOAK the beans in cold water overnight, then drain. Place in a large saucepan and add the wine, onion, cloves, half the olive oil and 3¹/₂ cups water. Cover and bring to a boil. Reduce the heat, remove the lid and simmer for 1 hour.

HEAT the remaining oil in a small saucepan. Strip the leaves off the rosemary sprig and chop finely. Place in the oil with the garlic and chile flakes and cook for 1 minute. Add to the beans and simmer for 30 minutes–1 hour, until the beans are tender.

DRAIN the beans, reserving cooking liquid. Return cooking liquid to the saucepan and simmer until it thickens. Season. Return beans to the saucepan and simmer for another 5 minutes. Stir in the parsley and cool for 15 minutes before serving.

# CHAR-GRILLED RADICCHIO

2 heads radicchio
1/4 cup olive oil
1 teaspoon balsamic vinegar

SERVES 4

TRIM the radicchio, discarding the outer leaves. Slice into quarters lengthwise and rinse well. Drain, then pat dry with paper towels.

PREHEAT a skillet to hot. Lightly sprinkle the radicchio with some of the olive oil and season. Cook for 2–3 minutes, until the under leaves soften and darken, then turn to cook the other side. Transfer to a dish and sprinkle with the remaining oil and vinegar. Serve hot with grilled meats, or cold as part of an antipasto platter.

There are several types of radicchio available in Italy, all from the North. This round variety, *rossa di Verona*, is from Chioggia. The longer-leaved type is from Treviso.

# CARDOONS WITH PARMESAN

CARDOONS, LIKE ARTICHOKES, ARE A TYPE OF THISTLE, GROWN FOR THEIR STALKS. THEY BROWN WHEN CUT, SO USE A STAINLESS STEEL KNIFE AND KEEP THEM IN ACIDULATED WATER. THE SICILIANS ALSO CALL THE YOUNG STALKS OF ARTICHOKES CARDOONS AND COOK THEM IN THE SAME WAY.

juice of 1 lemon
1 1/2 lb. cardoons
1 tablespoon all-purpose flour
4 tablespoons butter
1 small onion, thinly sliced
4 tablespoons grated Parmesan

SERVES 4

PUT HALF the lemon juice in a large bowl of cold water. Discard the green leaves, outer stalks and tough parts of the cardoons, leaving the tender white stalks. Cut into 3-inch lengths and toss into the bowl of water.

BRING a large saucepan of water to a boil. Add the remaining lemon juice, the flour and a large pinch of salt. Add the cardoons. Simmer for 50 minutes, or until tender. Drain and plunge into a bowl of cold water. Remove the strings with a knife, as you would with celery.

PREHEAT the oven to 350°F and grease a shallow 10 x 6 inch casserole or baking pan. Melt the butter in a small frying pan and add the onion. Cook over low heat for 10 minutes until soft and golden.

LAYER HALF the cardoons over the bottom of the casserole and season with pepper. Spoon half the onion over the top and sprinkle with half the Parmesan. Repeat these layers and bake in the oven for 30 minutes.

CARDOONS WITH PARMESAN

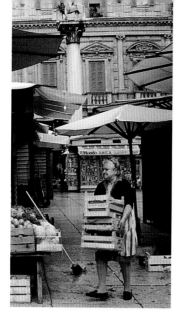

# POTATO CAKE

THE SOUTH OF ITALY CHERISHES ITS PASTA, WHILE THE NORTH PREFERS RICE AND POLENTA. ALTHOUGH THE POTATO HAS NEVER BECOME QUITE THE STAPLE IN ITALY THAT IT IS IN OTHER COUNTRIES, THERE ARE STILL SOME TRADITIONAL RECIPES.

1 small onion, thinly sliced into rings
5 tablespoons butter
2 garlic cloves, crushed
2 lb. potatoes, thinly sliced
2/3 cup mozzarella, grated
1/2 cup Parmesan, grated
2 tablespoons milk

SERVES 4

PLACE the onion in a bowl, cover with cold water and leave for 1 hour. Drain well. Preheat the oven to 415°F. Line an 8-inch springform pan with aluminum foil. Grease the foil.

MELT the butter in a small saucepan, add the garlic and set aside. Place a layer of potato over the bottom of the pan, followed by layers of onion, butter, mozzarella and Parmesan. Repeat the layers until you have used up all the ingredients, finishing with potato and keeping a bit of butter to drizzle on at the end. Season the layers as you go. Spoon the milk over the top.

BAKE for 1 hour, or until the top is golden brown and the potatoes are tender. If the top is overbrowning before the potatoes are done, cover with foil. Cool for 10 minutes before serving. Unclip the bottom of the pan, peel off the foil and transfer to a warm plate for serving.

# ROASTED ROSEMARY POTATOES

1/3 cup extra virgin olive oil
1 1/2 lb. baby potatoes or baking
   potatoes, cut into 1 1/2-inch cubes
long rosemary sprig
sea salt

SERVES 4

PREHEAT the oven to 325°F. Pour the oil into a shallow casserole or baking pan. Toss the potatoes into the casserole, turning to coat thoroughly in oil, then spread out so that the pieces aren't touching. Scatter the rosemary leaves over the potatoes.

ROAST for 30 minutes, then turn and sprinkle generously with sea salt. Return to the oven and roast for another 30–40 minutes, or until crisp and golden. Serve hot or cold.

ROASTED ROSEMARY
POTATOES

# POTATO AND LEEK GRATIN

3 tablespoons butter
3/4 lb. leeks, trimmed, halved and
   sliced
3 garlic cloves, thinly sliced
1 tablespoon chopped thyme
2 lb. potatoes, thinly sliced
1 1/2 cups mascarpone
1 cup vegetable stock

SERVES 4

PREHEAT the oven to 375°F. Heat the butter in a saucepan and cook the leeks for 10 minutes until soft. Season, add the garlic and thyme and cook for a couple of minutes. Grease an 8-inch round gratin dish with butter.

ARRANGE a layer of potato on the bottom of the dish and season with salt and pepper. Scatter with 3 tablespoons of leek and a few dollops of mascarpone. Continue layers, finishing with a potato layer and dollops of mascarpone. Pour stock over the top and cover with aluminum foil.

BAKE for 45 minutes, then remove the foil and bake for another 15 minutes to brown the top.

# POTATO AND PUMPKIN GRATIN

1 lb. potatoes, thinly sliced
leaves from 3 large thyme or
   rosemary sprigs, finely chopped
1 1/2 lb. pumpkin, thinly sliced
1 large garlic clove, crushed
2 cups heavy cream

SERVES 4

PREHEAT the oven to 375°F. Lightly grease a 10 x 9 inch gratin dish with a little butter. Arrange a layer of potato in the dish, season with salt, pepper and herbs, then top with a layer of pumpkin. Continue the layers, finishing with pumpkin. Mix the garlic with the cream and pour over the top. Cover the dish with buttered foil and bake in the oven for 45 minutes.

TEST TO see if the gratin is cooked by inserting a knife into the center. If the slices seem soft, it is cooked. Remove the foil and increase the oven temperature to 375°F. Cook for another 15 minutes, until there is a good brown crust on top. Allow to rest for at least 10 minutes before serving. Delicious with grilled meats or on its own with just a green salad.

POTATO AND PUMPKIN GRATIN

# VEGETABLE TORTE

1/4 lb. asparagus
4 tablespoons olive oil
1 onion, chopped
1 zucchini, halved lengthwise and
   finely sliced
2 large garlic cloves, crushed
1/4 lb. spinach, stalks removed
   if necessary
1 tablespoon chopped basil
3/4 cup Parmesan, grated
1 cup ricotta
1 1/3 cups mascarpone
4 eggs

SERVES 4

WASH the asparagus and remove the woody ends (hold each spear at both ends and bend it gently—it will snap at its natural breaking point). Remove the spear tips of the asparagus and slice the remaining stems. Bring a small saucepan of salted water to a boil and cook the asparagus stems for 2 minutes. Add the tips and cook for 1 minute. Drain the asparagus and set aside.

PREHEAT the oven to 375°F. Heat the olive oil in a saucepan and cook the onion until soft. Increase the heat and add the zucchini. Cook until the zucchini is soft and golden brown, stirring occasionally. Add the garlic and cook for 1 minute more. Finally, add the spinach and mix briefly until just wilted.

REMOVE the saucepan from the heat, add the asparagus and the basil, season with salt and pepper and set aside to cool.

GREASE an 8-inch springform pan with butter and dust with about 1 tablespoon of the Parmesan. Mix together the ricotta, mascarpone, eggs and 1/2 cup Parmesan and add it to the cooled vegetables. Mix well and taste for seasoning.

SPOON the mixture into the pan and scatter with the remaining Parmesan. Place in the oven, on a baking sheet to catch any drips, and cook for 30 minutes. The top should be light golden brown and the mixture still wobble slightly in the center. Leave to cool for 30 minutes, then chill in the fridge for about 3 hours, until the torte has set. Serve with a simple arugula or mixed leaf salad.

PIZZAS & BREADS

Naples in the shadow of Vesuvius.

# PIZZA SPINACI

2 tablespoons olive oil
2 garlic cloves, crushed
2 tablespoons pine nuts
2 lb spinach, roughly chopped
1 x 12-inch pizza dough circle
   (page 281)
cornmeal
1 batch tomato sauce (page 285)
1 1/2 cups mozzarella, chopped
15 very small black olives, such as
   Ligurian
3 tablespoons grated Parmesan
1/2 tablespoon olive oil

MAKES ONE 12-INCH PIZZA

PREHEAT the oven to 475°F. Heat the oil in a frying pan and lightly fry the garlic and pine nuts over low heat until golden. Add the spinach, increase the heat and stir until wilted. Season with salt and pepper.

PLACE the circle of pizza dough on a baking sheet dusted with cornmeal and spoon the tomato sauce onto the dough, spreading it up to the rim. Sprinkle with half the mozzarella. Spread the spinach and olives over the top, followed by the rest of the mozzarella and the Parmesan.

BAKE for 12–15 minutes, or until golden and puffed. Brush the rim with the oil before serving.

# PIZZA MARGHERITA

THIS CLASSIC PIZZA WAS SUPPOSEDLY INVENTED IN 1889 BY RAFFAELE ESPOSITO IN HONOR OF QUEEN MARGHERITA. THE QUEEN HAD HEARD SO MUCH OF THE FABLED PIZZAS OF NAPLES THAT SHE REQUESTED ONE TO EAT WHEN SHE VISITED THE CITY.

1 x 12-inch pizza dough circle
   (page 281)
cornmeal
1 batch tomato sauce (page 285)
1 cup mozzarella, chopped
9 small basil leaves
1 1/2 tablespoons olive oil

MAKES ONE 12-INCH PIZZA

PREHEAT the oven to 475°F. Place the pizza dough circle on a baking sheet dusted with cornmeal and spoon the tomato sauce onto the dough, spreading it up to the rim. Scatter with the mozzarella and basil and drizzle with a tablespoon of the oil.

BAKE for 12–15 minutes, or until golden and puffed. Remove from the oven and brush the rim with the remaining oil before serving.

PIZZA MARGHERITA

## MAKING A PIZZA

THE DOUGH (*impasto*) for the Brandi pizza is made with 00 (*doppio zero*) flour, water, salt and a piece of the previous day's dough as a leavening agent. The dough is risen slowly over 12 hours before being shaped. Each piece of dough (*pagnotte*) is stretched and flattened by hand to a diameter not more than 12 inches across. A true Neapolitan pizza is never tossed or rolled with a rolling pin and needs to be shaped gently to retain more air so that it puffs up in the oven. As the dough sits on the surface, it shrinks back slightly.

The pizza dough circle is spread with a fresh tomato sauce made from the pulp of tomatoes picked in the San Marzano region near Naples. The sauce is never cooked—like the rest of the ingredients it cooks only in the oven. The pizza is then scattered with shredded fresh buffalo mozzarella (*mozzarella di buffala*) or a cows milk mozzarella called *fior di latte*. Salt is scattered over the surface, followed by a drizzle of extra virgin olive oil from a brass can and fresh basil leaves. This is the classic combination for a pizza Margherita or Napoletana.

The pizza base is then stretched out a little further as it is placed on the long-handled wooden paddle used to move it into the brick-lined, wood-burning oven. The pizza is transferred from the paddle onto the floor of the oven and cooked for just 1 or 2 minutes at a red-hot temperature of about 750ºF. The extreme heat of the oven melts together the ingredients and causes the pizza to puff up and crispen. The pizza is then removed, sprinkled with a little more olive oil and served immediately.

PIZZA MARGHERITA had its birthplace at the famous Antica Pizzeria Brandi, still operating over 100 years later in Naples. Here pizza is made by hand, following the traditional methods. The kitchen is open so customers can see the work of the *pizzaiolo* and the brick-lined wood-fired pizza oven is kept at such a high temperature and is so thick that it retains its heat overnight. Each pizza takes only 1 or 2 minutes to brown and puff up.

# PIZZA

PIZZA BEGAN LIFE AS A FAST FOOD, EATEN HOT ON THE BACK STREETS OF NAPLES. TODAY IT IS FOUND ALL OVER THE WORLD, BUT IT IS STILL IN NAPLES THAT SKILLED *PIZZAIOLI* (PIZZA-MAKERS) USE WONDERFUL LOCAL TOMATOES, MOZZARELLA AND BASIL TO PRODUCE THE FINEST OF PIZZAS.

A pizza, in the sense of a flatbread covered with toppings, has probably been around since the Greeks and Romans, and many regions developed their own versions. However, it is the pizza of Naples that has come to be regarded as the true pizza. The first Neapolitan pizzas were white, made with garlic, lard, salt and anchovies. It was the tomato that was to transform pizza and the Neapolitans who were the first Europeans to embrace this new fruit, successfully growing them from seeds brought from the New World. The first tomato pizza was probably the classic *marinara*.

## PIZZA MARGHERITA

By the mid-nineteenth century, pizzerias had opened in Naples and wandering vendors sold slices to people on the streets. A way of life was born for the Neapolitans and their pizza began to achieve wider notoriety, with visitors venturing into poor neighborhoods to sample this new food. When Queen Margherita visited in 1889, she too wanted to try the famous pizza. A *pizzaiolo*, Raffaele Esposito, was summoned and created a pizza of mozzarella, tomatoes and basil based on the colors of the Italian flag—later to be named after her.

# PIZZA QUATTRO STAGIONI

1 x 12-inch pizza dough circle
(page 281)
cornmeal
1 batch tomato sauce (page 285)
1 tablespoon grated Parmesan
1/3 cup mozzarella, chopped
1 oz thinly sliced prosciutto, cut into
small pieces
1 plum tomato, thinly sliced
3 basil leaves, shredded
4 small artichoke hearts, marinated
in oil, drained and quartered
4 button mushrooms, sliced
pinch of dried oregano
1/2 tablespoon olive oil

MAKES ONE 12-INCH PIZZA

PREHEAT the oven to 475°F. Place the pizza dough circle on a baking sheet dusted with cornmeal and spoon the tomato sauce onto the dough, spreading it up to the rim. Sprinkle the Parmesan on top.

VISUALLY divide the pizza into quarters. Scatter the mozzarella over two opposite quarters. Spread the prosciutto over one of these, and arrange the tomato over the other. Lightly salt the tomato and sprinkle the basil over both sections.

ARRANGE the artichokes over the third quarter, and the mushrooms over the final quarter. Sprinkle the oregano over both these sections.

DRIZZLE the olive oil over the pizza. Bake for 12–15 minutes, or until golden and puffed.

Italy is the world's largest producer of artichokes, with 98 percent of the crop being grown for export. This beautiful vegetable, which varies in color from green to vibrant purple, is actually a thistle.

# PIZZA MELANZANA

1/2 lb long thin eggplants, thinly
sliced
1/4 cup olive oil
1 x 12-inch pizza dough circle
(page 281)
cornmeal
1 batch tomato sauce (page 285),
made with a pinch of dried red
chile flakes
1 1/4 cups mozzarella, chopped
15 black olives
1 tablespoon baby capers
4 tablespoons grated pecorino
1/2 tablespoon olive oil

MAKES ONE 12-INCH PIZZA

LAYER the eggplant in a colander, sprinkling salt on each layer. Leave to drain for 1 hour. Wipe off the salt with paper towels. Preheat the oven to 475°F.

HEAT the olive oil in a large frying pan and quickly brown the eggplant on both sides, cooking in batches. Drain on paper towels.

PLACE the pizza dough on a baking sheet dusted with cornmeal and spoon the tomato sauce onto the dough, spreading it up to the rim. Arrange the eggplant in a circular pattern over the top, then scatter with mozzarella. Scatter with the olives, capers and pecorino, then drizzle with oil. Bake for 12–15 minutes, or until golden and puffed.

PIZZA MELANZANA

# CALZONE

CALZONE IS UNLIKE OTHER PIZZAS IN THAT THE BASE IS FOLDED OVER THE TOPPING. THIS
NEAPOLITAN SPECIALTY MEANS "PANTS", PRESUMABLY BECAUSE THERE IS A RESEMBLANCE. EACH OF
THE FOLLOWING FILLINGS MAKES A 10-INCH CALZONE—ENOUGH FOR ONE TO TWO PERSONS.

cornmeal
1/2 batch pizza dough (page 281)
  for each calzone
1 1/2 tablespoons olive oil

MOZZARELLA AND PROSCIUTTO
1 cup mozzarella, cut into 1-inch
  cubes
2 thin slices prosciutto, cut in half
1 artichoke heart, marinated in oil,
  drained and cut into 3 slices from
  top to bottom

POTATO, ONION AND SALAMI
2 tablespoons vegetable oil
1 small onion, very thinly sliced
2 small red potatoes, unpeeled,
  very thinly sliced
1/2 cup mozzarella, chopped
2 oz sliced salami
2 tablespoons grated Parmesan

EACH RECIPE MAKES
ONE 10-INCH CALZONE

PREHEAT the oven to 450°F. Lightly grease a
baking sheet and dust with cornmeal.

ON a lightly floured surface roll out the dough
into a 7-inch circle. Now, using the heels of your
hands and working from the center outwards,
press out the circle to a diameter of about
12 inches. Transfer to the baking sheet. Brush
the entire surface lightly with olive oil.

TO MAKE the mozzarella and prosciutto calzone,
spread the mozzarella over one half of the pizza
dough, leaving a narrow border around the edge.
Roll the half slices of prosciutto into little tubes
and place on top of the cheese. Top with the
artichoke slices, then season well.

TO MAKE the potato, onion and salami calzone,
heat the oil in a frying pan and add the onion
slices. Cook for 1 minute, then scatter the potato
on top. Cook, stirring, for 3–4 minutes, until it is
beginning to brown. Season with salt and pepper.
Spread over one half of the pizza dough, leaving a
narrow border around the edge. Scatter the
mozzarella on top, followed by the salami slices
and Parmesan.

WHICHEVER calzone you make, fold the plain
side of the dough over the filling to make a half-
moon shape. Match the cut edges and press
them firmly together to seal. Fold them over and
press into a scrolled pattern to thoroughly seal in
the filling. Brush the surface with a little more oil,
then transfer to the oven. Bake for 20 minutes,
until the crust is golden.

PIZZA IS THE CLASSIC fast food and in Naples traditional round pizzas are baked to order, then folded into quarters and wrapped in paper to go. Elsewhere, it is more usual to find *pizza a tagglio,* pizza that has been baked on a large baking sheet and then sold by the slice. Probably originating in Rome, *pizza a tagglio* can be ordered by weight in many places and is then reheated as a fast snack or lunch.

## ASSOCIAZIONE VERA PIZZA NAPOLETANA

The True Neapolitan Pizza Association has been set up to safeguard the pizza. Their guidelines include making the dough only from flour, yeast, salt and water and by hand, not machine. The pizza is to be cooked directly on the floor of a brick or stone-lined wood-fired oven and the temperature must exceed 750°F. The *cornicione* (edge) must be high and soft and the whole crust not too crisp. A pizza should take only 2 minutes to cook and be brown and crispy with all the ingredients melted together.

Emigrating Neapolitans took pizza with them to America and, by the 1950s, it could probably be found more easily in North America than in northern Italy. When the rest of Italy did finally take to pizza, they adapted it to their own tastes: the Roman pizza has more topping, is thinner and crisper and does not have a *cornicione.*

**PISSALADEIRA** a Ligurian pizza that has a topping of onion, anchovy, tomato, garlic and black olives. It is also known as pizza all'Andrea.

**PIZZETTE** these miniature pizzas can often be found as part of an antipasto selection to be eaten with drinks in an Italian bar. They are also sold in bakeries as snacks.

**PIZZA BIANCA** means "white pizza" and is a pizza without a tomato base. Toppings vary from onions, peppers, olives, cheese and herbs to a simple garlic, rosemary and olive oil pizza.

**ROMANA** similar to a Margherita but with added anchovies and oregano. Romana is one of the classic pizzas that are recognized by the Associazione Vera Pizza Napoletana.

**SPINACI** often has a *bianca* base topped with spinach and garlic, though some varieties do include tomatoes or cheese as well.

**QUATTRO FORMAGGIO** four cheeses are used on this pizza, usually a mixture of mozzarella, fontina, Parmesan, Gorgonzola or pecorino.

**QUATTRO STAGIONE** the name means "four seasons", and the seasons are represented by ingredients in each quarter, from prosciutto, mushrooms and artichokes to clams or olives.

**MARINARA** is topped with tomato sauce, olive oil, garlic and oregano and sometimes other herbs. Despite its name, this pizza never has seafood—Marinara refers to the sauce.

**PROSCIUTTO E RUCOLA** a modern pizza topping where the base is baked with cream and Parma ham and then scattered with fresh arugula as soon as it comes out of the oven.

**MARGHERITA** the pizza invented for Queen Margherita. In Naples, it is made with San Marzano tomatoes topped with buffalo mozzarella or *fior di latte* and fresh basil.

**CALZONE** also called a *pizza ripieno,* this classic pizza is made by folding the pizza dough over the filling. The word *calzone* means pant leg—supposedly a reflection of its shape.

**SICILIANA** a pizza from Sicily that is baked in a rectangle and has a thicker crust than a Neapolitan pizza. It is often topped with tomatoes and anchovies.

# FOCACCIA WITH GREEN OLIVES AND ROSEMARY

ONE QUANTITY OF OUR FOCACCIA DOUGH RECIPE (PAGE 282) MAKES TWO FOCACCIA. EACH OF THE FOLLOWING RECIPES IS FOR ONE FOCACCIA, SO YOU CAN MAKE A COUPLE OF DIFFERENT TYPES WITH EACH BATCH OF DOUGH.

1/2 batch focaccia dough (page 282), rolled out, on a baking sheet
1 cup green olives
olive oil
2 teaspoons coarse sea salt
leaves of 2 rosemary sprigs

MAKES 1 FOCACCIA

PREHEAT the oven to 425°F. When the dough has risen a second time, scatter the olives over the surface and press them firmly down into the dough.

BRUSH WITH olive oil and sprinkle with the salt and rosemary. Bake for about 20 minutes, or until golden.

FOCACCIA WITH GREEN OLIVES AND ROSEMARY

# FOCACCIA WITH PANCETTA AND PARMESAN

1/2 batch focaccia dough (page 282), rolled out, on a baking sheet
3 oz pancetta, diced
10 basil leaves, torn in half
olive oil
2 tablespoons grated Parmesan

MAKES 1 FOCACCIA

PREHEAT the oven to 425°F. When the dough has risen a second time, scatter the pancetta over the surface and press the pieces firmly into the dough. Press a piece of basil into each indentation. Brush the surface of the dough with olive oil, sprinkle with Parmesan and bake for about 20 minutes, or until golden.

# FOCACCIA WITH GORGONZOLA AND PINE NUTS

1 cup Gorgonzola, or other creamy blue cheese
1–3 tablespoons mascarpone
1/2 batch focaccia dough (page 282), rolled out, on a baking sheet
10 sage leaves, roughly chopped
2 tablespoons pine nuts

MAKES 1 FOCACCIA

PREHEAT the oven to 425°F. Roughly mash the Gorgonzola with a fork, then mix in enough mascarpone to make the cheese spreadable, but not thin. When the dough has risen a second time, spread the Gorgonzola over the surface. Scatter the sage and pine nuts on top and bake for 20 minutes, or until golden.

FOCACCIA WITH GORGONZOLA AND PINE NUTS

FOCACCIA WITH PANCETTA AND PARMESAN

# COUNTRY-STYLE BREAD

THIS IS ONE OF THE BASIC LOAVES OF ITALY (ALTHOUGH NOT TUSCANY, WHERE THE REGIONAL *PANE TOSCANO* IS MADE WITHOUT SALT). IF YOU'RE SERVING IT FRESH WITH BUTTER, IT'S BEST EATEN ON BAKING DAY, BUT THE DAY-OLD BREAD IS EXCELLENT FOR MAKING BRUSCHETTA AND CROSTINI.

STARTER
3/4 cup milk, warmed
2 teaspoons honey
1 teaspoon dried yeast or
   1/4 oz. fresh yeast
1 cup all-purpose flour

DOUGH
1 teaspoon dried yeast or
   1/4 oz. fresh yeast
2 1/2 teaspoons salt
1 lb. all-purpose flour

MAKES 2 LOAVES

TO MAKE the starter, mix the milk and honey in a large bowl with 3 tablespoons warm water. Sprinkle the yeast over the top and stir to dissolve. Leave in a draft-free spot to activate. If the yeast does not bubble and foam in 5 minutes, throw it away and start again. Add the flour and whisk to form a thick paste. Cover loosely with plastic wrap and leave at room temperature overnight.

TO MAKE the dough, sprinkle the yeast over the starter. Using your fingertips, break up the starter by squeezing it between your fingers. Gradually add 1 cup water, combining it with the starter. Mix in the salt and flour with your fingers until the mixture comes together to form a soft dough.

TURN out the dough onto a lightly floured work surface and knead for 10 minutes or until smooth and elastic. Place the dough in a lightly oiled bowl and cover with a damp kitchen towel. Leave to rise in a draft-free place for 1–1 1/2 hours or until doubled in size. Knock back, turn out onto a lightly floured surface and knead for 1–2 minutes until smooth.

DIVIDE the dough into two and shape into round loaves, then flatten them slightly. Lightly grease a large baking sheet with oil and dust with flour. Put the loaves on the sheet and score a criss-cross pattern about 1/4 inch deep on top of each loaf. Dust lightly with more flour.

COVER with a damp kitchen towel and leave to rise in a draft-free place for about 40 minutes, or until doubled in size. Preheat the oven to 400°F. Bake for 30–35 minutes or until the bread sounds hollow when tapped underneath. Transfer to a wire rack to cool.

# PIZZETTE

1/2 batch pizza dough (page 281)
cornmeal
1³/4 cups mozzarella, grated

### GARLIC AND ROSEMARY PIZZETTE
4 garlic cloves, crushed
2 teaspoons chopped rosemary
1¹/2 tablespoons extra virgin olive oil
1/2 cup Parmesan, grated
3 garlic cloves, thinly sliced

### TOMATO AND OLIVE PIZZETTE
1¹/2 cups pitted black olives, diced
2 cups plum tomatoes, diced
3 garlic cloves, crushed
2 tablespoons finely shredded basil
3 tablespoons extra virgin olive oil
5 small basil sprigs

MAKES 10 PIZZETTE

PREHEAT the oven to 475°C. Form the pizza dough into 10 circles. Put the pizza circles on two baking sheets dusted with cornmeal. Brush with a little olive oil, then sprinkle the circles with mozzarella. Make five garlic and rosemary pizzette and five tomato and olive pizzette.

TO MAKE the garlic and rosemary pizzette, scatter five bases with the garlic and rosemary and drizzle the oil over the top. Sprinkle with Parmesan and garnish each pizzette with some slices of garlic.

TO MAKE the tomato and olive pizzette, mix together the olives, tomatoes, garlic and basil and spoon over the remaining dough circles. Drizzle with the oil and garnish with a basil sprig.

BAKE the pizzette for 10 minutes, or until the crusts are crisp and golden.

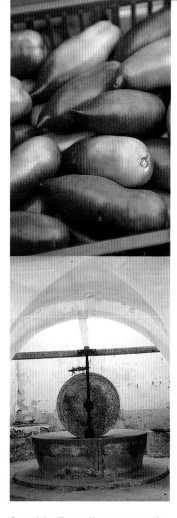

An old olive oil press at the Ravida estate in Menfi in Sicily. This stone was turned by a donkey who walked around it in a circle. Olives were ground between the two stones before being pressed to extract the oil.

# GRISSINI

1 tablespoon malt syrup (or honey)
2 teaspoons dried yeast or
  1/2 oz. fresh yeast
2¹/2 tablespoons olive oil
1 lb. all-purpose flour
1¹/2 teaspoons salt
fine semolina

MAKES 20

PUT 1¹/3 cups warm water in a small bowl and stir in the malt (or honey) and yeast. Leave until the yeast foams. Sift the flour and salt into a bowl, add the yeast mixture and 2 tablespoons olive oil and mix until the dough clumps together.

FORM into a ball and knead on a lightly floured surface for 5–6 minutes, or until smooth and elastic. Put the dough on a lightly oiled baking sheet and flatten out to fill the shape of the sheet. Brush with the remaining oil. Slide into a plastic bag and leave for 1 hour, or until doubled in size.

PREHEAT the oven to 450°F and lightly oil two baking sheets. Sprinkle the dough with semolina. Cut into four portions lengthwise, then slice each portion into five strips. Pick up each strip by both ends and stretch out to 8 inches long. Place on the baking sheet, 2 inches apart.

BAKE for 20 minutes, or until crisp and golden. Cool slightly on the sheets, then on wire racks.

GRISSINI

# POLENTA, RICE
# & PASTA

The fresh porcini is considered the king of mushrooms. Several different varieties are available and appear during the summer and autumn. Porcini are also dried and preserved in oil for the months they are not available.

Santa Maria della Salute, Venice.

# POLENTA WITH WILD MUSHROOMS

POLENTA, MADE FROM COARSE-GROUND CORN, WAS KNOWN AS THE FOOD OF THE POOR IN ROMAN TIMES. TODAY, ESPECIALLY AMONG ITALIANS LIVING ABROAD, IT HAS A WIDE AND LOVING AUDIENCE. SOMETIMES POLENTA IS SO FINE IT IS ALMOST WHITE; MORE OFTEN IT IS GOLDEN YELLOW.

POLENTA
1 tablespoon salt
2 cups coarse-grain polenta
3 tablespoons butter
3/4 cup Parmesan, grated

1/4 cup olive oil
1 lb. selection of wild mushrooms,
    particularly fresh porcini, sliced
    if large, or chestnut mushrooms
2 garlic cloves, crushed
1 tablespoon chopped thyme
3/4 cup mascarpone

SERVES 6

BRING 6 cups water to a boil in a heavy-bottomed saucepan and add the salt. Add the polenta to the water in a gentle stream, whisking or stirring vigorously as you pour it in. Reduce the heat immediately so that the water is simmering. Stir continuously for the first 30 seconds to avoid any lumps appearing—the more you stir, the better the texture will be. Once you have stirred well at the beginning you can leave the polenta to mildly bubble away, stirring it every few minutes to prevent it from sticking. Cook for 40 minutes.

MEANWHILE, prepare the mushrooms. Heat the olive oil in a large saucepan or frying pan. When the oil is hot, add just enough mushrooms to cover the bottom of the pan and cook at quite a high heat, stirring frequently. Season with salt and pepper. Sometimes the mushrooms can become watery when cooked: just keep cooking until all the liquid has evaporated. Add a little of the garlic at the last minute to prevent it from burning and then add a little thyme.

REMOVE THIS batch of mushrooms from the pan and repeat the process until they are all cooked. Return all the mushrooms to the pan (if the polenta isn't yet cooked, leave all the mushrooms in the pan and then reheat gently). Add the mascarpone and let it melt into the mushrooms.

ADD the butter and 1/2 cup of the Parmesan to the cooked polenta and season with pepper. Spoon the polenta onto plates and then spoon the mushrooms on top. Sprinkle with the remaining Parmesan and serve immediately.

# BAKED POLENTA WITH FOUR CHEESES

USE "PROPER" POLENTA INSTEAD OF THE QUICK-COOK VARIETY. IT MIGHT SEEM LABOR INTENSIVE, AS YOU HAVE TO STIR CONSTANTLY, BUT THE FLAVOR IS MUCH BETTER. IN ITALY THEY SOLVE THE PROBLEM BY HAVING SPECIAL "SELF-STIRRING" POLENTA PANS WITH A REVOLVING SPOON.

POLENTA
1 tablespoon salt
2 cups coarse-grain polenta
5 tablespoons butter

TOMATO SAUCE
3 tablespoons extra virgin olive oil
2 garlic cloves, thinly sliced
large sprig rosemary or thyme,
 roughly chopped
28 oz. can tomatoes

1 cup Gorgonzola, cubed
1 1/2 cups Taleggio, cubed
1 1/4 cups mascarpone
1 cup Parmesan, grated

SERVES 6

BRING 6 cups water to a boil in a heavy-bottomed saucepan and add the salt. Add the polenta to the water in a gentle stream, whisking or stirring vigorously as you pour it in. Reduce the heat immediately so that the water is simmering. Stir continuously for the first 30 seconds, to avoid any lumps appearing—the more you stir, the better the texture will be. Once you have stirred well at the beginning you can leave the polenta to mildly bubble away, stirring it every few minutes to prevent it from sticking. Cook for 40 minutes. Add the butter and mix well.

POUR the polenta into a shallow casserole or baking sheet about 2 inches deep (you want the polenta to come no more than halfway up the side of the dish). Leave to cool completely.

TO MAKE the tomato sauce, heat the olive oil in a saucepan and cook the garlic gently until light brown. Add half the rosemary or thyme and then the tomatoes. Season with salt and pepper and cook gently, stirring occasionally, until reduced to a thick tomato sauce.

PREHEAT the oven to 350°F. Turn the polenta out of the casserole and onto a board, then slice it horizontally in two. Pour half the tomato sauce into the bottom of the empty dish. Place the bottom slice of the polenta on top of the sauce and season. Scatter the Gorgonzola and Taleggio over the top. Dot the mascarpone over the polenta with a teaspoon, and sprinkle with half the Parmesan and the remaining herbs.

PUT the other layer of polenta on top and pour over the remaining tomato sauce. Sprinkle with the remaining Parmesan and bake for 30 minutes. Leave to rest for 10 minutes before serving with a simple arugula salad.

Arrange the first layer of polenta carefully in the dish but don't worry if you break it—it will seal again as it cooks. Lay the cheese in an even layer on top of the polenta before finishing with the final layers.

Risotto rice comes in different types, all varying in absorbency. For this reason cooking times cannot be entirely accurate—just keep stirring until it is done.

At Antica Riseria Ferron in the Veneto, rice is polished by hand to produce perfect wihite grains.

# MILANESE RISOTTO

MILANESE RISOTTO, THE CLASSIC ACCOMPANIMENT TO OSSO BUCO, TAKES ITS BRILLIANT YELLOW COLOR FROM SAFFRON AND ITS RICH FLAVOR FROM BEEF MARROW. IF BEEF MARROW IS HARD TO FIND, YOU CAN USE A FATTY PIECE OF LARDO, PROSCIUTTO OR PANCETTA, FINELY CHOPPED.

$3/4$ cup dry white vermouth or white wine
large pinch of saffron threads
6 cups chicken stock
$1/2$ cup butter
$2^1/2$ oz. beef marrow
1 large onion, finely chopped
1 garlic clove, crushed
$1^2/3$ cups risotto rice (arborio, vialone nano or carnaroli)
$1/2$ cup Parmesan, grated

SERVES 6 AS A SIDE DISH

PUT the vermouth in a bowl, add the saffron and let it soak. Put the stock in a saucepan, bring to a boil and then maintain at a low simmer.

MELT the butter and beef marrow in a large wide heavy-bottomed saucepan. Add the onion and garlic and cook until softened but not browned. Add the rice and reduce the heat to low. Season and stir briefly to thoroughly coat the rice.

ADD the vermouth and saffron to the rice. Increase the heat and cook, stirring, until all the liquid has been absorbed. Stir in a ladleful of the simmering stock and cook over moderate heat, stirring continuously. When the stock has been absorbed, stir in another ladleful. Continue like this for 20 minutes, until all the stock has been added and the rice is *al dente*. (You may not need to use all the stock, or you may need a little extra—every risotto will be slightly different.)

STIR IN a handful of Parmesan and serve the rest on the side for people to help themselves.

# SEAFOOD RISOTTO

AS WITH MOST SEAFOOD DISHES, DON'T SERVE THIS RISOTTO WITH PARMESAN. IN LOMBARDIA AND PIEMONTE, RISOTTO IS CREAMY BUT THE GRAINS RETAIN A "BITE". VENETIANS MAKE THEIR RISOTTOS *ALL'ONDA*, ALMOST LIQUID LIKE SOUPS, TO BE EATEN WITH A SPOON. YOU CAN CHOOSE EITHER STYLE.

6 oz. squid tubes
1/2 lb. shrimp
4 tablespoons olive oil
2 garlic cloves, crushed
6 oz. firm white fish fillets, such as
  monkfish or sea bass, skinned
  and cut into bite-sized pieces
16 scallops, cleaned
4 cups fish stock
1 leek, white part only, thinly sliced
1²/₃ cups risotto rice (arborio,
  vialone nano or carnaroli)
1/2 cup dry white wine
3 plum tomatoes, chopped
1 tablespoon butter
1¹/₂ tablespoons finely chopped
  parsley
1¹/₂ tablespoons finely chopped dill

SERVES 4

CUT the squid tubes into thinner rings. Peel and devein the shrimp.

HEAT HALF the olive oil in a large wide heavy-bottomed saucepan. Add the garlic and cook gently without browning for 20–30 seconds. Add the squid and shrimp and season lightly. Increase the heat and cook until they turn opaque. Remove the squid and shrimp from the pan and set aside.

ADD the fish and scallops to the saucepan and cook until the fish changes color. Remove from the saucepan and set aside.

PUT the stock in a saucepan, bring to a boil and then maintain at a low simmer.

ADD the remaining oil to the large wide saucepan. Add the leek and cook for 3–4 minutes, or until softened but not browned. Add the rice and reduce the heat to low. Season and stir briefly to thoroughly coat the rice, then add the white wine. Increase the heat and cook, stirring, until all the liquid has been absorbed.

STIR IN a ladleful of the simmering stock and cook over moderate heat, stirring continuously. When the stock has been absorbed, stir in another ladleful. Continue like this for 20 minutes, until all the stock has been added and the rice is *al dente*. (You may not need to use all the stock, or you may need a little extra—every risotto will be slightly different. If you prefer, add more stock to make the risotto more liquid.) Add the tomato and cooked seafood and toss lightly.

REMOVE the saucepan from the heat and gently stir in the butter and chopped herbs. Season with salt and black pepper. Spoon into warm serving bowls and serve at once.

Cooking the seafood quickly over high heat keeps it tender.

# ASPARAGUS RISOTTO

THIS RISOTTO IS PARTICULARLY FLAVORSOME BECAUSE THE ASPARAGUS STEMS ARE PUREED WITH THE STOCK AND SO ADDED TO THE RISOTTO DURING THE COOKING. THE ADDITION OF CREAM AT THE END GIVES A RICH CONSISTENCY.

2 lb. asparagus
2 cups chicken stock
2 cups vegetable stock
4 tablespoons olive oil
1 small onion, finely chopped
1²/₃ cups risotto rice (arborio, vialone nano or carnaroli)
³/₄ cup Parmesan, grated
3 tablespoons heavy cream

SERVES 4

WASH the asparagus and remove the woody ends (hold each spear at both ends and bend it gently—it will snap at its natural breaking point). Separate the tender spear tips from the stems.

COOK the asparagus stems in boiling water for 8 minutes, or until very tender. Drain and place in a blender with the chicken and vegetable stocks. Blend for 1 minute, then put in a saucepan, bring to a boil and maintain at a low simmer.

COOK the asparagus tips in boiling water for 1 minute, drain and refresh in iced water.

HEAT the olive oil in a large wide heavy-bottomed saucepan. Add the onion and cook over low heat until softened but not browned. Add the rice and reduce the heat to low. Season and stir briefly to coat the rice. Stir in a ladleful of the simmering stock and cook over moderate heat, stirring continuously. When the stock has been absorbed, stir in another ladleful. Continue like this for about 20 minutes, until all the stock has been added and the rice is *al dente*. (You may not need to use all the stock, or you may need a little extra—every risotto will be slightly different.)

ADD the Parmesan and cream and gently stir in the asparagus tips. Season and serve hot.

Gabriele Ferron cooking risotto at his restaurant in Isola della Scala.

For freshness, grate the Parmesan from a block as you need it. Take care as you fold in the asparagus tips—try not to break them.

# RED WINE RISOTTO

THE SECRET TO A REALLY SPECTACULAR RED WINE RISOTTO IS TO USE ONLY THE VERY BEST INGREDIENTS. AS THE DISH IS SO SIMPLE, A GOOD-QUALITY WINE IS REQUIRED—TRADITIONALLY THE DRY RED AMARONE OF VALPOLICELLA IS USED.

2 cups chicken stock
7 tablespoons butter
1 onion, finely chopped
1 large garlic clove, crushed
2 tablespoons chopped thyme
1 cup risotto rice (arborio, vialone nano or carnaroli)
2 cups dry red wine
1/2 cup Parmesan, grated

SERVES 4

PUT the stock in a saucepan, bring to a boil and then maintain at a low simmer.

HEAT the butter in a large wide heavy-bottomed saucepan. Add the onion and garlic and cook until softened but not browned. Add the thyme and rice and reduce the heat to low. Season and stir briefly to thoroughly coat the rice.

ADD HALF the red wine. Increase the heat and cook, stirring, until all the liquid has been absorbed. Stir in a ladleful of the simmering stock and cook over moderate heat, stirring continuously. When the stock has been absorbed, stir in another ladleful. Continue like this for 10 minutes, until you have added half the stock.

ADD the remaining red wine to the risotto, stirring continuously until it has been absorbed. Stir in another ladleful of the stock and then continue for 10 minutes until all the stock has been added and the rice is *al dente*. (You may not need to use all the stock, or you may need a little extra—every risotto will be slightly different.)

STIR IN half the Parmesan just before serving with the remaining cheese to be sprinkled on top.

Stir the rice into the butter and onion mixture, making sure that you coat all the grains. Add the red wine and stir continuously so the rice does not stick to the bottom of the pan and the grains are kept separate.

# RISOTTO NERO

YOU CAN SOMETIMES BUY THE INK SAC OF THE SQUID FROM YOUR FISHMONGER, ALTHOUGH MOST ARE LOST OR BURST BY THE TIME THE SQUID REACHES THE STORE. THE LITTLE SACHETS OF INK ARE MORE EASILY FOUND. SQUID INK QUALIFIES AS SEAFOOD, SO DON'T SERVE THIS RISOTTO WITH PARMESAN.

2 medium-sized squid
4 cups fish stock
7 tablespoons butter
1 red onion, finely chopped
2 garlic cloves, crushed
1²/₃ cups risotto rice (arborio, vialone nano or carnaroli)
3 sachets of squid or cuttlefish ink, or the ink sac of a large cuttlefish
¹/₂ cup white wine
2 teaspoons olive oil

SERVES 6

PREPARE the squid by pulling the heads and tentacles out of the bodies along with any innards. Cut the heads off below the eyes, leaving just the tentacles. Discard the heads and set the tentacles aside. Rinse the bodies, pulling out the transparent quills. Finely chop the bodies.

PUT the stock in a saucepan, bring to a boil and then maintain at a low simmer.

HEAT the butter in a large wide heavy-bottomed saucepan and cook the onion until softened but not browned. Increase the heat and add the chopped squid. Cook for 3–5 minutes, or until the squid turns opaque. Add the garlic and stir briefly. Add the rice and reduce the heat to low. Season and stir briefly to thoroughly coat the rice.

SQUEEZE OUT the ink from the sachets and add to the rice with the wine. Increase the heat and stir until it has all been absorbed.

STIR IN a ladleful of the simmering stock and cook over moderate heat, stirring continuously. When the stock has been absorbed, stir in another ladleful. Continue like this for 20 minutes, until all the stock has been added and the rice is *al dente*. (You may not need to use all the stock, or you may need a little extra—every risotto will be slightly different.)

HEAT the olive oil in a frying pan and fry the squid tentacles quickly. Garnish the risotto with the tentacles and serve immediately.

Adding the wine to the ink and rice helps the ink dissolve and spread evenly through the risotto.

# MUSHROOM RISOTTO

4 dried porcini mushrooms
4 cups vegetable or chicken stock
2 tablespoons olive oil
1 tablespoon butter
1 small onion, finely chopped
2 garlic cloves, crushed
1²/₃ cups risotto rice (arborio,
   vialone nano or carnaroli)
2²/₃ cups mushrooms, sliced
pinch of nutmeg
¹/₂ cup Parmesan, grated
3 tablespoons finely chopped
   parsley

SERVES 4

SOAK the porcini in 2 cups boiling water for 30 minutes. Drain, retaining the liquid. Chop the porcini mushrooms. Pass the liquid through a fine sieve. Put the stock in a saucepan, bring to a boil and then maintain at a low simmer.

HEAT the olive oil and butter in a large wide heavy-bottomed saucepan. Cook the onion and garlic until softened but not browned. Add the rice and reduce the heat to low. Season and stir briefly to thoroughly coat the rice. Toss in the fresh mushrooms and nutmeg. Season and cook, stirring, for 1–2 minutes. Add the porcini and their liquid, increase the heat and cook until the liquid has been absorbed.

STIR IN a ladleful of the stock and cook over moderate heat, stirring continuously. When the stock has been absorbed, stir in another ladleful. Continue for 20 minutes, until all the stock has been added and the rice is *al dente*. (You may not need to use all the stock, or you may need a little extra.) Remove from the heat and stir in the Parmesan and parsley. Season and serve.

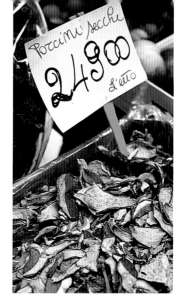

Dried porcini give an earthiness to dishes. When used with fresh mushrooms they add an attractive depth of flavor.

# RISI E BISI

RISI E BISI IS A THICK SOUP, HALFWAY BETWEEN RISOTTO AND SOUP IN TEXTURE AND APPEARANCE—
YOU CAN COOK IT THIN ENOUGH TO EAT WITH A SPOON, OR THICK ENOUGH TO USE A FORK. SOME
VERSIONS ARE VERY SIMPLE AND DO NOT EVEN INCLUDE PANCETTA.

6 cups chicken or vegetable stock
2 teaspoons olive oil
3 tablespoons butter
1 small onion, finely chopped
3 oz. pancetta, cut into small cubes
2 tablespoons chopped parsley
2¹/₂ cups shelled young peas
1 cup risotto rice (arborio, vialone
   nano or carnaroli)
¹/₂ cup Parmesan, grated

SERVES 4

PUT the stock in a saucepan, bring to a boil and then maintain at a low simmer. Heat the oil and half the butter in a large wide heavy-bottomed saucepan and cook the onion and pancetta over low heat for 5 minutes until softened. Stir in the parsley and peas and add 2 ladlefuls of the stock. Simmer for 6–8 minutes.

ADD the rice and the remaining stock. Simmer until the rice is *al dente* and most of the stock has been absorbed. Stir in the remaining butter and the Parmesan, season and serve.

RISI E BISI

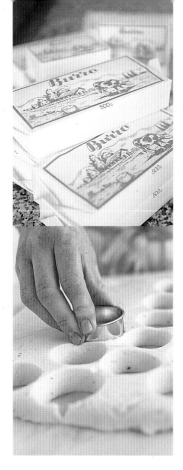

A biscuit cutter gives a good clean edge to the gnocchi. If you don't have one, use an upturned glass or teacup instead.

This cheesemaker has just opened a whole Parmesan. Traditionally Parmesan is "flaked", as shown here, rather than cut.

# ROMAN GNOCCHI

THESE *GNOCCHI ALLA SEMOLINA* CAN BE PREPARED A DAY OR TWO IN ADVANCE, WRAPPED WELL AND STORED IN THE REFRIGERATOR IN EITHER SLAB FORM OR CUT INTO CIRCLES. THEY ARE QUITE DIFFERENT FROM THE MORE WELL-KNOWN POTATO GNOCCHI SERVED WITH PASTA SAUCE.

3 tablespoons unsalted butter, melted
1/3 cup Parmesan, grated
3 egg yolks
4 cups milk
pinch of nutmeg
11/2 cups semolina flour

TOPPING
3 tablespoons butter, melted
1/3 cup heavy cream
1/3 cup Parmesan, grated

SERVES 4

LINE a 12 x 10 inch jelly roll pan with parchment paper. Beat together the butter, Parmesan and egg yolks and season lightly. Set aside.

HEAT the milk in a large saucepan. Add the nutmeg, and season with salt and pepper. When the milk is just boiling, pour in the semolina in a steady stream, stirring as you pour. Reduce the heat and continue to cook, stirring, for 10–12 minutes, or until all the milk has been absorbed and the mixture pulls away from the side of the saucepan in one mass.

REMOVE the saucepan from the heat and beat in the egg yolk mixture. When smooth, spoon quickly into the jelly roll pan. Smooth the surface to give an even thickness, using a knife dipped in cold water. Set aside to cool.

PREHEAT the oven to 350°F and grease a 10 x 7 inch shallow casserole or baking sheet.

LIFT the semolina slab out of the jelly roll pan and peel off the parchment paper. Cut the semolina into circles, using a 11/2-inch biscuit cutter dipped in cold water. Arrange the circles, slightly overlapping, in the greased casserole.

TO MAKE the topping, blend together the butter and cream. Pour this over the gnocchi and sprinkle the Parmesan on top. Transfer to the oven and bake for 25–30 minutes, or until golden. Serve at once.

# POTATO GNOCCHI WITH PANCETTA AND SAGE

WHEN COOKING THE POTATOES FOR GNOCCHI YOU WANT TO KEEP THEM AS DRY AS POSSIBLE—TOO MUCH MOISTURE WILL RESULT IN A HEAVY DOUGH. BAKING POTATOES HAVE A LOW MOISTURE CONTENT AND BAKING THE POTATOES IN THEIR SKINS KEEPS THEM DRIER THAN BOILING.

GNOCCHI
2 lb. baking potatoes, unpeeled
2 egg yolks
2 tablespoons grated Parmesan
1–1 1/2 cups all-purpose flour

SAUCE
1 tablespoon butter
3 oz. pancetta or bacon, cut into
 thin strips
8 very small sage or basil leaves
1/2 cup heavy cream
1/2 cup Parmesan, grated

SERVES 4

PRICK the potatoes all over, then bake for 1 hour, or until tender. Leave to cool for 15 minutes, then peel and mash, or put through a ricer or a food mill (do not use a blender or food processor).

MIX IN the egg yolks and Parmesan, then gradually stir in the flour. When the mixture gets too dry to use a spoon, work with your hands. Once a loose dough forms, transfer to a lightly floured surface and knead gently. Work in enough extra flour to give a soft, pliable dough that is damp to the touch but doesn't stick to your fingers.

DIVIDE the dough into six portions. Working with one portion at a time, roll out on the floured surface to make a rope about 1/2 inch thick. Cut the rope into 1/2-inch lengths. Take one piece of dough and press your finger into it to form a concave shape, then roll the outer surface over the tines of a fork to make deep ridges. Fold the outer lips in towards each other to make a hollow in the middle. Continue with the remaining dough.

BRING a large saucepan of salted water to a boil. Add the gnocchi in batches, about 20 at a time. Stir gently and return to a boil. Cook for 1–2 minutes, or until they rise to the surface. Remove them with a slotted spoon, drain and put in a greased shallow casserole or baking pan. Preheat the oven to 400°F.

TO MAKE the sauce, melt the butter in a small frying pan and fry the pancetta until crisp. Stir in the sage leaves and cream. Season and simmer for 10 minutes, or until thickened.

POUR the sauce over the gnocchi, toss gently and sprinkle the Parmesan on top. Bake for 10–15 minutes, or until the Parmesan melts and turns golden. Serve hot.

Knead enough to just bring the dough together and make it smooth. Keep the work surface, your hands and any baking sheets well floured. Roll and shape the dough quickly to stop it drying out.

Fold the filling into the crepes and place them at an angle in the dish, so the filling doesn't run out as it heats up.

# CRESPELLE

### CREPES
1¹/₂ cups all-purpose flour
3 eggs
³/₄ cup milk
3–4 tablespoons butter

### CHICKEN LIVER, SPINACH AND CHEESE FILLING
1 tablespoon butter
5 oz. chicken livers, trimmed
pinch of nutmeg
1¹/₃ cups spinach, shredded
1 cup ricotta
1 cup Parmesan, grated
2 tablespoons chopped parsley
1 batch tomato sauce (page 285)

### HAM, EGG AND ASPARAGUS FILLING
6 oz. asparagus, chopped
1 tablespoon butter
1 tablespoon all-purpose flour
¹/₂ cup hot milk
2 tablespoons grated Parmesan
1 teaspoon chopped basil
2 eggs, hard-boiled and chopped
4 oz. ham, cut into strips
3 tablespoons melted butter
³/₄ cup Parmesan, grated

MAKES 12 CREPES

TO MAKE the crepes, place the flour in a bowl. Make a well in the center and add the eggs and a good pinch of salt. Mix well with a wooden spoon. Gradually pour in the milk combined with ³/₄ cup water, whisking constantly until you have a smooth runny batter. Allow to rest for 2 hours.

STIR the batter and add a little more water, if necessary, to return it to the original consistency. Heat a little butter in a 7-inch crepe pan. Spoon in 2–3 tablespoons of batter, tilting the pan to cover the bottom. Cook for 1 minute, until brown but not set, then turn over with a spatula and cook for another 30 seconds until set. Slide onto a plate and cook the rest of the batter. Preheat the oven to 350°F.

TO MAKE the chicken liver, spinach and cheese filling, heat the butter in a saucepan and cook the chicken livers for 3 minutes. Season with salt, pepper and the nutmeg, then chop. Put the spinach in the pan and cook until wilted. Mash the ricotta with a fork and add the Parmesan. Stir in the parsley, chicken livers and spinach, and season. Place a spoonful of filling in the center of each crepe and roll up, or fold it in half and then half again. Place in a greased shallow flameproof dish, pour the tomato sauce over the top and bake for 20 minutes.

TO MAKE the ham, egg and asparagus filling, simmer the asparagus in boiling salted water for 3 minutes. Melt the butter in a saucepan, stir in the flour, then add the hot milk, stirring until you have a thick sauce. Stir in the Parmesan, basil, eggs, asparagus and ham, and season well. Place a spoonful of filling in the center of each crepe and roll up, or fold it in half and then half again. Place in a greased shallow casserole or baking pan, sprinkle the melted butter and Parmesan on top and bake for 20 minutes.

**SPAGHETTI** these "little strings" are a specialty of Naples, where they're also known as vermicelli. Traditionally 16–20 inches long (as shown here) it is now usually sold half that size.

**ORZO** tiny pieces of pasta shaped like barley that are used in clear soups such as *pasta in brodo*.

**BAVETTE** a long pasta formed like a slightly flattened, oval spaghetti. This shape goes particularly well with pesto. There is also a larger Genovese version called *trenette*.

**BUCATINI** a long straight noodle with a *buco* (hole) down the center that makes it cook a little more quickly. Usually eaten with meat ragù.

**CAPELLI D'ANGELO** meaning "angel hair", and looking like long blond hair, this is the thinnest spaghetti you can buy. Goes well with delicate sauces.

**STRANGOZZI** a specialty of Mantova, this egg pasta is usually served with Norcia truffles or wild boar sauce in Umbria. Egg, spinach and peperoncino versions are shown.

**CAPPELLETTI** this egg pasta from Emilia-Romagna looks like a *cappello*, the Italian for hat, hence its name. The filling is ground meat with prosciutto and Parmesan.

**GEMELLI** meaning "the twins", this pasta is folded into two strands and picks up plenty of sauce at the seams.

**MAFALDINE** the curled edges of this dried ribbon pasta prevent it sticking to other ribbons when cooking, and collect more sauce.

**FUSILLI** spiral-shaped dried pasta originally from Campania. The shape goes well with a tomato sauce or meat ragù.

**DITALI** like the smaller *ditalini* and the larger *ditaloni*, these thimble-shaped pasta pieces can be smooth or ridged. Ditali are used in soups while ditalini are used in broths.

**LASAGNE** refers to the pasta sheet, rather than the actual dish. Most lasagna sheets are flat, but *lasagne riccia* has a frilled edge to incorporate more air and give a lighter dish.

**MAKING PASTA SECCA** Pastificio Faella, near Naples, is owned by Signore Mario Faella (pictured) and is one of the few *pastificios* (artisan pasta factories) to still use the traditional methods for making dried pasta. Italian farmers cannot grow enough wheat to meet demand, so Italian durum wheat semolina flour (the *Pasta di Semola di Grano Duro* shown) is mixed with drier imported flour and water to create *pasta alimentare*. The high

# PASTA

PASTA WAS ORIGINALLY A SOUTHERN ITALIAN, PARTICULARLY SICILIAN, DISH, WITH THE FIRST PASTA INDUSTRY LOCATED IN NAPLES TO TAKE ADVANTAGE OF ITS PURE WATER, LOCAL GRAIN AND ABUNDANT SUNSHINE.

It was Mussolini who moved the cultivation of wheat, and therefore pasta, to other areas of Italy, and emigrating Italians who made it famous throughout the world. Nowadays, northern Italy tends to eat fresh egg and filled pastas (*pasta fresca*), often with rich meat or cream sauces or sometimes with just melted butter and Parmesan. Emilia-Romagna in the North now rivals Naples as the center of pasta production, with its fresh pasta made daily by hand. The

South specializes in dried durum wheat semolina pasta made without egg (*pasta secca*). The hard durum wheat is needed to form the pasta into shapes and also to maintain its *al dente* consistency. This dried pasta is usually eaten with less rich and vegetable sauces. In Italy, pasta tends to be eaten as a *primo piatti*, or first course, rather than as a main course, and is always cooked fresh to order.

## TYPES OF PASTA SECCA (DRIED PASTA)

PASTA CORTA short shapes, from the tiny ones used in soups to the familiar penne, farfalle and fusilli. Many of these pastas are hollow so that they cook evenly.

PASTA LUNGA long shapes such as spaghetti and tagliatelle, or any variety over about 4 inches.

PASTA ALL'UOVO SECCA this dried egg pasta is made from a combination of durum wheat semolina and eggs and can only be made by machine because of the toughness of the dough. The shapes vary from ribbons, sold in nests, to filled pasta shapes such as tortellini or ravioli.

**MAKING PASTA FRESCA** The chefs at Borgo San Felice, Tuscany, make fresh pasta daily, just as many other restaurants in Italy do. Fresh pasta is made using 00 (*doppio zero* or double zero) flour and free-range eggs, rather than the harder durum wheat semolina used for making dried pasta. The flour and eggs are poured into the top of the pasta machine, which mixes the dough before extruding it through variously sized

amount of protein in the grain means there is no need for any other binding agents and it allows the pasta to easily pass through a die (the traditional brass die shown makes a whiter pasta and adds a roughness that helps it pick up sauce). As the pasta passes through the die, it is shaped and cut to length, then dried slowly in hot rooms. Finally, it is packaged up and sold by weight from the small store in front of the factory.

## TYPES OF PASTA FRESCA (FRESH PASTA)

**PASTA FRESCA ALL'UOVO** made from eggs and 00 flour (a soft wheat flour), this pasta is eaten mostly in the North and can be molded easily into shapes such as tortellini and cappelletti, as well as being rolled out to make sheets of lasagna and pasta ribbons.

**PASTA DI SEMOLA FRESCA** unlike fresh pasta from the North, this homemade pasta from the South is created from just durum wheat semolina and water. The most common shapes are fusilli, orecchiette and *strozzapreti*.

## MATCHING SAUCES TO PASTA

Pastas are crafted to complement certain sauces. Shapes are often available as *lisci* (smooth) and *rigati* (ridged) and should be served with just enough sauce to coat them. The drained cooking water from the pasta can be added to the sauce if it is too thick.

**SMALL PASTA SHAPES** (alfabeto, *ditalini*, orzo and *stelline*) known as *pastina,* these pastas are added to soups. There are many different shapes, ranging from letters and numbers to stars, rings and tiny shells.

**LONG PASTA** (*trenette*, linguine, spaghetti, *bucatini*, ziti) best eaten with fine-textured sauces such as pesto, tomato sauce or a meat ragù that will cling to their lengths. They are also used in *pasticcios*.

**PASTA RIBBONS** (tagliatelle, fettuccine) serve with simple, fresh flavorings such as truffles or with creamy mushroom or ham sauces. When yellow and green ribbons are served together they are known as "straw and hay".

**PASTA SHAPES** (fusilli, *lumache*, orecchiette) serve with thicker, chunkier sauces, which are trapped by their shape. Pasta shapes also go well with sauces that have pieces of sausage, seafood or vegetable in them or with thicker soup in dishes such as *pasta e fagioli*.

**STUFFED PASTAS** (cappelletti, tortelli, ravioli) as they already have flavored fillings such as meat, pumpkin or spinach, filled pastas go well with simple sauces such as butter and sage, a fresh tomato sauce or in a *pasta in brodo*.

dies. As the pasta passes through the machine, lengths of it are cut and laid out to dry on a baking sheet that has been sprinkled with semolina to stop it sticking. More semolina is sprinkled on as the layers build up, before the whole batch is tossed together to thoroughly coat it. The same pasta dough is also rolled out thin and cut into sheets for lasagne or used to make filled pastas such as tortellini and ravioli.

**MACCHERONI** can refer to any pasta in the south of Italy, though it usually means a smooth or ridged tube shape. Eaten with a tomato sauce or meat ragù.

**STELLINE** these little stars are a *pastina per brodo* (pasta for soups), which look very pretty when cooked.

**RUOTE** a wheel-shaped pasta that is usually served with tomato sauce. Sometimes also known as *rotelline*.

**TORTELLI** is a fresh pasta, originally from Bologna, that has different fillings such as pumpkin, meat or spinach. Tortellini are a smaller version and tortelloni a larger one.

**PIZZOCCHERI** a thick noodle made with a mixture of wheat and buckwheat flours. It is eaten with potato, winter greens, cabbage and cheese in a type of pasta bake.

**RIGATONI** the ribbed outside (*rigati*) of this tube-shaped pasta helps to pick up more sauce than penne. Eaten with a tomato sauce or baked.

**TAGLIATELLE** fresh or dried ribbons also known as fettuccine, particularly the slightly thicker ribbons in central and southern Italy. Traditionally eaten with a meat ragù.

**PENNE RIGATE** quill-shaped tubes popular in Campania and Liguria, where they are served with chile sauces, such as *penne all'arrabbiata*.

**CANDELE** large tubes that are broken or cut to form shorter lengths. Sometimes made as one of the Faella factory's specialties, they are served with strong cheese or meat ragùs.

**CONCHIGLIE** a pasta shell originating in Campania. Smaller shells are eaten with sauces, while larger ones are stuffed with spinach and ricotta.

**RAVIOLI** these stuffed pasta are also known as *agnolotti*. Smaller ravioli are eaten in soups, while larger ones are served with butter or a simple sauce. The filling is usually meat.

**ZITI** long tubes of dried, smooth pasta that are a specialty of the South, especially Naples. A larger version of ziti is known as *candele*.

201

# SPAGHETTI CARBONARA

THE ORIGIN OF THIS DISH IS HOTLY DISPUTED. WAS IT BROUGHT TO ROME BY THE *CARBONARI* (COAL MEN) FROM UMBRIA? OR INSPIRED BY THE EGG AND BACON RATIONS OF THE AMERICAN GI'S? OR PERHAPS NAMED AFTER THE NINETEENTH-CENTURY RADICAL GROUP, *I CARBONARI*.

13 oz. spaghetti
2 eggs
2 egg yolks
2/3 cup Parmesan, grated, plus
   extra for serving
2 tablespoons olive oil
2 tablespoons butter
2 garlic cloves
7 oz. pancetta, cut into small strips

SERVES 4

COOK the pasta in a large saucepan of boiling salted water until *al dente*. Meanwhile, mix the eggs, egg yolks and Parmesan together in a bowl and season lightly.

HEAT the oil and butter in a large frying pan. Squash the garlic cloves with the back of a knife and add to the pan with the pancetta. Cook over moderate heat until the pancetta is crisp, discarding the garlic when it becomes golden.

DRAIN the spaghetti, add to the frying pan and toss well. Remove from the heat and stir in the egg mixture. Serve immediately, with Parmesan.

SPAGHETTI CARBONARA

# TAGLIATELLE WITH WALNUT SAUCE

2 cups shelled walnuts
1/3 cup roughly chopped parsley
3 tablespoons butter
3/4 cup extra virgin olive oil
1 garlic clove, crushed
1/3 cup Parmesan, grated
1/2 cup heavy cream
13 oz. pasta, such as tagliatelle

SERVES 4

LIGHTLY TOAST the walnuts in a dry frying pan over moderately high heat for 2 minutes, or until browned. Set aside to cool for 5 minutes.

PUT the walnuts in a food processor with the parsley and blend until finely chopped. Add the butter and mix together.

GRADUALLY pour in the olive oil in a steady stream with the motor running. Add the garlic, Parmesan and the cream. Season with salt and black pepper.

COOK the pasta in a large saucepan of boiling salted water until *al dente*. Toss through the sauce to serve.

Walnuts grow all over Italy, with the best coming from Campania and Liguria. Green walnuts are used to make a *digestif* called *nocino*.

# TAGLIATELLE WITH TRUFFLES

IF YOU ARE GOING TO THE EXTRAVAGANCE OF USING TRUFFLES, DON'T SKIMP ON THE PARMESAN—USE PARMIGIANO REGGIANO FOR THE BEST FLAVOR. IF YOU CAN'T GET A FRESH TRUFFLE, USE ONE FROM A JAR, PRESERVED IN BRINE.

9 tablespoons butter
1 garlic clove
13 oz. fresh tagliatelle
2/3 cup Parmesan, grated
1 small white Alba truffle or black
   Norcia truffle

SERVES 4 AS AN APPETIZER

MELT the butter in a saucepan over moderately low heat. Add the garlic clove and heat until the butter bubbles, separates and turns lightly golden. Strain the butter.

MEANWHILE, cook the pasta in a large saucepan of boiling salted water until *al dente*. Drain and return to the saucepan. Add the browned butter and the Parmesan. Season with salt and black pepper and toss lightly.

PLACE ON warmed plates and take to the table. Using a mandoline or potato peeler, shave a few very thin slices of the truffle onto each serving.

Black truffles are found around Norcia in Umbria. When they're not in season, use preserved truffles.

# SPAGHETTI VONGOLE

2 tablespoons olive oil
3 cloves garlic, crushed
2 pinches of dried red chile flakes
1 teaspoon chopped parsley
1/2 cup dry white wine
2 x 14 oz. cans diced tomatoes
2 lb. clams
3 tablespoons finely chopped
   parsley
13 oz. spaghetti or linguine
1/2 teaspoon grated lemon zest
lemon wedges

SERVES 4

HEAT the oil in a large deep frying pan. Add the garlic and chile flakes and cook over low heat for 30 seconds. Add the parsley, wine and tomatoes. Increase the heat and boil, stirring occasionally, for 8–10 minutes until the liquid is reduced by half.

CLEAN the clams by scrubbing them thoroughly. Rinse well under running water. Discard any that are broken or cracked or do not close when tapped on the work surface. Add to the saucepan. Cover the pan, increase the heat and cook for 3–5 minutes until the clams open. Shake the pan often. Remove the clams from the pan, discarding any that stay closed. Stir in the parsley and season. Uncover the pan and boil until thick. Set 12 clams aside and extract the meat from the rest.

COOK the pasta in a large saucepan of boiling salted water until *al dente*. Drain and stir through the sauce. Add the lemon zest, reserved clams and clam meat and toss well. Serve with the lemon wedges.

SPAGHETTI VONGOLE

# PASTA WITH BORLOTTI BEANS

1 cup dried borlotti (cranberry)
  beans
2 tablespoons olive oil
4 oz. pancetta, diced
1 celery stalk, chopped
1 onion, finely chopped
1 carrot, diced
1 garlic clove, crushed
3 tablespoons chopped parsley
1 bay leaf
14 oz. can diced tomatoes, drained
6 cups vegetable stock
1 1/2 cups ditalini or macaroni
drizzle of extra virgin olive oil
grated Parmesan

SERVES 4

PLACE the beans in a large saucepan, cover with cold water and soak overnight. Drain and rinse under cold water.

HEAT the olive oil in a large saucepan and add the pancetta, celery, onion, carrot and garlic and cook over moderately low heat for 5 minutes until golden. Season with black pepper. Add the parsley, bay leaf, tomatoes, stock and borlotti beans and bring slowly to a boil. Reduce the heat and simmer for 1–1 1/2 hours, or until the beans are tender, adding a little boiling water every so often to maintain the level.

ADD the pasta and simmer for 6 minutes, or until the pasta is just *al dente*. Remove from the heat and allow to rest for 10 minutes. Serve warm with a drizzle of extra virgin olive oil over each bowl. Serve the Parmesan separately.

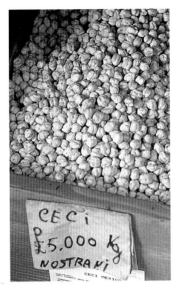

Chickpeas are grown in the south of Italy but appear in the cuisines of all regions, either whole or ground into *farinata* (flour).

# PASTA WITH CHICKPEAS

1 cup dried chickpeas
3 tablespoons olive oil
1 large onion, finely chopped
1 celery stalk, finely chopped
1 carrot, finely chopped
2 garlic cloves, crushed
1 rosemary sprig
pinch of crushed dried red chile
2 tablespoons tomato paste
6 cups vegetable stock
3/4 cup small pasta shells
drizzle of extra virgin olive oil
grated Parmesan

SERVES 4

PUT the chickpeas in a large saucepan, cover with cold water and soak overnight. Drain and rinse under cold water.

HEAT the olive oil in a large saucepan, add the chopped vegetables, garlic and rosemary and cook over moderately low heat for 8 minutes. Add the chile and season. Stir in the tomato paste and stock, then add the chickpeas. Bring to a boil. Reduce the heat and simmer for 1–1 1/2 hours, or until the chickpeas are tender, adding a little boiling water every so often to maintain the level.

ADD the pasta and continue cooking until it is *al dente*. Remove the rosemary sprig. Drizzle with extra virgin olive oil and sprinkle with Parmesan.

PASTA WITH CHICKPEAS

Specialty pastas are still produced by small family firms, using old-fashioned methods and bronze dies for shaping.

# PASTA PRIMAVERA

PASTA (MEANING "DOUGH" IN ITALIAN, FROM THE SAME ROOT AS "PASTRY" AND THE FRENCH "PATE") HAS A LONG HISTORY AND WAS PROBABLY ENJOYED BY BOTH THE ANCIENT GREEKS AND ETRUSCANS. THIS FAVORITE SAUCE, WITH ITS FRESH YOUNG VEGETABLES, HERALDS THE ARRIVAL OF SPRINGTIME.

3/4 cup fava beans, fresh or frozen
5 oz. asparagus, cut into short
   lengths
12 oz. fresh tagliatelle
1 cup green beans, cut into short
   lengths
3/4 cup peas, fresh or frozen
2 tablespoons butter
1 small fennel bulb, thinly sliced
1 1/2 cups heavy cream
2 tablespoons grated Parmesan,
   plus extra to serve

SERVES 4

BRING a large saucepan of water to a boil. Add 1 teaspoon of salt, the fava beans and the asparagus and simmer for 3 minutes.

REMOVE the vegetables with a slotted spoon and set aside. Add the tagliatelle to the saucepan and, when it has softened, stir in the green beans and the peas (if you're using frozen peas add them a few minutes later). Cook for about 4 minutes, or until the pasta is *al dente*.

MEANWHILE, heat the butter in a large frying pan. Add the fennel and cook over moderately low heat without coloring for 5 minutes. Add the cream, season with salt and pepper and cook at a low simmer.

PEEL the skins from the fava beans. Drain the pasta, green beans and peas and add to the frying pan. Add 2 tablespoons of Parmesan and the fava beans and asparagus. Toss lightly to coat. Serve immediately, with extra Parmesan.

TOMATO AND
RICOTTA ORECCHIETTE

# TOMATO AND RICOTTA ORECCHIETTE

13 oz. orecchiette
1 lb. plum tomatoes
1 1/4 cups ricotta
1/2 cup Parmesan, grated, plus
   extra to serve
8 basil leaves, torn into pieces

SERVES 4

COOK the pasta in a large saucepan of boiling salted water until *al dente*.

SCORE a cross in the top of each tomato, plunge them into boiling water (you can use the pasta water) for 20 seconds, then drain and peel the skin away from the cross. Core and chop. Mash the ricotta, add the Parmesan and season.

DRAIN the pasta and return to the pan. Add the ricotta mixture, the tomato and basil. Season and toss. Serve at once, with Parmesan.

# TAGLIATELLE WITH RAGU

SPAGHETTI BOLOGNESE IS ONE OF THE MOST POPULAR AND WELL-KNOWN ITALIAN DISHES AROUND THE WORLD. HOWEVER, THE ITALIANS THEMSELVES WOULD NEVER DREAM OF SERVING THEIR TRADITIONAL BOLOGNESE SAUCE ON SPAGHETTI—TAGLIATELLE IS THE USUAL ACCOMPANIMENT.

4 tablespoons butter
1 onion, finely chopped
1 celery stalk, finely chopped
1 carrot, finely chopped
3 oz. pancetta or bacon, finely
  chopped
7 oz. ground beef
7 oz. ground pork
2 oregano sprigs, chopped, or
  $1/4$ teaspoon dried oregano
pinch of nutmeg
4 oz. chicken livers, trimmed and
  finely chopped
$1/2$ cup dry white wine
$3/4$ cup milk
14 oz. can diced tomatoes
1 cup beef stock
1 lb. tagliatelle
grated Parmesan

SERVES 4

The back streets of Bologna.

HEAT the butter in a saucepan and add the onion, celery, carrot and pancetta. Cook over moderate heat for 6–8 minutes, stirring from time to time.

ADD the ground beef, pork and oregano to the saucepan. Season with salt and pepper and the nutmeg. Cook for 5 minutes, or until the meat has changed color but not browned. Add the chicken liver and cook until it changes color.

POUR IN the wine, increase the heat and boil over high heat for 2–3 minutes, or until the wine has been absorbed. Stir in $1/2$ cup of the milk, reduce the heat and simmer for 10 minutes. Add the tomatoes and half the stock, partially cover the pan and allow to simmer gently over very low heat for 3 hours. Add more of the stock as it is needed to keep the sauce moist.

MEANWHILE, cook the pasta in a large saucepan of boiling salted water until *al dente.* Stir the remaining milk into the sauce 5 minutes before serving. Taste the sauce for seasoning, toss with the tagliatelle and serve with grated Parmesan.

# SPAGHETTINI AGLIO E OLIO

1 lb. spaghettini
1/3 cup olive oil
5 garlic cloves, crushed
pinch of dried red chile flakes
2 tablespoons finely chopped
   parsley
grated pecorino

SERVES 4

COOK the pasta in a large saucepan of boiling salted water until *al dente*.

MEANWHILE, heat the oil in a large frying pan over very low heat. Add the garlic and dried red chile flakes and gently fry for 2 minutes, or until the garlic has softened but not browned. Remove the frying pan from the heat.

LIGHTLY DRAIN the spaghettini. Don't shake it dry in the colander, as you need it to retain a little of the cooking water. Return the frying pan to the heat, add the spaghettini and parsley and toss to coat. Taste for seasoning and serve at once with the grated pecorino.

Growing olives that will later be pressed into olive oil.

# PENNE ALL'ARRABBIATA

BECAUSE THERE IS CHILE IN THE SAUCE, DON'T SERVE WITH PARMESAN—JUST A DRIZZLE OF GOOD-QUALITY EXTRA VIRGIN OLIVE OIL. THE CHILE IS WHAT GIVES THIS DISH ITS NAME: "ANGRY SAUCE". GOOD-TASTING FRESH TOMATOES CAN BE USED INSTEAD OF THE CANNED, BUT PEEL THEM FIRST.

2 tablespoons olive oil
2 large garlic cloves, thinly sliced
1–2 medium-sized dried red chiles
28 oz. can tomatoes
1 lb. penne or rigatoni
1 basil sprig, torn into pieces

SERVES 4

HEAT the olive oil in a saucepan and add the garlic and dried red chiles. Cook over low heat until the garlic is light golden brown. Turn the chiles over during cooking so both sides get a chance to infuse in the oil and turn slightly nutty in flavor. Add the tomatoes and season with salt. Cook gently, breaking up the tomatoes with a wooden spoon, for 20–30 minutes, or until the sauce is rich and thick.

MEANWHILE, cook the pasta in a large saucepan of boiling salted water until *al dente*. Drain.

ADD the basil to the sauce and season just before serving, tossed with the pasta. If you prefer a hotter sauce, break open the chiles to release the seeds.

PENNE ALL'ARRABBIATA

# PASTA IN BRODO

DIFFERENT PASTAS CAN BE SERVED *IN BRODO* (BROTH). TORTELLINI IN BRODO IS OFTEN SERVED AS THE *PRIMO PIATTO* AT CELEBRATIONS. AT OTHER TIMES, ANY PLAIN PASTA IS USED WITH VEGETABLES FOR A SIMPLE SOUP.

BROTH
2 tablespoons olive oil
1 large onion, chopped
2 carrots, chopped
1 celery stalk, chopped
3¹/₂ lb. chicken bones
4 large garlic cloves, unpeeled
1 bay leaf
small bunch of parsley stems and
	thyme sprigs
1 large wine glass of red or white
	wine

24 fresh tortellini or some large
	ravioli (wild mushroom or meat
	stuffings are particularly good)
grated Parmesan
3 tablespoons roughly chopped flat-
	leaf parsley

SERVES 6

TO MAKE the broth, heat the olive oil in a saucepan and lightly brown the onion, carrots and celery. Add the chicken bones and lightly brown (this will give a good flavor to your broth). Add the garlic, herbs and wine, cook for a few minutes to reduce, then add enough water to completely cover the bones. Bring slowly to a boil, skimming the top several times to get rid of any scum that rises to the surface of the broth.

GENTLY SIMMER the broth for at least 1 hour. Strain through a fine sieve, pour the broth back into a saucepan and return to the heat. Cook until the broth has reduced a little (this will give it a more concentrated, gutsy flavor). Taste the broth and remove from the heat when you feel the flavor is strong enough. This should produce about 5 cups of flavorsome broth.

FOR a clearer broth, allow to chill in the fridge overnight, then scrape the fat and sediment from the surface and pour off the broth, leaving the sediment behind.

(UP TO this point, the broth can be made in advance and frozen for a few months—any longer and the flavor will start to diminish.)

COOK the pasta in a large saucepan of boiling salted water until *al dente.* Meanwhile, heat the broth in another saucepan (don't be tempted to cook the pasta in the broth—the semolina used to prevent homemade pasta from sticking can spoil the flavor). Drain the pasta well and add to the heated broth. Remove from the heat and allow to infuse for a couple of minutes, then spoon the pasta into bowls and pour over the broth. Sprinkle with Parmesan and the parsley to serve.

Use the largest pot you have to make the broth so the bones and vegetables are fully covered with liquid. A conical sieve is easier to use for draining as it directs the liquid through in one stream. For a clear broth, make sure the mesh is fine enough to collect all the pieces.

The shrimp, squid and octopus are added first as they take marginally longer to cook than the scallops and clams.

# SPAGHETTI WITH SHRIMP, CLAMS AND SCALLOPS

SEAFOOD PASTA IN MANY RESTAURANTS AROUND THE WORLD IS ERRONEOUSLY TERMED *MARINARA*.
MARINARA IS TRADITIONALLY THE SAUCE MADE BY FISHERMEN (OR THEIR WIVES), TO WHICH THE
DAY'S CATCH WOULD BE ADDED. SO THE NAME, IN FACT, REFERS TO THE SAUCE, NOT THE SEAFOOD.

1 cup dry white wine
pinch of saffron threads
2 lb. clams
4 baby octopus
1/2 lb. small squid tubes
1 lb. shrimp
6 tomatoes
3/4 lb. spaghetti
4 tablespoons olive oil
3 garlic cloves, crushed
8–10 scallops, cleaned
6 tablespoons chopped parsley
lemon wedges

SERVES 4

PUT the wine and saffron in a bowl and allow to infuse. Clean the clams by scrubbing them thoroughly and scraping off any barnacles. Rinse well under running water and discard any that are broken or open and don't close when tapped on the work surface. Place them in a large saucepan with 3/4 cup water. Cover the saucepan and cook over high heat for 1–2 minutes, or until they open (discard any that stay closed after that time). Drain, reserving the liquid. Remove the clams from their shells and set aside.

CLEAN the octopus by slitting the head and pulling out the innards. Cut out the eyes and hard beak and rinse. Spread the squid out flat, skin side up, and score a criss-cross pattern into the flesh, being careful not to cut all the way through. Slice diagonally into 3/4 x 13/4 inch strips. Peel and devein the shrimp.

SCORE a cross in the top of each tomato, plunge them into boiling water for 20 seconds, then drain and peel the skin away from the cross. Core and chop. Cook the pasta in a large saucepan of boiling salted water until *al dente*.

MEANWHILE, heat the oil in a large frying pan and add the garlic and tomato. Stir over moderate heat for 10–15 seconds, then pour in the saffron-infused wine and the reserved clam liquid. Season and simmer for 8–10 minutes, or until reduced by half. Add the squid, shrimp and octopus and cook until the squid turns opaque. Add the scallops, clam meat and parsley and cook until the scallops turn opaque.

DRAIN the spaghetti and return to the pan. Add two-thirds of the sauce, toss well then transfer to a large serving platter. Spoon the remaining sauce over the top and serve with lemon wedges.

# SPAGHETTI ALLA PUTTANESCA

4 tablespoons olive oil
1 small onion, finely chopped
2 garlic cloves, finely sliced
1 small red chile, cored, seeded and sliced
6 anchovy fillets, finely chopped
28 oz. can diced tomatoes
1 tablespoon finely chopped oregano or $^1/_4$ teaspoon dried oregano
$^3/_4$ cup pitted black olives, halved
1 tablespoon capers, chopped if large
$^3/_4$ lb. spaghetti

SERVES 4

HEAT the olive oil in a large saucepan and add the onion, garlic and chile. Fry gently for about 6 minutes, or until the onion is soft. Add the anchovies and cook, stirring, until well mixed.

ADD the tomatoes, oregano, olives and capers and bring to a boil. Reduce the heat, season and leave to simmer.

MEANWHILE, cook the pasta in a large saucepan of boiling salted water until *al dente*. Drain, toss well with the sauce and serve at once.

# BUCATINI ALL'AMATRICIANA

THIS IS ROME'S MOST FAMOUS PASTA DISH. WHEN THE MEN OF AMATRICE IN ABRUZZI CAME TO ROME TO WORK AS CHEFS, THIS IS THE DISH THEY BROUGHT WITH THEM. IT IS PREPARED IN AMATRICE FOR THE LOCAL FAIR HELD ON THE SUNDAY AFTER THE AUGUST PUBLIC HOLIDAY.

1 tablespoon olive oil
5 oz. pancetta, in 2 thick slices
1 small onion, finely chopped
2 garlic cloves, crushed
$^3/_4$ teaspoon dried red chile flakes
20 oz. canned tomatoes, diced
$^3/_4$ lb. bucatini
2 tablespoons finely chopped parsley
grated Parmesan

SERVES 4

HEAT the oil in a large saucepan. Trim the fat from the pancetta and add the fat to the pan. Cook the pancetta fat over medium-high heat until it is crisp to extract the liquid fat, then discard the rinds. Dice the pancetta, add to the saucepan and cook until lightly browned.

ADD the onion and fry gently for about 6 minutes, or until soft. Add the garlic and chile flakes and cook, stirring, for 15–20 seconds then stir in the tomatoes. Season with salt and pepper.

SIMMER the sauce for about 15 minutes, or until it thickens and darkens.

MEANWHILE, cook the pasta in a large saucepan of boiling salted water until *al dente*. Stir the parsley into the sauce, drain the pasta, toss together well and serve with Parmesan.

BUCATINI ALL'AMATRICIANA

# RAVIOLI APERTO

### FILLING
2 tablespoons butter
1 small onion, finely chopped
1³/₄ cups baby spinach
1 cup ricotta
3 tablespoons heavy cream

1 batch pasta (page 278)
1 cup frozen spinach, thawed
1 cup chicken stock

SERVES 4

TO MAKE the filling, melt the butter in a frying pan and add the onion. Cook, stirring, for 5 minutes, or until softened. Add the baby spinach leaves and cook for 4 minutes. Remove from the heat, cool to room temperature and then chop. Add the ricotta and 2 tablespoons cream and stir well. Season with salt and pepper.

TO MAKE the ravioli, roll out the pasta thinly (roll out a small amount at a time and keep the rest covered with a kitchen towel to prevent the pasta drying out). Cut the pasta into sixteen 3-inch squares. Cook the pasta in a large saucepan of boiling salted water until *al dente*. Drain. Preheat the oven to 350°F.

LINE a baking sheet with parchment and lay out half the pieces of pasta on the baking sheet. Divide the filling into eight portions and spoon into the center of each square. Place the other eight pasta sheets on top to enclose the filling and cover with a damp kitchen towel.

TO MAKE a sauce, blend the spinach with a little of the chicken stock until smooth. Transfer to a saucepan with the remaining stock and heat for 2 minutes. Add the remaining cream, stir well, season and remove from the heat.

HEAT the ravioli in the oven for 5 minutes, or until just warm. Place two ravioli on each plate, reheat the sauce gently, pour over the ravioli and serve immediately.

Take time to place the filling carefully in the middle of each pasta square, so it doesn't ooze out of the sides when it cooks.

# PIZZOCCHERI

THIS BUCKWHEAT PASTA IS A CLASSIC RECIPE FROM VALTELLINA NEAR THE SWISS BORDER AND USES THE STAPLE FOODS OF THAT AREA. IT IS BEST EATEN AFTER STRENUOUS EXERCISE IN THE FRESH AIR—THIS IS A STURDY DISH.

PIZZOCCHERI
1 1/2 cups buckwheat flour
3/4 cup bread flour
1 egg
1/2 cup milk, warmed

CHEESE, POTATO AND
CABBAGE SAUCE
3/4 lb. Savoy cabbage, roughly
    chopped
6 oz. potatoes, cubed
4 tablespoons olive oil
1 tablespoon chopped sage
2 garlic cloves, crushed
3/4 lb. Italian cheeses, such as
    fontina, Taleggio, Gorgonzola and
    mascarpone, cubed
3/4 cup Parmesan, grated

SERVES 4

TO MAKE the pizzoccheri, sift the two flours into a bowl and add a pinch of salt. Make a well in the center and add the egg. Mix the egg into the flour and then gradually add the milk, mixing continuously until you have a soft dough (you may need more or less milk, depending on the dryness of your flour).

KNEAD the dough for a few minutes, or until it is elastic, and then cover it with a kitchen towel and allow to rest for an hour. Using a pasta machine or a rolling pin, roll out the dough very thinly and cut into noodles about 1/2 inch wide.

TO MAKE the sauce, bring a large saucepan of salted water to a boil. Add the cabbage and potato and cook for about 3–5 minutes or until they are cooked through. Add the pizzoccheri and cook for another 2 minutes. Drain, reserving a cup of the cooking water.

HEAT the oil in a saucepan and gently cook the sage and garlic for 1 minute. Add the cheese cubes and mix briefly, then add the cabbage, potato and pizzoccheri and season with salt and pepper. Remove from the heat and gently stir the mixture together, adding some pasta water to loosen it a little. Serve immediately with the Parmesan sprinkled on top.

ALTERNATIVELY, if you prefer your cheese completely melted, spoon everything into a casserole and heat in the oven for 5 minutes.

# TORTELLINI FILLED WITH PUMPKIN AND SAGE

LEGEND HAS IT THAT VENUS, BARRED FROM HEAVEN, SOUGHT REFUGE IN AN INN IN BOLOGNA INSTEAD. THE INNKEEPER, FILLED WITH LUST, SPIED ON HER THROUGH THE KEYHOLE, THEN RUSHED TO HIS KITCHEN TO CREATE PASTA IN THE SHAPE OF HER NAVEL—TORTELLINI.

FILLING
2 lb. pumpkin or butternut squash,
  peeled and cubed
6 tablespoons olive oil
1 small red onion, finely chopped
1/3 cup ricotta
1 egg yolk, beaten
1/4 cup Parmesan, grated
1 teaspoon grated nutmeg
2 tablespoons chopped sage

1 batch pasta (page 278)
1 egg
2 teaspoons milk
semolina
grated Parmesan

SAGE BUTTER
1/2 lb. butter
1/4 cup sage leaves

SERVES 6–8

TO MAKE the filling, preheat the oven to 375°F. Put the pumpkin in a roasting pan with half the olive oil and lots of salt and pepper. Bake in the oven for 40 minutes, or until it is completely soft.

MEANWHILE, heat the remaining olive oil in a saucepan and gently cook the onion until soft. Put the onion and pumpkin in a bowl, draining off any excess oil, and mash well. Allow to cool, then crumble in the ricotta. Mix in the egg yolk, Parmesan, nutmeg and sage. Season well.

TO MAKE the tortellini, roll out the pasta thinly (roll out a small amount at a time and keep the rest covered with a kitchen towel to prevent the pasta drying out). Cut the pasta into 3-inch squares. Mix together the egg and milk to make an egg wash and brush lightly over the pasta as you use it. Put a small teaspoon of filling in the middle of each square and fold it over diagonally to make a triangle, pressing down the corners. Pinch together the two corners on the longer side.

COOK the tortellini, in small batches, in a large saucepan of boiling salted water until *al dente*. Remove and drain with a slotted spoon.

(IF YOU are not using the tortellini immediately, place them, well spaced out, on parchment dusted with semolina and then cover with a kitchen towel. They can be left for 1–2 hours before cooking—don't refrigerate or they will become damp.)

TO MAKE the sage butter, melt the butter slowly with the sage and leave to infuse for at least 5 minutes. Drizzle over the tortellini and serve with a sprinkling of Parmesan.

Brushing the pasta with egg wash will make sure it holds together when filled and shaped. Don't overfill the tortellini or the filling will ooze out as it cooks. Pinching the edges together on the fat side of the pasta makes tortellini. Pinching them away from the fat side makes cappelletti (bishops' hats).

# RAVIOLI

## FILLING
2 tablespoons butter
1/2 small onion, finely chopped
2 garlic cloves, crushed
3 oz. prosciutto, finely chopped
4 oz. finely ground pork
4 oz. finely ground veal
1/2 teaspoon finely chopped fresh
    oregano, or 1/8 teaspoon dried
    oregano
1 teaspoon paprika
1/2 tablespoon tomato paste
1/2 cup chicken stock
2 egg yolks

1 batch pasta (page 278)
semolina
1 egg, beaten

SERVES 4

TO MAKE the filling, heat the butter in a frying pan. Cook the onion, garlic and prosciutto over moderately low heat for 5–6 minutes without browning. Add the pork and veal, increase the heat and lightly brown, breaking up the lumps. Add the oregano and paprika, season well and stir in the tomato paste and chicken stock.

COVER the pan and cook for 50 minutes. Uncover, increase the heat and cook for another 10 minutes until the filling is quite dry. Cool, then chop to get rid of any lumps. Stir in the egg yolks.

TO MAKE the ravioli, roll out the pasta thinly and divide into four sheets: two sheets to be 12 x 8 inches, and the other two to be slightly larger. Dust the work surface with semolina and lay out one of the smaller sheets (keep the rest of the pasta covered with a damp kitchen towel to prevent it drying out). Lightly score the pasta sheet into 24 squares. Place a scant teaspoon of filling in the center of each square and flatten it slightly with the back of the spoon.

BRUSH BEATEN egg along the score lines around the filling. Take one of the larger pasta sheets and cover the first, starting at one end. Match the edges and press the top sheet onto the beaten egg as you go. Avoid stretching the top sheet; instead, let it settle into place. Run your finger firmly around the filling and along the cutting lines to seal well.

USE a pastry wheel or sharp knife to cut into 24 ravioli squares and place on a baking sheet dusted with semolina. Cook the ravioli, in small batches, in a large saucepan of boiling salted water until *al dente*. Remove and drain with a slotted spoon. Serve with melted butter or a drizzle of olive oil.

(IF YOU are not using the ravioli immediately, place them, well spaced out, on parchment dusted with semolina and then cover with a kitchen towel. They can be left for 1–2 hours before cooking—don't refrigerate or they will become damp.)

Making ravioli by scoring the pasta, adding the filling, covering it and then cutting it is much easier than cutting the pasta first. You can also use a special fluted ravioli wheel to cut the edges, giving a crimped effect.

The steep streets of Naples.

Layer the meat, pasta and cheese in the pastry, smoothing the layers to keep them even.

# PASTICCIO OF MACARONI AND RAGU

FILLING
2 tablespoons butter
1 tablespoon olive oil
1 onion, finely chopped
2 garlic cloves, crushed
1 lb. ground beef
2/3 cup button mushrooms, finely sliced
4 oz. chicken livers, trimmed and finely chopped
pinch of nutmeg
1 tablespoon dry Marsala
3 tablespoons dry white wine
2 tablespoons tomato paste
1 cup chicken stock
3 tablespoons grated Parmesan
1 egg

PASTRY
2 1/2 cups all-purpose flour
2 teaspoons superfine sugar
7 tablespoons butter, cubed
1 egg
about 2 tablespoons chilled water

1 1/2 cups macaroni
1/3 cup ricotta
1/2 cup Parmesan, grated
2 tablespoons milk
pinch of cayenne pepper
1 egg, beaten
3/4 cup mozzarella, grated

SERVES 6

TO MAKE the filling, heat the butter and oil in a large frying pan and cook the onion and garlic over moderately low heat for 5–6 minutes until golden. Add the beef, increase the heat and cook until browned, breaking up any lumps.

ADD the mushrooms, chicken livers and nutmeg, season well and then cook until the livers change color. Add the Marsala and white wine and cook over high heat until they have evaporated. Stir in the tomato paste and chicken stock. Reduce the heat and simmer for 30 minutes. Remove from the heat and taste for seasoning. Beat the Parmesan and egg together and quickly stir through the meat.

TO MAKE the pastry, sift the flour, sugar and 1 teaspoon salt into a bowl and rub in the butter. Add the egg and the cold water, a little at a time, stirring until the dough comes together. Transfer to a lightly floured board and knead lightly until smooth. Put in a plastic bag and refrigerate.

COOK the macaroni in a large saucepan of boiling salted water for 8–10 minutes or until *al dente,* then drain. Meanwhile, blend together the ricotta, Parmesan, milk, cayenne and half the beaten egg. Season well and stir in the macaroni. Preheat the oven to 350°F and grease a deep-dish pie pan.

DIVIDE the pastry into two balls, one larger than the other. On a lightly floured work surface, roll out the larger ball to line the pie pan with overlapping edges. Roll out the second ball large enough to cover the pie pan. Spread half the filling in the pastry-lined pie pan, then layer half the pasta over it. Top with half the grated mozzarella. Repeat the layers.

BRUSH the pie rim with beaten egg and cover with the pastry lid. Brush the top with egg and make three slits in the center with a sharp knife. Bake for 50 minutes, until golden, and allow to rest for 10 minutes before serving.

# PASTICCIO OF TORTELLINI, BROCCOLI AND RICOTTA

PASTICCIO IS A GENERIC TERM IN THE ITALIAN KITCHEN, MEANING A PIE MADE UP OF VARIOUS LAYERS.
THE PREPARATION IS TIME-CONSUMING, SO PASTICCIO IS OFTEN A SPECIAL OCCASION DISH. IT CAN BE
MADE WITH A PASTRY CRUST OR WITHOUT, BUT THESE DAYS IT ALWAYS TENDS TO CONTAIN PASTA.

FILLING
2²/₃ cups ricotta
pinch of nutmeg
1 cup Parmesan, grated
1 egg

1¼ lb. broccoli, trimmed into florets
1 lb. cheese-filled tortellini
3 eggs
1 batch béchamel sauce (page
   285)
1½ tablespoons tomato paste
1 cup mozzarella, grated
4 tablespoons grated Parmesan

SERVES 6

TO MAKE the filling, mash the ricotta with a fork,
or pass through a food mill (do not use a blender
or food processor). Mix in the nutmeg and salt
and pepper. Add the Parmesan, then mix in the
egg. Set aside.

PREHEAT the oven to 350°F and grease a large
deep casserole. Bring a large saucepan of water
to a boil. Add the broccoli florets and a teaspoon
of salt and simmer for 3 minutes. Remove the
broccoli with a slotted spoon and set aside. Stir
the tortellini into the boiling water and then gently
lower in the eggs. Cook until the pasta is *al dente*.
Drain and rinse under cold water. Take out the
eggs after about 6 minutes when they are hard-
boiled, remove the eggshells and slice thinly.

PUT HALF of the béchamel sauce into a large
bowl and stir in the tomato paste. Add the
tortellini and toss to coat. Pour half of this mixture
into the casserole. Spread half of the ricotta filling
over it, then top with half the egg slices. Layer all
the broccoli on top of this, pressing it in firmly,
then spoon the remaining béchamel sauce over
the top. Sprinkle with the mozzarella. Finish with a
final layer of tortellini, the remaining egg slices and
finally the rest of the ricotta filling.

SPRINKLE the Parmesan over the top and bake
for 30–40 minutes. Remove from the oven and
allow to rest for 10 minutes before serving.

Ricotta is made from the whey left over from cheese-making. These ricotta are made from the whey of Parmesan cheese.

Bakeries and speciality shops make pasta daily. Here, tortellini and caramelle are made at Paolo Atti e Figli bakery in Bologna.

# LASAGNE AL FORNO

## MEAT SAUCE

2 tablespoons butter
1 onion, finely chopped
1 small carrot, finely chopped
1/2 celery stalk, finely chopped
1 garlic clove, crushed
4 oz. pancetta, sliced
1 lb. ground beef
1/4 teaspoon dried oregano
pinch of nutmeg
3 oz. chicken livers, trimmed and
   finely chopped
1/4 cup dry vermouth or dry white
   wine
1 1/3 cups beef stock
1 tablespoon tomato paste
2 tablespoons heavy cream
1 egg, beaten

1 batch béchamel sauce (page
   285)
1/2 cup heavy cream
4 oz. fresh lasagne verde or
   6 sheets dried lasagna
1 cup mozzarella, grated
2/3 cup Parmesan, grated

SERVES 6

Lasagna is traditionally made with lasagne verde. Make sure the layers fit without overlapping too much or the lasagna will be stodgy. Leave enough béchamel for a good thick layer on top.

TO MAKE the meat sauce, heat the butter in a frying pan and add the chopped vegetables, garlic and pancetta. Cook over moderately low heat for 5–6 minutes, or until softened and lightly golden. Add the ground beef, increase the heat a little and cook for 8 minutes, or until colored but not browned, stirring to break up the lumps. Add the oregano and nutmeg and season well.

STIR IN the chicken livers and cook until they change color. Pour in the vermouth, increase the heat and cook until it has evaporated. Add the beef stock and tomato paste and simmer for 2 hours. Add a little hot water, if necessary, during this time to keep the mixture moist, but towards the end allow all the liquid to be absorbed. Stir in the cream, remove from the heat and allow to cool for 15 minutes. Stir in the egg.

PUT the béchamel in a saucepan, heat gently and stir in the cream. Remove from the heat and cool slightly. Preheat the oven to 350°F and grease a 9 x 6 x 3 inch flameproof dish.

IF YOU are using fresh pasta, cut it into manageable sheets and cook in batches in a large saucepan of boiling salted water until *al dente*. Scoop out each batch with a slotted spoon as it is done and drop into a bowl of cold water. Spread the sheets out in a single layer on a kitchen towel, turning them over once to blot dry each side. Trim away any torn edges.

SPREAD HALF the meat sauce in the dish. Scatter with half the mozzarella, then cover with a slightly overlapping layer of pasta sheets. Spread half the béchamel over this and sprinkle with half the Parmesan. Repeat the layers, finishing with a layer of béchamel and Parmesan.

BAKE for 40 minutes until golden brown and allow to rest for 20 minutes before serving.

# VINCISGRASSI

MEAT SAUCE

3 tablespoons butter

2 cotechino sausages, casings
    removed, chopped

1³/₄ lb. chicken thigh fillets, cut into
    thin strips

³/₄ lb. chicken livers, trimmed and
    chopped

¹/₄ cup dry Marsala

³/₄ cup chicken stock

MUSHROOM SAUCE

3 dried porcini mushrooms

3 tablespoons butter

1 onion, finely chopped

1 cup button mushrooms,
    finely sliced

pinch of nutmeg

1 tablespoon chicken stock

1¹/₂ batches béchamel sauce (page
    285)

4 oz. fresh lasagna or
    6 sheets dried lasagna

³/₄ cup Parmesan, grated

SERVES 6

TO MAKE the meat sauce, heat the butter in a large frying pan and cook the sausage meat until browned, stirring to break up any lumps. Add the chicken and lightly brown. Increase the heat, add the liver and fry quickly, stirring, until darkened. Season, pour in the Marsala and stir until almost evaporated, then add the stock. Cover, reduce the heat and simmer for 25 minutes.

TO MAKE the mushroom sauce, soak the dried porcini in ¹/₄ cup warm water for 30 minutes. Drain and finely chop the porcini. Heat the butter in a saucepan and soften the onion over low heat for 5–6 minutes. Add the porcini and button mushrooms and cook over high heat for 2–3 minutes. Add the nutmeg and chicken stock. Season and simmer for 8–10 minutes, or until all the liquid has evaporated.

POUR ONE THIRD of the béchamel sauce into a bowl and refrigerate. Add the mushroom sauce to the remaining béchamel and mix well.

IF YOU are using fresh pasta, cook in batches in a large saucepan of boiling salted water until *al dente*. Scoop out each batch with a slotted spoon and drop into a bowl of cold water. Spread out the sheets in a single layer on a kitchen towel, turning them over once to blot dry each side. Trim away any torn edges.

GREASE a large flameproof dish and arrange an overlapping layer of pasta on the bottom. Top with half the meat sauce, then spread half of the mushroom sauce over the top. Sprinkle with one third of the Parmesan. Repeat the layers, then finish with a layer of pasta. Refrigerate the last of the Parmesan. Cover the vincisgrassi with plastic wrap and refrigerate for at least 6 hours.

PREHEAT the oven to 400°F. Spoon the reserved béchamel sauce over the top and sprinkle the remaining Parmesan over this. Bake for 30 minutes, or until golden, and allow to rest for 10 minutes before serving.

Grease the dish and line with pasta before spooning in the meat and mushroom sauces.

Roll the pasta around the filling fairly tightly, then lay the cannelloni seam side down in the dish.

# CANNELLONI

### MEAT SAUCE

3 tablespoons olive oil
1 onion, finely chopped
2 garlic cloves, crushed
4 oz. bacon, finely chopped
2/3 cup button mushrooms, finely
   chopped
1/4 teaspoon dried basil
1/2 lb. ground pork
1/2 lb. ground veal
1 tablespoon finely chopped parsley
7 oz. canned diced tomatoes
1 cup beef stock
3 tablespoons dried bread crumbs
1 egg

### TOMATO SAUCE

2 tablespoons olive oil
1 small onion, finely chopped
2 garlic cloves, crushed
2 x 14 oz. cans diced tomatoes
1 teaspoon chopped basil

10 sheets fresh lasagna, about
   7 x 5 inches (the grain of the
   pasta should run with the width
   not the length, or the pasta will
   split when rolled up), or
   1 1/2 batches pasta (page 278)
   rolled and cut into 10 sheets
   as above
4 large slices prosciutto, cut in half
1/2 cup fontina, grated
3/4 cup heavy cream
2/3 cup Parmesan, grated

SERVES 4

TO MAKE the meat sauce, heat the oil in a frying pan and cook the onion, garlic and bacon over moderate heat for 6 minutes, or until the onion is soft and golden. Stir in the mushrooms and basil, cook for 2–3 minutes, then add the pork and veal. Cook, stirring often to break up the lumps, until the meat has changed color. Season well, add the parsley, tomatoes and stock, partially cover the pan and simmer for 1 hour. Remove the lid and simmer for another 30 minutes to reduce the liquid. Cool slightly then stir in the bread crumbs, then the egg.

TO MAKE the tomato sauce, heat the oil in a frying pan and cook the onion and garlic for 6 minutes, or until the onion has softened but not browned. Stir in the tomatoes and basil. Add 1 cup water and season well. Simmer for 30 minutes, or until you have a thick sauce.

COOK the lasagna in batches in a large saucepan of boiling salted water until *al dente*. Scoop out each batch with a slotted spoon and drop into a bowl of cold water. Spread the sheets out in a single layer on a kitchen towel, turning them over once to blot dry each side. Trim away any torn edges. (We have allowed two extra sheets of fresh lasagna in case of tearing.)

PREHEAT the oven to 375°F. Grease a shallow 12 x 7 inch flameproof dish and spoon the tomato sauce over the bottom of the dish.

PLACE half a slice of prosciutto over each pasta sheet. Top with a sprinkling of fontina. Spoon an eighth of the meat filling across one end of the pasta sheet. Starting from this end, roll the pasta up tightly to enclose the filling. Place the filled rolls, seam side down, in a row in the dish.

BEAT TOGETHER the cream and Parmesan and season well. Spoon over the cannelloni so that it is covered. Bake for 20 minutes, or until lightly browned on top. Allow to rest for 10 minutes before serving.

# TIMBALLO

THE ELABORATE BAKED PIES OF RENAISSANCE ITALY, CALLED *PASTICCI* OR *TORTE*, WERE EMBRACED BY FRENCH CUISINE AND RENAMED *TIMBALES*. TWO CENTURIES LATER, THE ITALIANS RECLAIMED THE TIMBALE AS THEIR OWN AND IT WAS CHRISTENED THE TIMBALLO.

6 tomatoes
2 tablespoons olive oil
1 large onion, finely chopped
2 garlic cloves, crushed
5 chicken breast fillets
4 chicken thighs
1 bay leaf
2 thyme sprigs
3 tablespoons white wine
2 cups mushrooms, sliced
1/2 cup provolone, grated
9 eggs, beaten
2 tablespoons heavy cream
3 tablespoons chopped parsley
1 lb. 10 oz. ziti

SERVES 6

SCORE a cross in the top of each tomato, plunge into boiling water for 20 seconds, then drain and peel the skin away from the cross. Dice the flesh.

HEAT the oil in a large saucepan, add the onion and garlic and cook, stirring, for 7 minutes or until softened. Add the tomato and cook for 5 minutes over low heat. Add the chicken breasts and thighs, the bay leaf and thyme and stir well. Add the wine, cover the saucepan and cook over moderate heat for 20 minutes.

ADD the mushrooms to the saucepan and cook for another 10–15 minutes, turning the chicken once or twice until it is cooked through. Remove the chicken from the saucepan and cook the sauce until it has reduced and thickened. Remove the bay leaf and thyme and allow the sauce to cool to room temperature.

REMOVE the chicken meat from the bones, shred the meat and return to the sauce. Stir in the cheese, eggs, cream and parsley. Season with salt and pepper.

PREHEAT the oven to 350°F and grease a round 5-cup flameproof dish with a little butter or oil.

COOK the pasta in a large saucepan of boiling salted water until *al dente*. Drain well and place in the dish, one by one, in a single layer, starting in the middle and spiralling outwards to cover the bottom and side. Make sure there are no gaps.

FILL the center with the chicken sauce and bake for 1 hour. Allow to rest for a few minutes, then invert onto a plate to serve.

Start coiling the ziti in the center of the base and work your way to the outer edge. Then build up the side, without leaving any gaps.

# DESSERTS & BAKING

# TIRAMISU

*TIRA MI SU* MEANS "PICK ME UP" IN ITALIAN AND THIS IS HOW THE DESSERT STARTED LIFE—AS A NOURISHING DISH TO BE EATEN WHEN FEELING LOW. YOU CAN ALSO MAKE A FRUIT VERSION, USING FRAMBOISE AND PUREED RASPBERRIES INSTEAD OF BRANDY AND COFFEE.

5 eggs, separated
3/4 cup superfine sugar
11/3 cups mascarpone
1 cup cold strong coffee
3 tablespoons brandy or sweet
  Marsala
36 small ladyfingers (sponge
  fingers)
23/4 oz. dark chocolate, finely
  grated

SERVES 4

BEAT the egg yolks with the sugar until the sugar has dissolved and the mixture is light and fluffy and leaves a ribbon trail when dropped from the whisk. Add the mascarpone and beat until the mixture is smooth.

WHISK the egg whites in a clean dry glass bowl, using a wire whisk or hand beaters, until soft peaks form. Fold into the mascarpone mixture.

POUR the coffee into a shallow dish and add the brandy. Dip enough ladyfingers to cover the bottom of a 10-inch square dish into the coffee. The ladyfingers should be fairly well soaked but not so much so that they break up. Arrange the ladyfingers in one tightly packed layer on the bottom of the dish.

SPREAD half the mascarpone mixture over the layer of ladyfingers. Add another layer of soaked ladyfingers and then another layer of mascarpone, smoothing the top layer neatly. Dust with the grated chocolate to serve. The flavors will be better developed if you can make the tiramisu a few hours in advance or even the night before. If you have time to do this, don't dust with the chocolate, but cover with plastic wrap and chill. Dust with chocolate only at the last minute or it will melt.

Made from cream rather than milk and a specialty of southern Lombardia, mascarpone is usually found as an ingredient in dishes rather than eaten as a cheese.

# PANNA COTTA

MEANING "COOKED CREAM", THIS PIEMONTESE DESSERT SHOULD BE SOFTLY SET WITH A YELLOW COLOR AND A RICH CREAMY TEXTURE. DON'T BE TEMPTED TO PUT ANY MORE GELATIN IN THE MIXTURE OR YOUR PANNA COTTA MIGHT BECOME RUBBERY.

1³/₄ cups heavy cream
4 tablespoons superfine sugar
vanilla extract
3 sheets or 1¹/₄ teaspoons gelatin
1²/₃ cups fresh berries

SERVES 4

PUT the cream and sugar in a saucepan and stir over gentle heat until the sugar has dissolved. Bring to a boil, then simmer for 3 minutes, adding a few drops of vanilla extract to taste.

IF YOU are using the gelatin sheets, soak in cold water until they are floppy, then squeeze out any excess water. Stir the sheets into the hot cream until they are completely dissolved. If you are using powdered gelatin, sprinkle it onto the hot cream in an even layer and leave it to sponge for a minute, then stir it into the cream until dissolved.

POUR the cream mixture into four ¹/₂-cup individual pudding molds, cover each with a piece of plastic wrap and refrigerate until set.

UNMOLD the panna cotta by wrapping the molds in a cloth dipped in hot water and tipping them gently onto individual plates. Serve with the berries.

# STRAWBERRIES WITH BALSAMIC VINEGAR

DURING THEIR SEASON, WILD STRAWBERRIES ARE ABUNDANT THROUGHOUT ITALY. AN ACIDIC DRESSING OF CITRUS JUICE OR RED WINE LIFTS THEIR FLAVOR AND AROMA. IN LATIUM AND EMILIA-ROMAGNA STRAWBERRIES HAVE BEEN SERVED WITH BALSAMIC VINEGAR SINCE RENAISSANCE TIMES.

1 lb. strawberries, hulled and halved
¹/₄ cup good-quality balsamic
   vinegar
2 tablespoons superfine sugar
2 teaspoons lemon juice
¹/₄ cup small mint leaves

SERVES 6

PLACE the strawberries in a glass bowl. Heat the balsamic vinegar, superfine sugar and lemon juice in a small saucepan, stirring until combined. Remove from the heat and leave to cool.

POUR the balsamic vinegar over the strawberries, add the mint leaves and toss together. Cover with plastic wrap and marinate in the fridge for at least 1 hour. Delicious served over vanilla ice cream.

STRAWBERRIES WITH
BALSAMIC VINEGAR

# BAKED PEACHES

THE PEACH IS ONE OF ITALY'S FAVORITE FRUITS, WITH THE BEST BEING PRODUCED IN LE MARCHE, EMILIA-ROMAGNA AND CAMPANIA. THIS RECIPE ALSO WORKS WELL WITH FRESH APRICOTS. ALLOW THREE APRICOTS PER PERSON.

4 ripe peaches
1 1/2 oz. amaretti (imported Italian macaroons)
1 tablespoon sweet Marsala
1 tablespoon ground almonds
1 egg yolk
1 tablespoon sugar
1 2/3 tablespoons unsalted butter
confectioners' sugar

SERVES 4

PREHEAT the oven to 350°F. Halve the peaches and remove the pits. Crush the amaretti in a food processor or with the end of a rolling pin and then mix them with the Marsala, almonds, egg yolk and sugar.

FILL the peaches with the amaretti mixture, spreading the filling in an even layer over the entire surface. Dot each peach with butter and arrange in a shallow flameproof dish or on a baking sheet. Bake for 20–30 minutes or until the peaches are tender right through. Dust lightly with confectioners' sugar before serving.

# ZABAIONE

ZABAIONE (ALSO KNOWN AS ZABAGLIONE) IS ONE OF THOSE HAPPY OCCURRENCES, A DISH CREATED PURELY BY ACCIDENT WHEN, IN SEVENTEENTH CENTURY TURIN, A CHEF POURED FORTIFIED SWEET WINE INTO EGG CUSTARD. IN RURAL AREAS, ZABAIONE IS EATEN HOT FOR BREAKFAST.

6 egg yolks
3 tablespoons superfine sugar
1/2 cup sweet Marsala
1 cup heavy cream

SERVES 4

WHISK the egg yolks and sugar together in the top of a double boiler or in a heatproof bowl set over a saucepan of simmering water. When the mixture is tepid, add the Marsala and whisk for another 5 minutes, or until it has thickened.

WHIP the cream until soft peaks form. Gently fold in the egg yolk mixture. Cover and refrigerate for 3–4 hours before serving.

ZABAIONE

# CASSATA

THERE ARE TWO DIFFERENT DISHES NAMED CASSATA, ONE A CAKE MADE WITH RICOTTA AND CANDIED FRUIT, THE OTHER AN ICE-CREAM DESSERT. THIS CASSATA IN ITS CAKE FORM IS A CLASSIC SICILIAN DISH DECORATED WITH BRIGHTLY COLORED FROSTINGS, MARZIPAN AND CANDIED FRUIT.

14 oz. Madeira or pound cake
4 tablespoons sweet Marsala
1<sup>1</sup>/3 cups ricotta
<sup>1</sup>/3–<sup>1</sup>/2 cup superfine sugar
½ teaspoon vanilla extract
³/4 cup mixed candied fruit (orange, lemon, cherries, pineapple, apricot), chopped
2 oz. dark chocolate, chopped
green food coloring
7 oz. marzipan
2 tablespoons apricot jelly
2<sup>1</sup>/2 cups confectioners' sugar

MAKES ONE 8-INCH CAKE

LINE an 8-inch round cake pan with sloping sides with plastic wrap. Cut the cake into thin slices to line the pan, reserving enough pieces to cover the top at the end. Fit the slices of cake carefully into the pan, making sure there are no gaps. Sprinkle the Marsala over the cake in the pan.

PUT the ricotta in a bowl and beat until smooth. Add the sugar and vanilla extract and mix well. Add the candied fruit and chocolate and mix well. Spoon into the mold, smooth the surface and then cover with the reserved slices of cake. Cover with plastic wrap and press the top down hard. Put the cassata in the fridge for at least two hours or preferably overnight, then unmold onto a plate.

KNEAD enough green food coloring into the marzipan to color it light green. Roll out the marzipan in a circle until it is large enough to completely cover the cassata. Melt the jelly in a saucepan with a tablespoon of water and brush over the cassata. Lift the marzipan over the top and trim it to fit around the edge.

MIX the confectioners' sugar with a little hot water to make a smooth frosting that will spread easily. Either pipe the icing onto the cassata in a decorative pattern, or drizzle it over the top in a crosshatch pattern.

The pieces of cake need to be fitted into the mold as neatly as possible. Cut smaller pieces of cake to fill any gaps. Sprinkle the Marsala over the cake evenly so no one patch gets too moist. Fill the mold with ricotta and smooth any air bubbles as you go.

# ZUCCOTTO

ZUCCOTTO IS A SPECIALTY OF THE CITY OF FLORENCE—ITS SHAPE PERHAPS INSPIRED BY THE ROUNDED ROOF OF THE LOCAL *DUOMO*. ZUCCOTTO IS A VARIANT OF *ZUCCHETTO*, THE NAME OF THE CARDINALS' SKULLCAPS.

When filling the zuccotto, try not to disturb the pieces of cake you have arranged. The easiest way is to smooth the filling up the side and then fill the middle afterwards.

10 oz. Madeira or pound cake
3 tablespoons maraschino liqueur
3 tablespoons brandy
2 cups heavy cream
3/4 cup confectioners' sugar
5 oz. dark chocolate, roughly
   chopped
1/3 cup blanched almonds
2 tablespoons skinned hazelnuts
2 tablespoons candied peel,
   chopped
cocoa powder, to dust
confectioners' sugar, to dust

SERVES 6

CUT the cake into 1/2-inch slices, then cut each slice into two triangles. Combine the maraschino and brandy and sprinkle them over the cake.

LINE a round 6-cup bowl with a layer of plastic wrap and then with the cake slices. Arrange the slices with the narrow point of each triangle pointing into the bottom of the bowl to form a star pattern, fitting each piece snugly against the others so you don't have any gaps. Cut smaller triangles to fit the gaps along the top and keep the rest of the cake for the top.

WHIP the cream until soft peaks form and then whisk in the confectioners' sugar until you have a stiff mixture. Add about a third of the chocolate and the almonds, hazelnuts and candied peel. Mix together thoroughly, then fill the cake-lined bowl with half the mixture, making a hollow in the middle and drawing the mixture up the sides. Leave in the fridge.

MELT the rest of the chocolate in a heatproof bowl over a saucepan of simmering water, or in a microwave, and fold it into the remaining cream mixture. Spoon this into the bowl and then cover the top with a layer of cake triangles, leaving no gaps. Cover the bowl with plastic wrap and refrigerate overnight.

TO SERVE, unmold the zuccotto and use a triangular piece of cardboard as a template to dust the top with alternating segments of cocoa and confectioners' sugar.

# LEMON GELATO

GELATO IS THE ITALIAN NAME FOR AN ICE CREAM BASED ON AN EGG CUSTARD MIXTURE, THOUGH IT HAS NOW COME TO MEAN ALL ICE CREAMS, INCLUDING SORBETS. ITALIANS ARE DISCERNING ABOUT ICE CREAM AND FLAVORS TEND TO BE FRESH AND AROMATIC, OFTEN BASED ON FRUIT.

5 egg yolks
1/2 cup sugar
2 cups milk
2 tablespoons grated lemon zest
3/4 cup lemon juice
3 tablespoons heavy cream

SERVES 6

WHISK the egg yolks and half the sugar together until pale and creamy. Place the milk, lemon zest and remaining sugar in a saucepan and bring to a boil. Pour over the egg mixture and whisk to combine. Pour the custard back into the saucepan and cook over low heat, stirring continuously until the mixture is thick enough to coat the back of a wooden spoon—do not allow the custard to boil.

STRAIN the custard into a bowl, add the lemon juice and cream and then cool over ice. Churn in an ice-cream maker following the manufacturer's instructions. Alternatively, pour into a plastic freezer box, cover and freeze. Stir every 30 minutes with a whisk during freezing to break up the ice crystals and give a better texture. Keep in the freezer until ready to serve.

# COFFEE GELATO

5 egg yolks
1/2 cup sugar
2 cups milk
1/2 cup freshly made espresso
1 tablespoon Tia Maria

SERVES 6

WHISK the egg yolks and half the sugar together until pale and creamy. Place the milk, coffee and remaining sugar in a saucepan and bring to a boil. Pour over the egg mixture and whisk to combine. Pour back into the saucepan and cook over low heat, stirring continuously until the mixture is thick enough to coat the back of a wooden spoon—do not allow the custard to boil.

STRAIN the custard into a bowl and cool over ice. Stir in the Tia Maria. Churn in an ice-cream maker following the manufacturer's instructions. Alternatively, pour into a plastic freezer box, cover and freeze. Stir every 30 minutes with a whisk during freezing to break up the ice crystals and give a better texture. Keep in the freezer until ready to serve.

COFFEE GELATO

## PRALINE SEMIFREDDO

5 oz. croccante (candied almonds)
2¹/₂ cups heavy cream
2 eggs, separated
³/₄ cup confectioners' sugar
2 tablespoons Mandorla (almond-
   flavored Marsala) or brandy

SERVES 6

FINELY CRUSH the almonds in a food processor or with a rolling pin. Pour the cream into a large bowl and whisk until soft peaks form. Beat the egg yolks with a quarter of the confectioners' sugar until pale. Whisk the egg whites in a clean dry glass bowl until stiff peaks form, then gradually add the rest of the confectioners' sugar and whisk until glossy stiff peaks form. Gently fold the egg yolks into the cream, then fold in the egg whites. Fold in the almonds and Mandorla.

LINE six 1-cup individual pudding molds or a 6-cup loaf pan with two long strips of aluminum foil each. Spoon in the mixture, level the surface and tap each mold on the counter a few times. Cover the surface with more foil and freeze for at least 24 hours. To unmold, leave at room temperature for 5 minutes, then use the foil strips as handles to lift out the semifreddos. Serve with zabaione (page 246).

## CHOCOLATE SEMIFREDDO

2 cups heavy cream
²/₃ cup superfine sugar
¹/₃ cup cocoa powder
4 eggs, separated
3 tablespoons brandy
3 tablespoons confectioners' sugar
1¹/₄ cups skinned hazelnuts,
   roughly chopped

SERVES 10

LINE a 6-cup loaf pan with aluminum foil. Heat ³/₄ cup of the cream in a small saucepan. Combine the superfine sugar, cocoa powder and egg yolks in a bowl. Pour the hot cream on top and mix well. Pour back into the saucepan and cook over low heat, stirring continuously until the mixture is thick enough to coat the back of a wooden spoon—do not allow the custard to boil. Stir in the brandy and remove from the heat. Cover the surface with plastic wrap and cool for 30 minutes.

WHIP the egg whites in a clean dry glass bowl until stiff peaks form. Whip the remaining cream in a large bowl until soft peaks form. Add the confectioners' sugar and continue whipping until stiff and glossy. Lightly fold the chocolate custard into the whipped cream, then fold in the egg whites. Gently fold in the hazelnuts. Spoon into the pan, smooth the surface and cover with foil. Freeze for at least 24 hours. Leave at room temperature for 5 minutes before serving in slices.

## MAKING A CAPPUCCINO

THE BLEND of roasted beans chosen by a cafè to make its coffee must be freshly ground to release the full flavor of the coffee. The grinder is positioned to a specific setting as the size of the grounds will affect the speed at which the water goes through the coffee. If the grounds are too fine, the water runs through slowly and the coffee will be too dark; if they are too coarse, the coffee will taste weak. There are two different-sized filter holders—a one- or a two-cup—and the holder needs to be filled to the top with the fresh coffee.

The coffee in the filter holder is packed down to level it off, then the holder is secured in place on the machine. A lever is then released to allow the water to run through the coffee under pressure. The temperature of the water must be very hot but not quite boiling, about 190–200°F, and compressed to about 9 atmospheres so that it travels through the coffee in no more than 30 seconds. The coffee will be bitter if it takes longer; and taste too weak if it is quicker.

The resulting espresso should be almost black, with just a light brown *crema* (froth) on top. If the *crema* is lighter, the water has been passed through the machine at too low a temperature or under too much pressure; if it is too dark, the temperature is too high or the pressure too low. The milk is frothed using steam released from the machine down the steam nozzle. The steam heats and aerates the milk until it becomes *schiuma* (foam). This is then poured and spooned onto an espresso to make a cappuccino.

CAFFE FLORIAN in Venice's Piazza San Marco was established in 1720 and modeled on the coffee houses of Constantinople, which were "schools of wisdom" for academics and literary figures. Set in a square ringed on three sides by cafès and once described by Napoleon as the Drawing Room of Europe, many of the world's most famous figures have taken coffee at Florian's while discussing art, literature and

# COFFEE

FOR A COUNTRY THAT DOESN'T ACTUALLY PRODUCE COFFEE, THIS DRINK IS ENORMOUSLY IMPORTANT TO ITALIAN CULTURE. ITALIANS INSIST THEIR COFFEE IS PREPARED PROPERLY, AND THE RITUALS OF MAKING A GOOD ESPRESSO AND OF CAFE LIFE ARE AS IMPORTANT AS THE DRINK ITSELF.

Coffee was first brought to Italy in the sixteenth century by the Arabs. By the seventeenth century, Venice had become the gateway through which the drink spread into Europe, and it was here that the beans were roasted before being dispersed throughout the Continent. As a result of the trade, coffee shops sprang up in Venice for people to enjoy this new drink and the most famous, Caffé Florian, established in 1720, is still there today.

## COFFEE BLENDS

The best Italian coffee is made just from high-quality arabica beans, though some brands may be a blend of arabica and the less delicate robusta beans. For the roast, Italians tend to prefer a dark, almost burnt, roast. This gives a very concentrated flavor and aroma and many Italians balance out the edge of bitterness by adding sugar. Surprisingly, the darker the roast, the less caffeine, as caffeine is lost during the roasting process. Italian coffee made in bars in fact has very little caffeine, as not only does it use dark beans but also the preparation process is so short that the water does not come into contact with the coffee grounds for very long.

# RASPBERRY SORBET

SORBETS ARE ICE CREAMS WITHOUT CREAM OR MILK. IF YOU FREEZE A SORBET MIXTURE WITHOUT CHURNING OR WHISKING YOU CAN MAKE A GRANITA—THE ICE CRYSTALS ARE BROKEN UP WITH A FORK FOR A ROUGHER TEXTURE.

$^1/_2$ cup sugar
1 tablespoon liquid glucose or
  superfine sugar
$^1/_4$ teaspoon lemon juice
$1^2/_3$ cups raspberries

SERVES 4

HEAT the sugar, glucose, lemon juice and 1 cup water in a small saucepan for 4 minutes or until dissolved. Purée the raspberries in a blender or food processor or by mashing with the back of a spoon, add the syrup and process until puréed. Pass through a plastic sieve to remove the seeds.

CHURN in an ice-cream maker following the manufacturer's instructions. Alternatively, pour into a plastic freezer box, cover and freeze. Stir every 30 minutes with a whisk during freezing to break up the ice crystals and give a better texture. Keep in the freezer until ready to serve.

# WATERMELON GRANITA

1 lb. watermelon, rind and seeds
  removed
1 tablespoon liquid glucose or
  superfine sugar
$^1/_2$ teaspoon lemon juice

SERVES 4

PUREE the watermelon in a blender or food processor, or chop it finely and push it through a metal sieve. Heat the glucose, lemon juice and $^1/_4$ cup water in a saucepan until dissolved. Add the watermelon and stir well.

POUR into a plastic freezer box, cover and freeze. Stir every 30 minutes with a fork during freezing to break up the ice crystals and give a better texture. Keep in the freezer until ready to serve, then roughly fork to break up the ice crystals.

WATERMELON GRANITA

Choose pears that have a nice rounded shape and arrange them so they fit neatly against each other in the tart.

# FRESH PEAR TART

PASTRY
1 1/4 cups all-purpose flour
1/4 cup superfine sugar
1 teaspoon grated lemon zest
4 tablespoons unsalted butter, chilled and cut into small cubes
1 egg yolk

MASCARPONE CREAM
2/3 cup mascarpone
1/4 cup superfine sugar
1 egg
1/4 teaspoon vanilla extract
1 tablespoon all-purpose flour
2–3 tablespoons milk, as necessary

4 ripe pears
juice of 1/2 lemon
1/3 cup toasted hazelnuts, roughly chopped
1 1/2 tablespoons superfine sugar
1 tablespoon apricot jelly
1 teaspoon pear liqueur, or other fruit-flavored liqueur

SERVES 6

TO MAKE the pastry, mix the flour, sugar, lemon zest and a pinch of salt in a bowl. Rub in the butter, then add the egg yolk and 2–3 teaspoons cold water and mix until the dough gathers in a loose clump. Transfer to a lightly floured surface and knead until smooth, adding more flour if needed. Chill in a plastic bag for 30 minutes.

PREHEAT the oven to 375°F and grease a 9-inch loose-bottomed tart pan. Lightly dust the work surface with flour and roll out the pastry until large enough to fit the pan. Line the pan neatly, trimming the pastry edges with a knife. Cover the pastry with parchment and fill with pie weights or uncooked rice or beans. Bake for 15 minutes then allow to cool. Reduce the oven to 325°F.

TO MAKE the mascarpone cream, blend the mascarpone, sugar, egg, vanilla extract and flour together until smooth (you can also use a food processor). Add a little milk if necessary to make the cream spreadable. Spoon the mascarpone cream into the pastry shell and smooth the surface.

PEEL, HALVE and core the pears, brushing the cut surfaces with lemon juice as you prepare each one. Arrange the pear halves like wheel spokes in the tart shell, with the wide base of each pear half to the outside. You may need to trim the last couple so they fit snugly. Place a round piece of pear in the center. Scatter the hazelnuts over the pears, then sprinkle the sugar over the top. Bake for 45 minutes, or until golden and set and the pears are soft.

HEAT the apricot jelly and liqueur in a small saucepan with 2 tablespoons water. Simmer, stirring, for 3–4 minutes until the jelly has melted. Strain and brush over the pears. Serve the tart warm or at room temperature.

politics. One of the great historic coffee houses of Europe, Caffé Florian still retains its stylish elegance. Patrons of the cafè can sit on chairs stretching outside into the square with their cappuccinos and watch the world go by to music from the live orchestra. In winter, people can choose instead to settle inside on one of the plush banquettes to enjoy their espressos or perhaps a grappa or Campari from the bar.

## MAKING ESPRESSO

To make a coffee, the beans are freshly ground and very hot water is forced through measured amounts of this ground coffee under pressure. This produces the basic espresso— a small amount of coffee topped with a foamy brown *crema*, which can then have milk added to make a cappuccino, latte or *macchiato*.

In Italy, coffee is drunk in a bar (also known as a caffè bar). People visit for a cappuccino and *cornetto* (a croissant-shaped pastry) on their way to work, or pop in for a quick espresso pick-me-up in the mid-morning or afternoon, all of which are cheaper if taken standing at the bar. In Italy, ordering a *caffè* will always mean you get an espresso. Coffee made at home is usually made in an espresso pot or *moka*, a double jug that boils water and forces it through the coffee grounds under pressure.

**ESPRESSO** made by forcing very hot, but not boiling, water through ground coffee to give a concentrated coffee. Espressos are drunk at any time through the day and especially after meals.

**LATTE MACCHIATO** a cup of hot milk that has been tinted with coffee—the opposite of a caffè macchiato. Usually served in a long glass.

**AMERICANO/CAFFE LUNGO** a weak espresso, with the same amount of coffee but diluted with extra water. It is served in a larger cup than an espresso.

**CAFFE MACCHIATO** a shot of espresso tinged with a little bit of cold milk or a dot of hot foamed milk.

**CAFFE FREDDO** an iced coffee based on a shot of sweetened espresso. Also sometimes made with cold milk to produce a *caffè latte freddo*.

**ESPRESSO DOPPIO** a double shot of espresso served in a slightly larger cup.

**CAFFE LATTE** a shot of espresso topped up with lots of hot milk. This is considered a breakfast drink.

**CAFFE CORRETTO** a shot of espresso fortified with a shot of alcohol, usually grappa or brandy. The type of alcohol added depends on the region.

**CAFFE RISTRETTO** a "restricted coffee", this extra-strong espresso is made with a little less water.

**AFFOGATO** a scoop of vanilla ice cream that has had a shot of espresso and a shot of alcohol poured over it.

**CAPPUCCINO** a shot of espresso topped with steamed milk and sometimes dusted with cocoa. It takes its name from its brown surface, which matches the habits worn by Capucin monks.

**COFFEE GRANITA** a grainy iced dessert served when it begins to melt to an almost soupy texture. To make it, freeze sweetened coffee, stirring every few hours until you have a slushy texture.

# CANNOLI

IDEALLY YOU SHOULD USE METAL CANNOLI TUBES FOR THIS RECIPE. YOU'LL FIND THESE IN GOURMET KITCHEN STORES. ALTERNATIVELY, YOU COULD USE 3/4-INCH WIDE WOODEN OR CANE DOWEL, CUT INTO 5-INCH LENGTHS.

## PASTRY
2 cups all-purpose flour
2 teaspoons cocoa powder
1 teaspoon instant coffee
1 tablespoon superfine sugar
1 tablespoon unsalted butter, chilled
    and cut into small cubes
3 tablespoons dry white wine
1 teaspoon dry Marsala

1 egg, beaten
oil for deep-frying

## FILLING
1 1/4 cups ricotta
2/3 cup superfine sugar
1/4 teaspoon vanilla extract
1/2 teaspoon grated lemon zest
1 tablespoon candied peel, finely
    chopped
6 candied cherries, chopped
2 tablespoons dark chocolate,
    grated
confectioners' sugar

SERVES 6

TO MAKE the pastry, mix the flour, cocoa powder, coffee and sugar in a bowl. Rub in the butter, then add the wine and Marsala and mix until the dough gathers in a loose clump. Transfer to a lightly floured surface and knead until smooth (the dough will be quite stiff). Chill in a plastic bag for 30 minutes.

LIGHTLY DUST the work surface with flour and roll the pastry out to 13 x 10 inches. Trim the edges, then cut the pastry into twelve 3-inch squares. Lightly grease the metal cannoli tubes. Wrap a pastry square diagonally around each tube, securing the overlapping corners with beaten egg and pressing them firmly together.

HEAT the oil in a deep-fat fryer or deep frying pan to about 350°F, or until a scrap of pastry dropped into the oil becomes crisp and golden, with a slightly blistered surface, in 15–20 seconds. If the oil starts to smoke it is too hot. Add the cannoli, a couple at a time, and deep-fry until golden and crisp. Remove with tongs and drain on paper towels. As soon as the tubes are cool enough to handle, slide them out and leave the pastries on a rack to cool.

TO MAKE the filling, mash the ricotta with a fork. Blend in the sugar and vanilla extract, then mix in the lemon zest, candied peel, candied cherries and chocolate. Fill the pastries, either with a pastry bag or a spoon. Arrange on a plate and dust with confectioners' sugar for serving. The cannoli should be eaten soon after they are filled.

Traditional cannoli molds need to be lightly greased before use. Wrap a pastry square around each tube, then deep-fry.

Almonds are native to the Mediterranean. In Italy, fresh almonds are picked while they still have their green coating and the kernel is soft and a bit wet. They are then eaten on their own or served with cheese.

# BISCOTTI

3 cups all-purpose flour
2/3 cup superfine sugar
3 eggs
1/2 teaspoon baking powder
1/2 teaspoon vanilla extract
1 cup blanched almonds

MAKES 20

PREHEAT the oven to 350°F and line two baking sheets with parchment. Sieve the flour into a large bowl or food processor, add the sugar, eggs, baking powder, vanilla extract and a pinch of salt and mix or process until you have a smooth dough. Transfer to a floured surface and knead in the almonds.

DIVIDE the dough into two pieces and roll each one into a log about 8 inches long. Put on the baking sheets and press down gently along the top to flatten the logs slightly. Bake for 25 minutes until the dough is gold in color. Take the logs out of the oven and allow to cool slightly while you turn down the oven to 325°F.

CUT EACH log into 1/2-inch thick diagonal slices, lay these back on the baking sheet and return the biscotti to the oven for 15 minutes until they start to brown and are dry to the touch. Store in an airtight container.

# AMARETTI

3/4 cup blanched almonds
1 cup confectioners' sugar
3 teaspoons all-purpose flour
2 egg whites
1/4–1/3 cup superfine sugar
1 teaspoon almond extract

MAKES 15

PREHEAT the oven to 350°F. Grind the almonds, confectioners' sugar and flour to a fine powder with a pestle and mortar or food processor (be careful not to overwork the mixture or it will become oily).

WHISK the egg whites in a clean dry glass bowl until soft peaks form. Add the superfine sugar a tablespoon at a time and beat continuously until you have a stiff shiny mixture. Fold in the almond mixture and the almond extract until just blended.

SPOON the mixture into a pastry bag with a 1/2-inch plain tip and pipe 1 1/4-inch wide mounds, well spaced, onto a baking sheet. Smooth the tops of each amaretti with a damp finger and bake for 40 minutes until they are light brown. Turn off the oven, leave the door ajar and allow the amaretti to cool and dry out. Store in an airtight container.

# SCHIACCIATA CON UVA

THIS BREAD IS A FLORENTINE SPECIALTY, TRADITIONALLY MADE IN TUSCANY DURING THE GRAPE HARVEST. THE RAISINS, REPRESENTING LAST SEASON'S GRAPES, ARE COMBINED WITH THE NEW SEASON'S GRAPES TAKEN FROM THE PRESENT HARVEST.

3/4 cup raisins
1/3 cup sweet Marsala
1/2 cup milk
2 teaspoons dried yeast or
  1/2 oz. fresh yeast
1/2 cup superfine sugar
2 1/2 cups all-purpose flour
olive oil
2 3/4 cups black seedless grapes

SERVES 6

PUT the raisins and Marsala in a bowl to soak. Warm the milk to hand hot and place in a small bowl. Stir in the yeast and 1 teaspoon of the sugar and set aside in a draft-free spot. If the yeast does not bubble and foam in 5 minutes, throw it away and try again.

PUT the flour, 1/3 cup of the sugar and a pinch of salt in a bowl and mix together. Add the yeast mixture and mix until the dough starts to come together in a clump. Transfer to a lightly floured surface and knead for 6–8 minutes. Add a little more flour or a few drops of warm water if necessary to give a soft, but not sticky, dough.

RUB the inside of a large bowl with olive oil. Roll the ball of dough around in the bowl to coat it with oil, then cut a cross on the top of the ball with a sharp knife. Leave the dough in the bowl, cover with a kitchen towel or put in a plastic bag and leave in a draft-free spot for 1–1 1/2 hours until doubled in size.

DRAIN the raisins and squeeze them dry. Lightly dust a baking sheet with flour. Punch down the dough (give it one good blow in the center with your fist to expel the air) and then divide it in two. Shape each portion into a disk about 8 inches in diameter and place one disk on the baking sheet. Scatter half the grapes and half the raisins on top, then cover with the second disk of dough. Scatter the remaining grapes and raisins over the top. Cover again and leave for 1 hour to rise again and double in size.

PREHEAT the oven to 350°F. Sprinkle the surface of the bread with the remaining sugar. Bake for 40–50 minutes, or until golden.

Pile the grapes and raisins into the center of the bottom layer, so that when the top goes on they are almost covered and stay soft when they are cooking. Scatter the raisins and grapes on top and press them into the dough so they don't burn as they cook.

# PANFORTE

PANFORTE MEANS "STRONG BREAD", AN APT DESCRIPTION FOR THIS DENSE, FRUITY LOAF THAT STILL RETAINS ITS MEDIEVAL FLAVOR. PANFORTE IS ALSO KNOWN AS SIENA CAKE—SIENA POSSIBLY BEING THE FIRST ITALIAN CITY TO USE SUGAR AND SPICES SUCH AS WHITE PEPPER.

3/4 cup hazelnuts
2/3 cup almonds
2/3 cup candied mixed peel, chopped
1/2 cup candied pineapple, chopped
grated zest of 1 lemon
2/3 cup all-purpose flour
1 teaspoon ground cinnamon
1/4 teaspoon ground coriander
1/4 teaspoon ground cloves
1/4 teaspoon grated nutmeg
pinch of white pepper
2/3 cup sugar
4 tablespoons honey
3 tablespoons unsalted butter
confectioners' sugar

MAKES ONE 9-INCH CAKE

LINE a 9-inch springform pan with rice paper or parchment and grease well with butter. Toast the nuts under a hot broiler, turning them so they brown on all sides, then allow to cool. Put the nuts in a bowl with the mixed peel, pineapple, lemon zest, flour and spices and toss together. Preheat the oven to 300°F.

PUT the sugar, honey and butter in a saucepan and melt them together. Cook the syrup until it reaches 250°F on a sugar thermometer, or a little of it dropped into cold water forms a soft ball when molded between your finger and thumb.

POUR the syrup into the nut mixture and mix well, working fast before it stiffens too much. Pour straight into the pan, smooth the surface and bake for 35 minutes. (Unlike other cakes this will neither firm up as it cooks or color at all so you need to time it carefully.)

COOL IN the pan until the cake firms up enough to remove the side of the pan. Peel off the paper, turn the cake over onto another piece of parchment paper and allow to cool completely. Dust the top heavily with confectioners' sugar.

The hills around Siena.

# POLENTA CAKE

IN THE MOUNTAINOUS REGIONS OF NORTH ITALY POLENTA WAS TRADITIONALLY THE STAPLE DIET OF THE POOR. TODAY IT IS HAVING A RESURGENCE OF POPULARITY. COARSE- OR FINE-GRAINED POLENTA WILL GIVE THIS CAKE DIFFERENT TEXTURES, BUT EITHER IS FINE. ENJOY WITH A GLASS OF VIN SANTO.

$^1/_3$ cup golden raisins
2 tablespoons brandy
1 cup ricotta
1 cup superfine sugar
$1^1/_2$ cups polenta
pinch of grated nutmeg
$^1/_2$ teaspoon grated lemon zest
$^1/_4$ teaspoon vanilla extract
1 tablespoon unsalted butter, chilled
  and cut into small cubes
2 tablespoons pine nuts
confectioners' sugar

MAKES ONE 10-INCH CAKE

PUT the golden raisins and brandy in a small bowl with enough water to cover them and leave for 30 minutes. Drain and dry well on paper towels.

PREHEAT the oven to 315°F and grease a 10-inch loose-bottomed or springform pan with a tight-fitting bottom.

Put the ricotta in a large bowl and add $1^3/_4$ cups cold water. Beat with a wire whisk or electric beaters until smooth. Don't be alarmed by the thinness of the mixture—it can be very liquid, depending on the brand of ricotta used. Add the sugar and beat until smooth, then stir in the polenta, nutmeg, lemon zest, vanilla extract and golden raisins.

POUR the mixture into the pan. Dot the surface with butter and sprinkle the pine nuts on top. Put the pan on a baking sheet to catch any drips and bake for about $1^1/_2$ hours until golden and set. Serve warm or cold with whipped cream, dusted with confectioners' sugar.

Sprinkling the polenta in from a height distributes it evenly and makes it easier to whisk in. Tip the mixture into the pan so that the golden raisins are spread evenly. Dotting the top of the cake with butter gives it a golden finish.

# HAZELNUT AND CHOCOLATE CAKE

1 cup skinned hazelnuts
3 tablespoons cocoa powder
1/2 cup all-purpose flour
1/4 cup self-rising flour
3/4 cup light brown sugar
1 cup unsalted butter, softened
4 eggs, separated
confectioners' sugar

SERVES 8

TOAST the hazelnuts under a hot broiler, turning them so they brown on all sides. Allow them to cool, then put in a food processor and process until fine (don't overprocess or they will become oily), or chop finely with a knife. Transfer to a bowl with the cocoa powder and sifted flours. Preheat the oven to 350°F.

BEAT TOGETHER the sugar and butter until very creamy. Add the egg yolks one at a time, mixing well after each addition. Add hazelnut mixture and stir well. Whisk the egg whites in a clean dry glass bowl until stiff peaks form, then fold into mixture. Pour into the pan and bake for 50 minutes or until a skewer inserted in the center comes out clean. Rest for 15 minutes, then turn out onto a rack to cool completely. Dust with confectioners' sugar.

In Tuscany chestnuts are grown in quantity. The season is short— early November until Christmas— so they are also dried for year-round use. The dried chestnuts are soaked in water, then boiled in milk for soups or sweet desserts.

# CHESTNUT CAKE

1 lb. chestnuts or 1/2 lb. cooked peeled chestnuts
5 egg yolks
3/4 cup superfine sugar
1/3 cup unsalted butter, softened
1 tablespoon grated lemon zest
3/4 cup ground almonds
2 tablespoons all-purpose flour
4 egg whites

SERVES 8

PREHEAT the oven to 350°F, and grease and flour an 8-inch cake pan.

BOIL the chestnuts in a saucepan of water for 25 minutes, or until they are tender. Drain, peel and, while still hot, purée and sieve. (If you are using the cooked chestnuts, simply purée them.)

WHISK the egg yolks and sugar until light and fluffy. Add the butter, lemon zest, chestnut purée, ground almonds and flour and stir well. Whisk the egg whites until soft peaks form and fold into the mixture. Pour into the pan and bake for 50–60 minutes. Cool on a wire rack and serve with whipped cream.

CHESTNUT CAKE

# VENETIAN RICE PUDDING

2½ cups milk
1 cup heavy cream
1 vanilla bean, split
¼ cup superfine sugar
¼ teaspoon ground cinnamon
pinch of grated nutmeg
1 tablespoon grated orange zest
⅔ cup golden raisins
2 tablespoons brandy or sweet
  Marsala
½ cup arborio or vialone nano rice

SERVES 4

PUT the milk, cream and vanilla bean in a heavy-bottomed saucepan and bring just to a boil, then remove from the heat. Add the sugar, cinnamon, nutmeg and orange zest and set aside.

PUT the golden raisins and brandy in a small bowl and leave to soak. Add the rice to the infused milk and return to the heat. Bring to a simmer and stir slowly for about 35 minutes, or until the rice is creamy. Stir in the golden raisins and remove the vanilla bean at the end. Serve warm or cold.

Rice grown in Italy is much more absorbent than that grown elsewhere. It is ideal for risotto, and also for rice-based desserts.

# BAKED FIGS

WHEN NOT IN ITALY, YOU'LL HAVE TO BUY CANTUCCI AT ITALIAN SPECIALTY STORES, ALTHOUGH SOME LARGER SUPERMARKETS DO STOCK THEM. DON'T WASTE THE REST OF THE PACKET—SERVE THEM AFTER THE FIGS, FOR DIPPING IN AFTER-DINNER DRINKS LIKE VIN SANTO OR ESPRESSO.

3 cantucci (*biscotti di Prato*)
1 teaspoon grated lemon zest
¼ cup heavy cream
4 purple figs, ripe but firm
juice of ½ lemon
1 tablespoon brown sugar

SERVES 4

PREHEAT the oven to 415°F and lightly grease a shallow flameproof dish large enough to hold eight fig halves, overlapping slightly. Crush the cantucci with a heavy rolling pin. Combine the crumbs with half the lemon zest and half the cream.

SLICE EACH fig in half lengthwise and drizzle the lemon juice over the cut surfaces. Fill the figs with the cantucci filling, pressing it loosely onto the centers of the cut surfaces. Arrange the figs in the dish, with each stem end slightly overlapping the bottom of the fig in front. Pour the remaining cream over the top and sprinkle with the remaining lemon zest, then the sugar.

BAKE FOR 10 minutes or until the sugar melts and a little syrup forms in the dish. Serve warm with a little of the syrup spooned on top, with mascarpone or whipped cream and the rest of the packet of cantucci.

BAKED FIGS

BASICS

Pasta is traditionally made on the work surface and not in a bowl. Roll it by hand or with a pasta machine—whichever method you choose, it must be thin enough to read a newspaper through.

# PASTA

1 lb. 00 *(doppio zero)* or
   all-purpose flour
4 eggs
chilled water

MAKES 1¹/₂ LB.

MOUND the flour on a work surface or in a large bowl. Make a well in the center. Break the eggs into the well and whisk with a fork, incorporating the flour as you whisk. You may need to add a little chilled water (¹/₄ teaspoon at a time) to make a loosely massed dough. Turn the dough onto a lightly floured surface—it should be soft, pliable and dry to the touch. Knead for 6–8 minutes, or until smooth and elastic with a slightly glossy appearance. Cover with a kitchen towel and leave for 30 minutes. It is then ready to roll out.

TO MAKE the dough in a processor, mix the flour for 2–3 seconds, then add the eggs with the motor running. Mix again for 5 seconds, or until the mixture looks like coarse meal. Mix until a loose ball forms, then continue for 4–5 seconds until the machine slows down and stops. If the dough seems too sticky to form a smooth ball, add 2 teaspoons flour, mix briefly and continue adding small amounts of flour until the ball forms. If the mixture is too dry, add chilled water, a teaspoon at a time. Transfer to a lightly floured surface and knead for 2–3 minutes until smooth and elastic. Cover with a kitchen towel and leave for 30 minutes.

TO ROLL OUT the dough, divide into two or three manageable portions. Work with one portion at a time, keeping the rest covered. Flatten the dough onto a lightly floured surface and roll out from the center to the outer edge, rotating the dough often. When you have a ¹/₄-inch thick circle of dough, fold it in half and roll it out again. Do this eight times to give a smooth circle of pasta, then roll to a thickness of 1 inch (mend any tears with a little pasta from the outside of the circle and a little water). Transfer to a lightly floured kitchen towel. If the pasta is to be filled, keep it covered and don't allow it to dry out. If the sheets are to be cut into lengths or shapes, leave them uncovered while you roll out the other portions, so that the surface moisture will dry slightly before cutting.

IF YOU have a pasta machine, work the dough through the rollers, making the setting smaller each time until the dough is the correct thickness.

# PIZZA DOUGH

1 tablespoon superfine sugar
2 teaspoons dried yeast or
   1/2 oz. fresh yeast
3/4 cup lukewarm water
1 lb. all-purpose flour
1/2 teaspoon salt
3 tablespoons olive oil
cornmeal

MAKES TWO 12-INCH PIZZAS

PUT the sugar and yeast in a small bowl and stir in 1/3 cup of the water. Leave in a draft-free spot to activate. If the yeast does not bubble and foam in 5 minutes, throw it away and start again.

MIX the flour and salt in a bowl or in a food processor fitted with a plastic blade. Add the olive oil, remaining water and the yeast mixture. Mix until the dough loosely clumps together. Transfer to a lightly floured surface and knead for 8 minutes, adding a little flour or a few drops of warm water if necessary, until you have a soft dough that doesn't stick but is dry to the touch.

RUB the inside of a large bowl with olive oil. Roll the ball of dough around in the bowl to coat it with oil, then cut a shallow cross on the top of the ball with a sharp knife. Leave the dough in the bowl, cover with a kitchen towel or put in a plastic bag and leave in a draft-free spot for 1–1 1/2 hours until doubled in size (or leave in the fridge for 8 hours to rise slowly). Punch down the dough to its original size, then divide into two portions. (At this stage the dough can be stored in the fridge for up to 4 hours, or frozen. Bring back to room temperature before continuing.)

WORKING with one portion at a time, push the dough out to make a thick circle. Use the heels of your hands and work from the center of the circle outwards, to flatten the dough into a 12-inch circle with a slightly raised rim. (If you find it difficult to push the dough out by hand you can use a rolling pin.) The pizza dough is now ready to use, as instructed in the recipe. Cook on a lightly greased tray, dusted with cornmeal, and get it into the oven as quickly as possible.

Knead the dough by stretching it away from you and then folding it back on itself until it is soft and springy. The dough is ready when a finger indent springs out quickly.

Make the dough in a large bowl so you have enough room to bring it together. Knead on a well-floured surface until the dough is really elastic. Use the heel of your hand to stretch it into a rectangle.

# FOCACCIA DOUGH

1/2 teaspoon superfine sugar
2 teaspoons dried yeast or
   1/2 oz. fresh yeast
3 cups lukewarm water
2 lb. all-purpose flour
2 teaspoons salt
3 tablespoons olive oil
cornmeal

MAKES 2 FOCACCIAS

PUT the sugar and yeast in a small bowl and stir in 1/4 cup of the water. Leave in a draft-free spot to activate. If the yeast does not bubble and foam in 5 minutes, throw it away and start again.

MIX the flour and salt in a bowl or in a food processor fitted with a plastic blade. Add 2 tablespoons of the olive oil, the yeast mixture and three-quarters of the remaining water. Mix, then add the rest of the water, a little at a time, until the dough loosely clumps together. Transfer to a lightly floured surface and knead for 8 minutes until smooth, or until the impression made by a finger springs back immediately.

RUB the inside of a large bowl with the remaining olive oil. Roll the ball of dough around in the bowl to coat it with oil, then cut a shallow cross on the top of the ball with a sharp knife. Leave the dough in the bowl, seal it in a plastic bag and leave in a draft-free spot for 1–1 1/2 hours until doubled in size (or leave in the fridge for 8 hours to rise slowly).

PUNCH DOWN the dough to its original size, then divide into two portions. (At this stage the dough can be stored in the fridge for 4 hours, or frozen. Bring back to room temperature before continuing.) Roll out each portion of dough to an 11 x 8 inch rectangle, then use the heels of your hands, working from the center of the dough outwards, to make a 15 x 11 inch rectangle.

LIGHTLY GREASE 2 baking sheets and dust with cornmeal. Put a portion of dough in the center of each baking sheet and press out to fill the sheet. Slide the baking sheets inside a plastic bag. Seal and leave in a draft-free spot for 2 hours to rise again. The focaccia dough is now ready to use, as instructed in the recipe.

# BECHAMEL SAUCE

4 tablespoons butter
1/3 cup all-purpose flour
pinch of grated nutmeg
2 1/2 cups milk
1 bay leaf

MAKES 3 CUPS

HEAT the butter in a saucepan over low heat. Add the flour and nutmeg and cook, stirring, for 1 minute. Remove from the heat and gradually stir in milk. Add the bay leaf, return to the heat and simmer, stirring often, until the sauce thickens. Season, cover with plastic wrap to prevent a skin forming, and cool. Discard the bay leaf.

BECHAMEL SAUCE

# TOMATO SAUCE

1/4 lb. plum tomatoes
3 basil leaves
2 garlic cloves, crushed
1 tablespoon strained tomatoes
2 teaspoons extra virgin olive oil

MAKES 3/4 CUP

CORE the tomatoes and purée in a food processor with the basil leaves (or chop tomatoes and basil very finely and stir together). Stir in the garlic, strained tomatoes and olive oil and season well. Allow to rest for at least 30 minutes before serving to allow the flavors to blend.

# PESTO

2 garlic cloves
1/3 cup pine nuts
2 1/2 cups basil leaves
4 tablespoons grated Parmesan
1/2 cup extra virgin olive oil

MAKES 3/4 CUP

POUND the garlic, pine nuts, basil and Parmesan using a mortar and pestle or mix to a paste in a food processor. Add the oil in a steady stream, mixing continuously. Add salt if necessary. Refrigerate in a sterilized jar, covered with a layer of olive oil.

TOMATO SAUCE

# SALSA VERDE

1 1/2 tablespoons fresh white
  bread crumbs
1 tablespoon milk
1 hard-boiled egg yolk
2 anchovy fillets
1 tablespoon capers
5 tablespoons finely chopped
  parsley, mint and basil
1 garlic clove, crushed
1/4 cup extra virgin olive oil

MAKES 3/4 CUP

SOAK the bread crumbs in the milk for 10 minutes. Finely chop together the egg yolk, anchovy and capers. Add the herbs, garlic and soaked bread crumbs and mix with a fork. Slowly blend in the olive oil until the sauce is smooth and thick. Season with pepper, then set aside for at least 1 hour before using.

SALSA VERDE

PESTO

OVEN-DRIED TOMATOES

GIARDINIERA

# VINAIGRETTE

2 tablespoons lemon juice
4 tablespoons olive oil
2 teaspoons finely chopped onion
   or 1 finely chopped shallot
1 tablespoon chopped parsley

MAKES ³/₄ CUP

MAKE the dressing by combining all the ingredients. Season with salt and pepper.

# OVEN-DRIED TOMATOES

24 plum tomatoes
sea salt
4 garlic cloves, crushed
¹/₂ tablespoon extra virgin olive oil
24 basil leaves
1 mild red chile, cut into 24 small
   pieces
¹/₂ tablespoon dried oregano
3 cups olive oil

MAKES 8 CUPS

PREHEAT the oven to 150°F. Core each tomato and slice almost in half lengthwise, with just the skin keeping it together. Open out butterfly-fashion and space out, cut side up, on wire racks. Sprinkle with sea salt and bake for 8 hours, until dark and almost leathery, but not crisp. Cool and store in sterilized jars for up to six months, or preserve as below.

MIX the garlic with the extra virgin olive oil. Brush one half of each tomato, then place a basil leaf, piece of chile and sprinkling of oregano on top. Fold the other half over to enclose and place in a sterilized jar. Pour in the olive oil to cover the tomatoes and push down firmly to expel any air. Seal and refrigerate for up to two months.

# GIARDINIERA (GARDEN PICKLES)

3 cups carrots, cut into short
   lengths
1¹/₄ cups pearl onions
1 cup small fresh gherkins
3¹/₂ cups white wine vinegar
1 tablespoon sea salt
2 tablespoons honey
1¹/₃ cups stringless green beans,
   cut into short lengths
10 black peppercorns
6 whole cloves
5 juniper berries
2 bay leaves

MAKES 5 CUPS

PREHEAT the oven to 250°F. Put the carrots, onions, gherkins, vinegar, salt and honey in a saucepan with 2¹/₂ cups water and then bring to a boil. Reduce the heat and simmer for 20 minutes. Add the green beans and simmer for 5 minutes, or until the vegetables are tender but still slightly crisp.

DRAIN the vegetables, reserving the liquid. Arrange the vegetables in a sterilized 5-cup jar and add the peppercorns, cloves, juniper berries and bay leaves. Pour in the liquid to cover the vegetables. Seal and refrigerate for 24 hours before use. Will keep for up to two months.

**BAROLO** made in Piemonte from Nebbiolo grapes, this excellent wine is a deep red color with a strong flavor best appreciated after aging and when eaten with meat and game.

**BRUNELLO DI MONTALCINO** this prestigious wine from Montalcino near Sienna is a full-bodied and fragrant partner to meat dishes. It is made from Sangiovese Grosso grapes.

**VALPOLICELLA** made around Verona from Corvina, Rondinella and Molinara grapes, this is a popular, easy-drinking wine. It is worth searching out the excellent versions from the hills of Verona.

**BARDOLINO** one of Italy's most exported wines, Bardolino is made from the same grapes and in the same region as Valpolicella. Light and often slightly sparkling, drink young and even cool.

**LAMBRUSCO** from Emilia-Romagna, this rich red, naturally fizzy wine is very different at home to the mass-produced export versions. Its acidity balances the region's rich foods.

**CHIANTI** no longer usually found in straw-covered bottles, the quality of Chianti is now governed by DOCG regulations. Made largely from Sangiovese grapes, it is best drunk young.

**BARBARESCO** another Piemonte wine, Barbaresco is very similar to, though more delicate than, Barolo and also best appreciated after aging and with the meat dishes of the region.

**VERDICCHIO** a light, dry wine made in Le Marche mostly from Verdicchio grapes and bottled in amphora-shaped bottles. Very good with the seafood of the region, it should be drunk young.

**SOAVE** made in Veneto, Soave is pale in color with a greenish tinge and light bouquet. Though much is mass-produced, there are some very good wines from the hilly *classico* area.

**FRASCATI** a well-known white wine made in the hills near Rome from Trebbiano Toscano and Malvasia Bianca grapes. Mostly dry, it is good with Rome's famous meat dishes.

**ORVIETO** a pale gold Umbrian wine made from Trebbiano Toscano grapes. Traditionally an *abboccato* (semi-sweet) wine, there are now more *secco* (dry) versions. Serve with antipasto.

**PROSECCO** made in Veneto from Prosecco grapes, this wine comes in *frizzante* and *spumante* (light and fully sparkling) versions and can be sweet or dry. The essential ingredient in a bellini.

IN TUSCANY, one of Italy's most famous wine-producing regions, you can see both the most traditional and the most innovative of Italian wine-making today. Agricola San Felice is a vineyard situated in the prestigious Chianti Classico area, where many of the vineyards proudly display a black rooster on their bottles—a sign that they are members of the Chianti Classico Consortium. The DOC regulations introduced

# WINE

THE HISTORY OF WINE IN ITALY STRETCHES BACK THOUSANDS

OF YEARS. THE ETRUSCANS MAY WELL HAVE ENJOYED WINE,

THOUGH IT WAS THE GREEKS AND LATER THE ROMANS WHO

SAW THE REAL POTENTIAL IN ITALY FOR CULTIVATING VINES.

A terrain that ranges from the Alps to the sunbaked south and a Mediterranean climate create a perfect environment for producing a huge variety of unique wines. While today's wines are very different from the rich, aged wines enjoyed by the Romans, there can still be found some continuation in wine-making methods and traditions, particularly in some of Italy's most classic wines—Recioto and Amarone della Valpolicella and Vin Santo, where grapes are dried out

before pressing. While traditional methods are respected and preserved, and many Italian wine producers still consist of a family working their own vineyards, the Italians have also been quick to modernize their cellars and innovative in producing new wines. French varieties have been planted alongside Italian varieties and new technology installed.

## DENOMINAZIONE DI ORIGINE CONTROLLATA

Italy's reputation worldwide for its wines was initially based on easy-drinking bottles of Soave, Frascati, Lambrusco, Asti Spumante and particularly the distinctive bottles of Chianti, which graced trattorias all over the world. While these wines were popular and profitable, the quality was variable, and in 1963 the Italian government introduced laws called the *denominazione di origine controllata (DOC)* to control wine production. This has led to a rise in standards and Italy's place as one of the world's leading wine exporters.

In Italy, wine is an important part of every meal and is seen as a partner for food, rather than a drink to be drunk on its own.

AS WELL AS producing traditional Chianti Classico, San Felice has long been involved in viticultural research, most notably with its *Vitiarium,* a small vineyard where about 300 less well-known Tuscan vines are being cultivated. It was this innovative approach to wine-making that led to *Vigorello,* a precursor to today's super-Tuscans, first being produced here in 1968. The super-Tuscans are inspired by the great wines of

# GLOSSARY OF ITALIAN FOOD AND COOKING

*al dente* Meaning "to the tooth". Pasta and risotto rice are cooked until they are *al dente*—the outside is tender but the center still has a little resistance or "bite". Pasta cooked beyond this point becomes soggy.

amaretti Small cookies like macaroons, made from sweet and bitter almonds. They vary, but are usually 3/4–1 1/4 inch wide.

artichoke (*carciofo*) The edible flower of a member of the thistle family. Some have thorns and the types vary greatly in size. The largest are usually boiled, but the smallest and most tender can be eaten raw as antipasto. Most common varieties include Romanesco (large and purple), Precoce di Chioggia (large and green), Violetto Toscano (small and tender enough to eat raw) and Spinoso di Palermo (a purple variety from Sicily).

bocconcini Means literally "small mouthful" and is used to describe various foods, but generally refers to small balls of mozzarella, about the size of walnuts.

bouquet garni A bundle of herbs used to flavor dishes. Made by tying sprigs of parsley, thyme, celery leaves and a bay leaf in either a piece of muslin or portion of leek.

bresaola Lean beef that is cured and air-dried for 2–3 months—a specialty of the Valtellina Valley in Lombardia. Has a dark red color and stronger flavor than prosciutto. Serve thinly sliced.

cantucci Tuscan almond cookies, also known as *biscotti di Prato*. These hard, double-baked cookies often contain whole almonds. They are usually eaten dipped into a dessert wine such as *vin santo*.

caperberries The fruit of the caper bush, which appear after the flowers. They are usually preserved in brine and served as an accompaniment, like olives.

capers The pickled flowers of the caper bush. These are available preserved in brine, vinegar or salt and should be rinsed well and squeezed dry before use.

cardoons Similar to the artichoke plant, cardoons have large leaves and long stems. Unlike artichokes, it is the stems that are eaten rather than the flowers. The stalks are usually blanched like celery.

casalinga Means "homemade" or "homey". When attributed to sausages or salami, it generally means having a coarse texture and earthy flavor.

cavolo nero Cabbage with long leaves that are so dark green they appear to be almost black. Used mainly in Tuscan cooking. If unavailable, Savoy cabbage can be used.

cetriolini Small gherkins. If unavailable, use cornichons or small cocktail gherkins.

ciabatta Slipper-shaped Italian bread with a rough, open texture, made from a very wet dough, which allows large bubbles to form and gives a thin crust. Ciabatta quickly goes stale and is best eaten on the day it is bought or made.

cipolline Small white onions, usually flattened in appearance rather than round.

coppa A type of cured pork made from half pork fat and half pig's neck and shoulder. It is rolled and cured in a casing and, when sliced, resembles a fatty sausage.

cotechino A sausage made from pork and pork rind, giving it a gelatinous texture. Cotechino is flavored with cloves and cinnamon and needs to be cooked before eating.

country-style bread Any bread that is bought as a whole loaf and has a rough texture. Pugliese, ciabatta and pane Toscano are all examples. Other white bread is not a suitable substitute.

croccante Caramelized nuts, usually almonds but sometimes hazelnuts (these are also known as pralines).

*doppio zero* (00) flour The finest grade of flour, made from soft wheat (*grano tenero*) and mainly used for making cakes and fresh egg pasta.

farro A type of spelt grain, farro is used in soups and stews in a similar way to barley. If farro is unavailable, spelt or barley can be used. Farro is most commonly used in the cuisines of the areas where it is grown—Tuscany, Umbria and Lazio.

finocchiona A type of salami from Tuscany, flavored with wild fennel seeds. The salami is very often large and is aged for up to a year before use. It also comes in a more crumbly version called *sbriciolona*.

flat-leaf parsley Also known as Italian or Continental parsley. Used as an ingredient rather than a garnish, unlike curly parsley.

fontina A traditional mountain cheese from the Valle d'Aosta in Piemonte. Full-fat and semi-soft with a sweetish flavor, fontina melts evenly and well and so is particularly good for cooking.

for Chianti in 1967 froze in time what was already a disputed "recipe" for that wine, allowing up to 30 percent white grapes to be added to the red Sangiovese grapes. Later DOCG regulations improved on this situation until, by 1996, Chianti could be made with very few, or even no, white grapes. Today San Felice produces some very high-quality Chianti Classico wines, including *Il Grigio, a* Chianti Classico Riserva.

## BUYING ITALIAN WINE

Good wines are produced in every one of Italy's regions. Even in the hot South, some excellent wines can be found, while Piemonte and Tuscany produce red wines of international repute. The *denominazione di origine controllata* (DOC) label on wines in Italy guarantees authenticity and certain minimum standards of quality by defining production processes. Some of the country's finest wines, such as Barolo, Barbaresco, Chianti and Brunello di Montalcino are controlled under the stricter *denominazione di origine controllata e garantita* (DOCG) regulations. However, some of Italy's wine-makers choose to produce wines that do not conform to the strict regulations required to obtain DOC status, particularly those regarding grape varieties. There are now attempts to classify these "super-table" wines, many rating among Italy's finest, under a new IGT (*Indicazione Geographica Tipica*) system, but many are still sold as just *vino da tavola*. In Italy, an *Enoteca* is a "wine library"—a specialist wine store that can give advice on buying wines.

## ORDERING ITALIAN WINE

In many restaurants in Italy, you may not even be passed a wine list. Instead, the choice is between the house red or white wine. If there is a wine list, you may still choose to pick a local wine, many of which are made to be the perfect partner for the food of their region.

## READING ITALIAN LABELS

ABBOCCATO medium dry
AMABILE medium sweet
AMARONE dry (literally bitter)
CLASSICO wines that come from the best part of a DOC area
DOLCE sweet
FRIZZANTE slightly fizzy, usually naturally fizzy from fermentation
RECIOTO wine made from selected (ie riper) bunches of grapes
RISERVA wine that has undergone a longer period of aging
SECCO dry
SPUMANTE fully sparkling
SUPERIORE higher degree of alcohol than normal

Bordeaux and choose to exist outside the DOC regulations. Marketed often to international acclaim, they are sold under the humble *vino da tavola* status. Vigorello is made from 70 percent Sangiovese mixed with 30 per cent of the foreign Cabernet Sauvignon. The grapes are fermented in stainless-steel tanks, then the wine aged for 18 months in French oak *barriques* in San Felice's cellars to give a smooth finish to the wine.

## MARSALA

FLORIO'S has produced the fortified wine, Marsala, in western Sicily for over 150 years. Not a traditional Italian drink, Marsala was in fact invented in 1773 by an Englishman, John Woodhouse, for export to the English market and the drink was named after the small Sicilian town that remains today the center of production. As a DOC-regulated wine, Marsala must be aged in wooden casks: at Florio's this is done first in large oak ones, then in small Slovenian red oak casks that add complexity and flavor, and finally in 450-gallon oak casks, where the

Marsala can rest for up to 10 years before being bottled. At the very least, a Marsala Fine must age for one year, but Florio's specializes in Marsala Superiore—wines aged for over 2 years. They also produce an outstanding dry Marsala Vergine—aged for over 5 years. Marsala is an important ingredient in Italian cooking, while dry Marsala can be drunk as an aperitif and sweet Marsala as a dessert wine.

## ITALIAN DRINKS

**LIMONCELLO** this southern liqueur from the Amalfi Coast is always served ice cold and is made from fresh lemons, sugar and alcohol.

**VIN SANTO** this Tuscan dessert wine is made from Malavasia and Trebbiano grapes left out to dry before being pressed and aged for 3 to 4 years. *Cantucci* are often dunked in the wine.

**GRAPPA AND NOCINO** grappa is produced by distilling the skins, seeds and pulp, the *vinacce,* left over from winemaking. *Nocino* is a sweet infusion of sugar, alcohol and green walnuts.

**AMARETTO** this is a sweet, bitter almond-flavored liqueur that is enjoyed as a *digestif* after a meal and is also added to many sweet recipes to give an almond flavor.

**Gorgonzola** A blue cheese, originally made in Gorgonzola in Lombardia but now produced in other regions as well. It melts well and is often used in sauces. If not available, use another full-fat blue cheese.

**juniper berries** Blackish-purple berries with a resin flavor. Used in stews and game dishes. Crush the berries slightly before use to release their flavor.

**Marsala** A fortified wine from Marsala in Sicily that comes in varying degrees of dryness and sweetness. Dry Marsalas are used in savory dishes, and sweet ones in desserts such as zabaione. Do not try to use sweet Marsala in savory dishes.

**mascarpone** A cream cheese originally from Lombardia. Made with cream rather than milk, it is very high in fat. Mascarpone is generally used in desserts such as tiramisù or instead of cream in sauces.

**misticanza** A Roman salad that was once made of wild greens. Today it is generally a mixture of arugula, purslane, sorrel, mint, dandelion, wild fennel and endive with some lettuce. In Umbria it also refers to a mixture of dried beans used for soups.

**mortadella** A large, finely textured pork sausage, with lengths of lard running through it. Some versions contain pistachio nuts and all should be eaten thinly sliced or in cubes and very fresh. Traditionally made in Bologna, the sausage is also known as bologna or baloney in the U.S.

**olive** Eating olives can be named after where they come from, such as Ligurian; their curing style, such as Sicilian; or their variety, such as Cerignola. Though green and black olives have a different flavor, they can be used interchangeably in recipes unless the final color is a factor.

**olive oil** Extra-virgin and virgin olive oils are pressed without any heat or chemicals and are best used in simple uncooked dishes and for salads. Pure olive oil can be used for cooking or deep-frying. Different varieties of olives are grown all over Italy and the oil of each region has a distinctive taste. Tuscan oil tends to be full-bodied and peppery; Ligurian oil pale and subtle; and Pugliese and Sicilian oil fruity and sharp.

**pancetta** Cured belly of pork, somewhat like streaky bacon. Available in flat pieces or rolled up (*arrotolata*), and both smoked and unsmoked. Generally used, either sliced or cut into cubes, as an ingredient in dishes like spaghetti carbonara.

**Parma ham** This prosciutto comes from traditionally reared pigs fed on the whey from making Parmigiano Reggiano. It has a sweet taste and is only flavored with salt. Parma hams can be identified by the stamp on the skin showing the five-pointed star of the Dukes of Parma. Other prosciutto can be used if Parma ham is unavailable.

**passata** Meaning "puréed", this most commonly refers to a smooth uncooked tomato pulp. Or, use "strained tomatoes". Best without added herbs and flavorings.

**pecorino** One of Italy's most popular cheeses, virtually every region produces a version. Made from sheeps milk and always by the same method, although the result varies according to the milk and aging process used. Pecorino Romano is a well-known hard variety from Lazio and Sardinia.

**peperoncini** The Italian name for chiles, these are popular in the cooking of the South, and are also served there as a condiment. The smallest are called *diavolilli*.

**polenta** The name of the dish and also the ingredient itself, which is ground corn. The cornmeal comes in different grades of coarseness. Finer varieties are better in cakes and coarse ones to accompany stews. A white cornmeal is also available.

**porcini** The Italian name for a *cep* or *boletus* mushroom. Usually bought dried and reconstituted in boiling water, but available fresh in the spring and autumn.

**prosciutto** Italian name for ham. *Prosciutto crudo* is cured ham and includes Parma ham and San Daniele. *Prosciutto cotto* is cooked ham.

**provolone** Curd cheese made from cows milk. The curds are spun and worked into large pear- or tube-shaped cheeses, then immersed in brine and bound with string. Available fresh or matured and eaten as a table cheese or used in cooking.

**radicchio** A salad leaf of the chicory family with slightly bitter red leaves. There are several varieties: radicchio di Castelfranco, di Chioggia and rosso di Verona are similar to a red cabbage with round leaves; radicchio di Treviso has longer, pointed leaves.

**risotto rice** Round-grained, very absorbent rice, mostly cultivated in northern Italy. Risotto rice comes in four categories, classified not by quality but by the size of each grain. The smallest, *Riso Comune* (common rice) is very quick to cook (12–13 minutes), and is ideal for rice pudding. *Semifino* rice includes varieties like *vialone nano* and cooks in about 15 minutes. *Fino* rice takes a minute longer and has more bite. The largest rice, *Superfino*, includes *arborio* and *carnaroli* and takes about 20 minutes.

**soffritto** The flavor base for many soups, stews and risottos. *Soffritto* is a mixture of fried ingredients like onion, celery, carrot, garlic, pancetta and herbs. It means literally to "under-fry" and the mixture should be sweated rather than colored.

**squid/cuttlefish ink** Used to color and flavor pasta and risotto. The ink is stored in a sac that can be removed from whole squid and cuttlefish or bought in sachets from fishmongers or delicatessens.

**Taleggio** A mountain cheese originally from the Italian Alps near Bergamo, but now also made in other regions. Taleggio is an excellent table and cooking cheese and should be eaten young as its flavor becomes more acidic with age. It is made in squares and has a pink-yellow crust and creamy center.

**truffles** Both black and white truffles can be found in Italy. The black ones come from Umbria (especially around Norcia), Piemonte and Emilia-Romagna. The white ones come from Alba (considered the best), Emilia-Romagna, Le Marche, Tuscany and Umbria. Fresh truffles are very expensive but only a tiny amount is needed. Preserved truffles are also available, as is truffle oil.

**vin santo** A golden dessert wine eaten with *cantucci* cookies. Now made all over Italy, but the best known is made in Tuscany.

# INDEX

# BIBLIOGRAPHY

Behr, Edward. *The Art of Eating*, nos. 22 and 41.

Bissell, Frances. *Sainsbury's Book of Food*. Websters International Publishers, 1989.

Capalbo, Carla. *The Food Lover's Companion to Tuscany*. Chronicle Books, 1998.

Carluccio, Antonio and Priscilla. *Complete Italian Food*. Quadrille Publishing, 1997.

Conran, Caroline and Terence, and Hopkinson, Simon. *The Conran Cookbook*. Conran Octopus, 1997.

David, Elizabeth. *Italian Food* (revised edition). Penguin Books, 1989.

Davidson, Alan. *The Oxford Companion to Food*. Oxford University Press, 1999.

Del Conte, Anna. *The Classic Food of Northern Italy*. Pavilion Books Ltd, 1995.

Del Conte, Anna. *Gastronomy of Italy*. Prentice Hall Press, 1988.

Evans, Matthew. *World Food Italy*. Lonely Planet, 2000.

Harris, Valentina. *Italian Regional Cookery*. BBC Books, 1990.

Hazan, Marcella. *The Essentials of Classic Italian Cooking*. Macmillan, 1995.

Mariani, John. *The Dictionary of Italian Food and Drink*. Broadway Books, 1998.

Millon, Marc and Kim. *The Food Lover's Companion to Italy*. Little, Brown and Company (UK), 1996.

Plotkin, Fred. *Italy for the Gourmet Traveller*. Kyle Cathie Ltd, 1997.

Roden, Claudia. *The Food of Italy*. Vintage 1999.

Sinclair, Charles. *International Dictionary of Food and Cooking*. Peter Collin Publishing Ltd 1998.

Stobart, Tom. *The Cook's Encyclopaedia*. Grub Street, 1998.

# THE FOOD OF ITALY

Published by Murdoch Books®

© Text, design, photography and illustrations Murdoch Books® 2000.
All rights reserved. First published 2000. Reprinted 2002.
National Library of Australia Cataloguing-in-Publication Data
Braimbridge, Sophie. Food of Italy. Includes index. ISBN 1-55285-148-6.
1. Cookery, Italian. I. Glynn, Joanne. II. Jones, Chris L. (Photographer) III. Title. 641.5945
A catalogue record of this book is available from the British Library.

Food Editor: Lulu Grimes
Design Concept and Art Direction: Marylouise Brammer
Designer: Susanne Geppert
Editor: Jane Price
Photographer: Chris L. Jones
Stylist: Mary Harris
Stylist's Assistant: Briget Palmer
Additional Photography: Howard Shooter
Additional Recipes: Sarah Randell, Maria Villegas
Map: Russell Bryant

Publisher: Kay Scarlett
Production Manager: Kylie Kirkwood
Chief Executive: Juliet Rogers

Murdoch Books® Australia
GPO Box 1203, Sydney, NSW 1045
Phone: (02) 4352 7000  Fax: (02) 4352 7026

Murdoch Books® UK
Ferry House, 51– 57 Lacy Road, London SW15 1PR
Phone: (020) 8355 1480  Fax: (020) 8355 1499

IMPORTANT: Those who might be at risk from the effects of salmonella food poisoning
(the elderly, pregnant women, young children and those suffering from immune deficiency
diseases) should consult their GP with any concerns about eating raw eggs.

## ACKNOWLEDGMENTS

The Publisher wishes to thank the following for all their help in making this book possible: Marcello Sicuro,
Palermo Fishmarket; Mario Spinnato, Palermo; Gaetano Tapinoso, Palermo; Antonino Biondo, Palermo;
Giuseppe Glaviano, Palermo; Antonino Dripola, Palermo; Bruno Parisi, Cantine Florio, Marsala; Natalia Ravidà,
Ravida Azienda Agricola, Menfi; Jolly Hotel, Palermo; Mario Faella-Titolare, Pastificio Faella, Naples; Eduardo Pagnani,
Brandi Pizzeria, Naples; Ferdinando Cozzolino, La Fenice, Presenzano; Berardino Lombardo, La Caveja; Luigi Richard,
Chiara Bosco, Grand Hotel Parker's, Naples; Giancarlo Padrichelli, Tutto Tartufo, Spoleto; Serafino Mazzocchi, Spoleto;
Ascenso Trappetti, Spoleto; Domenico Basco, Spoleto; Daniela Zuccari, Hotel San Luca, Spoleto; Mario Terenzi,
Boutique del Pecoraro, Norcia; Antica Macelleria Falorni, Greve in Chianti; Antica Drogheria Manganelli, Siena;
Lorenzo Righi, Hotel Relais Borgo SanFelice, Siena; Paolo Bonaga, Paolo Atti e Figli, Bologna; Giovanni Tamburini,
Bologna; Giovanni Montanini, Incas Alimentari, Bologna; La Baita, Bologna; Federica Rondelli, Consorzio
Parmigiano-Reggiano Sezione di Modena; Maeeini Rino, Coop Casearia Castelnovese, Modena; Luciano Stefani,
Giuseppe Giusti, Modena; Canalgrande Hotel, Modena; Davide Ponticelli, Vincenzo Dieci, San Nicola Prosciuttificio,
Parma; Hotel Verdi, Parma; Gabriele Ferron and Barbara Meneghello, Antica Riseria Ferron, Verona; Rita Ferrazzini,
Verona; Hotel Gabbia d'Oro, Verona; Michele Tossuti, Caffé Florian, Venice; Simone Moro, Venice; William Sfritto,
Venice; Claudio Staderini, Hotel Danieli, Venice; Francesca Forni, ITT Sheraton; Rod Johnson and Kayell Photographic;
Nicole Lawless and Kodak; Kylie Goodwin, Qantas; John Portelli, Enoteca Sileno, Melbourne; Simon Johnson,
Sydney; Sara Schwartz, Tasting Places, London; Mosaique Imports; Corso de Fiori; Max Pesch, Ilve Australia.